Food and Nutrition

Food and Nutrition

Late Dr. SHRINANDAN BANSAL (B.M.B.S)
Writer of Various Medical Books

Author of the following selected books

- Bansal's New Illustrated Medical Dictionary (Eng.-Eng.-Hindi)
- Bansal's New Medical Dictionary (Eng.-Eng.)
- Bansal's Medical Dictionary
  बंसल चिकित्सीय शब्दकोष
  (अंग्रेजी–हिन्दी)
- Bansal's Concise Medical Dictionary (English-English-Hindi)

A. I. T. B. S.

AITBS PUBLISHERS, INDIA

MEDICAL PUBLISHERS

J-5/6, Krishan Nagar, Delhi-110051 (INDIA)
Phone: 011-40167052, 49067602
E-mail: aitbsindia@gmail.com & aitbsindia@hotmail.com

First Edition : 2008
Second Edition : 2010
Reprint : 2014
Third Edition : 2027

ISBN : 978-81-7473-363-4

Published by:
Virender Kumar Arya for
AITBS Publishers, India
MEDICAL PUBLISHERS
J-5/6, Krishan Nagar, Delhi - 110051 (INDIA)
Phone: 011-40167052, 49067602
E-mail: aitbsindia@gmail.com & aitbsindia@hotmail.com

Printed by AITBS, Delhi

PREFACE TO THE THIRD EDITION

Lack of knowledge of the facts of food and nutrition causes various nutritional disorders, such as night blindness due to vit. A deficiency, Goitre formation due to iodine deficiency, marasmus in children due to protein deficiency and rickets in children due to calcium or vit. D deficiency, anemia due to iron deficiency, obesity and coronary heart disease due to excess of fat in the diet and diabetes mellitus due to excessive intake of carbohydrate or sugar etc., which can be prevented and cured by improving the nutrition. The purpose of writing this book is to provide the proper knowledge of the food and nutrition to the medical and paramedical persons, especially nursing students who may utilize it in the health-care of their patients.

Government of India has started several programmes to improve the nutritional status as :

(a) Applied Nutrition Programme

(b) Supplementary Feeding Programmes

(c) Mid-day Meal Programme for school children.

Programmes to overcome specific deficiency diseases as :

(a) National Goitre Control Programme

(b) Vitamin A Prophylaxis Programme

(c) Prophylaxis against Nutritional anemia.

A balanced diet is the best to consume, which contains different types of nutrients, i.e., protein, fats and carbohydrates, vitamins and minerals in proper quantity and proportion for maintaining the health, a vitality and general well being of the people, which is described in chapter 6.

The book also contains the chapters on constituents of food and their functions, different types of food, nutritional disorders, contamination of food, adulteration, food allergy, cooking and its effects on food, preservation and storage of food and nutrition education and gives an account of the diets consumed in different types of diseases and different group of people.

A new chapter "Food Hygiene" (No.10) has also been added in the second edition which contains food-borne diseases, hygiene of the vegetables, fruits, milk, eggs, fishes, meat and slaughter houses; sanitation of the eating places and food handlers and education of food handlers, to prevent food poisoning and other food-borne diseases.

The book has been thoroughly revised and the inadvertently occurring minor errors, if any, have been eradicated.

The book contains 25 chapters in which 382 pages are incorporated including 10 pages of index. It contains 12 figures and 8 coloured plates with the photographs of 18 fruits and 22 vegetables.

I hope that this book 'Food and Nutrition' will be very useful for medical and paramedical persons, especially nursing students.

I am very much indebted to Mr. Virender Kumar Arya for A.I.T.B.S. Publishers, India, who encouraged me by publishing this book.

Dr. Shrinandan Bansal

PREFACE TO THE FIRST EDITION

Lack of knowledge of the facts of food and nutrition causes various nutritional disorders, such as night blindness due to vit. A deficiency, Goitre formation due to iodine deficiency, marasmus in children due to protein deficiency and rickets in children due to calcium or vit. D deficiency, anemia due to iron deficiency, obesity and coronary heart disease due to excess of fat in the diet and diabetes mellitus due to excessive intake of carbohydrate or sugar etc., which can be prevented and cured by improving the nutrition. The purpose of writing this book is to provide the proper knowledge of the food and nutrition to the medical and paramedical persons, especially nursing students who may utilize it in the health-care of their patients.

Government of India has started several programmes to improve the nutritional status as :

(a) Applied Nutrition Programme

(b) Supplementary Feeding Programmes

(c) Mid-day Meal Programme for school children.

Programmes to overcome specific deficiency diseases as :

(a) National Goitre Control Programme

(b) Vitamin A Prophylaxis Programme

(c) Prophylaxis against Nutritional anemia.

A balanced diet is the best to consume, which contains different types of nutrients, i.e., protein, fats and carbohydrates, vitamins and minerals in proper quantity and proportion for maintaining the health, a vitality and general well being of the people, which is described in chapter 6.

The book also contains the chapters on constituents of food and their functions, different types of food, nutritional disorders, contamination of food, adulteration, food allergy, cooking and its effects on food, preservation and storage of food and nutrition education and gives an account of the diets consumed in different types of diseases and different group of people.

The book contains 24 chapters in which 344 pages are incorporated including 9 pages of index. It contains 12 figures and 8 coloured plates with the photographs of 18 fruits and 22 vegetables.

I hope that this book 'Food and Nutrition' will be very useful for medical and paramedical persons, especially nursing students.

I am very much indebted to Mr. Virender Kumar Arya for A.I.T.B.S. Publishers, India, who encouraged me by publishing this book.

Dr. Shrinandan Bansal

CONTENTS

CHAPTER 1

INTRODUCTION

Nutrition is the science of food and its relationship to health. It includes all the processes involved in the taking in and utilization of food substances by which body growth, development, repair and maintenance of activities in the body as a whole or in any of its parts are accomplished. These processes are ingestion, digestion, absorption and utilization.

Nutrition plays an important role in the promotion and maintenance of health and prevention of human diseases, especially the nutritional deficiency diseases. Malnutrition, undernutrition and the nutritional disorders are the greatest international health problems of today. Malnutrition causes certain specific nutritional deficiency diseases as kwashiorkor, marasmus, blindness due to vitamin A deficiency, anemia etc. Malnutrition predisposes to infection like tuberculosis. Infection in turn may aggravate malnutrition by affecting food intake and metabolism. Over nutrition, a form of malnutrition causes obesity, diabetes mellitus, hypertention, cardiovascular diseases, renal diseases and disorder of the liver and gallbladder. Undernutrition is the condition resulting from insufficient intake of food from any cause over an extended period of time. It is characterized by loss of weight, atrophy of muscles, weakness and edema. Hence a nurse should have the proper knowledge of nutrition.

Terms and their explanations associated with the nutrition—

Absorption — The transference of nutrients of the food present in the intestine, through the mucous membrane of the intestinal wall into the blood and lymph circulation.

Acidosis — An increase in the acidity of blood due to an accumulation of acids as in diabetes mellitus or renal disease, or an excessive loss of bicarbonate as in renal disease. pH is low in acidosis.

Aerobic — Living only in presence of oxygen.

Alkalosis — An increase in the alkalinity of the blood due to an accumulation of alkalies or reduction of acids. pH is high in alkalosis.

Allergen — Any substance causing allergy.

Anaerobic — Living in the absence of oxygen.

Anemia — A condition of the reduction in the number of red blood cells or the amount of hemoglobin in the circulating blood causing reduced oxygen carrying capacity of the blood. It is a symptom of various diseases characterized by pallor of the skin and mucous membrane, weakness, headache, vertigo, dyspnea, palpitation, amenorrhea, slight fever and edema on the ankles in severe cases.

Angina pectoris — The condition of sudden, severe, substernal pain and constriction of the chest due to insufficient blood supply to the heart caused by constriction of a coronary artery. The pain is increased on exertion, radiating usually to the left shoulder and down the left arm, or to the jaw.

Anthropometry — Science which deals with the measurement of all the parts of the human body.

Antibiotic — A chemical substance produced by a microorganism, which is capable of inhibiting the growth or to destroy the other micro-organisms. The antibiotics not toxic or allergic to the patient are used in the treatment of infectious diseases.

Antibody — A protein substance present in the blood serum, produced in response to a reaction with a specific antigen.

Antigen — A substance introduced into or formed within the body, induces the formation of antibody that specifically reacts with it, e.g., bacteria, toxins, foreign blood and some drugs etc.

Antioxidant — An agent that prevents or inhibits oxidation.

Antiseptic — 1. Peventing sepsis. 2. The substance which inhibits the growth and development of the causative micro-organisms but not necessarily kills them.

Apathy — Indifference, lack of feeling or emotion.

Arteriosclerosis — Thickening and hardening of the walls of the arteries with loss of elasticity and contractility.

Ascites — The accumulation of serous fluid in the abdominal cavity.

Astringent — An agent checking the hemorrhage by constricting the blood vessels or the secretion by coagulating its protein, e.g., ferric chloride, zinc oxide and tannic acid etc.

Atheroma — It is a mass found on the intima (inner wall) of the big arteries due to fatty degeneration occurring in atherosclerosis.

Atherosclerosis — Thickening and hardening of the arterial walls, due to the formation of atheromas in their intimas resulting in narrowness of thier lumens.

Autoclave — An apparatus for the sterilization of materials by steam under pressure, usually at 250°F (121°C) for specific period.

Autolysis — 1. Spontaneous disintegration of the cells or tissues by the enzymes present in the cells themselves, as occurs after death or in some pathological condition.

2. Destruction of the cells of the body by its own serum.

Base — A substance that combines with acid to form salt.

Bile acids — Glycocholic and taurocholic acids present in the bile which are important for the digestion of fats in the intestine.

Body mass index (BMI) or Quetelet's index — It is an index for estimating obesity, obtained by dividing the body weight in kilograms by height of the body in square meters.

$$\text{BMI}=\frac{\text{Weight in Kgs.}}{\text{Height in square meters}}$$

Ideal body mass index for an Indian woman = 19 – 24

Ideal body mass index for an Indian man = 20 – 26

If the body mass index exceeds the above normal limit, the person may be termed as obese or overweight.

Buerger's disease or thromboangitis obliterans — The disease in which there is arterial occlusion due to inflammation of the inner coat of the artery with clot formation in the leg in which the patient complains of pain in the leg on walking, which is due to diminution of blood supply. The disease is commonly seen in men of 20-40 years of age who smoke cigarettes.

Buffer — A substance of which the acidity or alkalinity is not changed upon adding a small amount of acid or alkali to it, e.g., hemoglobin in the blood.

Calcification — The process by which an organic tissue becomes hardened by the deposition of calcium salts in it.

Calorimeter — An instrument used for measuring the amount of heat produced in a chemical reaction.

Capillary — A minute blood vessel connecting the arteriols (small arteries) and venules (small veins). Exchange of materials between the blood and tissues, takes place through the walls of the capillaries.

Carrier — The person who harbors disease-producing organisms in his body in the absence of any sign and symptoms of the disease, so apparently looking healthy, but who is able to spread the organisms to others, thus acting as a carrier.

Catalyst — A substance which in minute quantity increases the speed of a chemical reaction without itself being affected in the reaction.

Cation — An ion that carries a positive charge opposite to an anion, e.g., calcium and sodium etc.

Coagulation — The process of clotting or the formation of a clot as in the coagulation of blood.

Coenzyme — An enzyme activator which activates a biochemical change.

Cofactor — A factor with which another factor must unite to function properly.

Conjunctiva — The mucous membrane covering the eyeball and lining the eyelids.

Constipation — Infrequent and difficult defecation with passage of hard and dry stools.

Cornea — The transparent anterior portion of the fibrous outer layer of the eyeball comprising about one sixth of its surface.

Cretinism — Arrested physical and mental development with dystrophy of bones and soft tissues and lowered basal metabolism, due to lack of thyroid secretion since birth.

1 cup = 150 mls.

Deamination — It is the process by which amino acids that are extra of the needs of the body are decomposed into the nitrogenous and non-nitrogenous substances in the liver. Ammonia is the main of the nitrogenous substances that is converted into urea which is excreted in the urine, i.e., deamination is the process by which ammonia is formed from amino acids.

Dementia — Deterioration of the mental faculties due to some organic disease of the brain with the reduction in intellectual function.

Denaturation — A change in the usual nature of a substance as by the addition of acetone to alcohol to make it unfit for drinking.

Deodourisation — Removal or absorption of foul smell.

Dermatitis — Inflammation of the skin.

Desaturation — The process by which a saturated organic compound is converted into an unsaturated one.

Desensitization — Treatment of an allergy by the administration of repeated graded doses of allergen causing allergy, orally or by injection.

Diarrhea — Frequent passage of loose or watery motions.

Diffusion — The tendency of molecules of a substance to move from the region of high concentration to one of low concentration.

Dyssebacea — A condition seen in riboflavine deficiency marked by greasy, excessive secretion of the sebaceous glands on the middle portion of the face.

Edema — A localized or generalized swelling resulting from excessive accumulation of fluid in the intercellular spaces of the body.

Elastin — An extracellular connective tissue protein that is the principal component of elastic fibres in the middle layers of the arteries.

Electrolyte — A substance which in solution is capable of conducting the electricity and is decomposed into ions by the passage of an electric current, e.g., acids, bases and salts.

Emaciation — Wasting of the body; the condition of being extremely lean.

Enamel — The white, dense and hardest substance in the body covering the crown of the teeth.

Enzyme — A complex protein substance produced by the living cells which speeds up the chemical reaction of the substance for which it often works specifically, and so acts as a catalyst. The substance acted upon by an enzyme is called substrate.

Excereta — Waste matter as feces, urine and perspiration etc., excreted from the body.

FAO — Food and agriculture organisation of the United Nations.

Fomes — Anything as clothes, towel and utensils etc., that harbor and transmit a disease-producing organism.

Fomites — Plural of fomes.

1 Glass = 200 mls.

Gliadin — A water-insoluble protein present in the gluten of wheat. The sticky mass resulting from mixing of wheat flour with water is due to gliadin.

Glossitis — Inflammation of the tongue.

Gluten — A protein of wheat and other cereals that gives elasticity to a dough.

Glycolysis — Conversion of glucose into pyruvic acid and lactic acid.

Gram — Metric unit of weight equal to 1000 milligrams.

Hemodialysis — Removal of certain chemical substances from the blood by passing it through the tubes made of semipermeable membrane, due to difference in rates of their diffusion through the semipermeable membrane. It is used to cleanse the blood in case where one or both kidneys are defective or absent.

Hemoglobin — The iron-containing and oxygen-carrying pigment of the red blood cells formed in the bone marrow, which gives red colour to the blood. It is found 12-16 gms. per 100 mls. of blood in adult females and 14-18 gms. per 100 mls. of blood in adult males and somewhat less in children.

Homeostasis — Stability in the normal physiological state of the body.

Hormone — Hormone is a chemical substance produced in a gland, organ or part of the body in a very minute quantity, which is carried through the blood to another part of the body, stimulating it by chemical action to increase or decrease its activity or to increase or decrease secretion of another hormone.

Hydrolysis — A chemical decomposition in which a substance is split into its components by the addition of water.

Hygroscopic — A substance which absorbs water readily.

Hyperemesis gravidarum — Excessive vomiting during pregnancy which causes dehydration and loss of weight.

Hyperparathyroidism — The condition caused by excessive activity of the parathyroid glands.

Hypogonadism — Decreased functional activity of the sex glands resulting in impairment of the sexual development.

Hypoparathyroidism — The condition caused by excessively diminished functional activity or removal of the parathyroid glands.

Ion — Carrying an electric charge.

Ketosis — Accumulation of ketone bodies (acetone, beta-hydroxybutyric acid and acetoacetic acid) in the body.

Legume — Fruit or pod of beans, peas, and lentils.

Lethargy — A condintion of sluggishness.

Lipid — Any one of a group of fats or fatlike substances, characterized by its insolubility in water and solubility in fat solvents such as alcohol, ether and chloroform.

Lipolysis — Decomposition of fat.

Lipotropic factors — The factors which promote the transportation and use of fats and help to prevent the accumulation of fat in the liver.

Lymph — A colourless, transparent, clear, alkaline fluid within the lymphatic vessels and the cisterna chyli, of which the lymphocytes are chief cellular component.

Malnutrition — It is a pathological condition resulting from a relative or absolute deficiency or excess of one or more essential nutrients in the diet. It includes.

Undernutrition — This is the condition resulting from insufficient food intake for a long period, e.g., protein-energy malnutrition (PEM) which causes the diseases marasmus and kwashiorkor in children.

Overnutrition — This is the pathological condition resulting from excessive intake of food for a long period. It causes obesity, diabetes mellitus and atheroma formation in the big arteries.

Matrix — 1. The intercellular substance of a tissue, as bone matrix. 2. The substance from which a structure as hair or nail develops.

Micro-organisms — Very small living beings, as bacteria.

Morbidity — The condition of being diseased.

Morbidity rate — Number of sick persons suffering from a specific disease per year per 1000 of population.

Mortality — Death.

Mortality rate — Death rate. Number of deaths per year per 1000 of population.

Murphy's sign — It is a sign for determining the inflammation of the gallbladder in which pain is produced on descending and striking of the gallbladder to the examining fingers, when it is palpated by passing the fingers under the right costal margin and the patient is asked to take a deep breath.

NIN — National Institute of Nutrition.

Normal flora of the intestine — Harmless bacteria present in the intestine which do not exist at birth but appear very shortly thereafter. These bacteria produce vitamins, especially vitamin K_1 and inhibit the growth of pathogenic organisms. Oral use of certain antibiotics for a long period, especially broad spectrum antibiotics kill these bacteria and may cause melena or bleeding per rectum due to destruction of vitamin K_1.

Nourish — To provide food or other substances necessary for life and growth.

Osmosis — The passage of the solution of low concentration toward that of high concentration through a semipermeable membrane, separating the solutions of different concentrations.

Osmotic pressure — The pressure that develops when two solutions of different concentrations are separated by a semipermeable membrane which varies with the concentration of the solution and with the variation in the temperature.

Oxidant — An agent that causes oxidation.

Oxidation — The process of combining with oxygen.

Parasite — A plant or animal that lives upon or within another living organism, known as the host from whom it derives its nourishment.

Parenteral — Not through the gastrointestinal route but by other means as by intramuscular, subcutaneous or intravenous injections.

Pathogenic — Producing disease.

Pellagra — A disease occurring due to niacin or nicotinic acid (vitamin B_7) deficeincy characterized by dermatitis, diarrhea and dementia, occurring mainly in the people who live upon maize only.

Peristalsis — A wavelike movement occurring in the intestines caused by their muscles by which their contents are propelled forward.

Phrenoderma or toad skin — A condition characterized by excessive dryness, wrinkling and scaling of the skin, sometimes seen in vitamin deficiences.

Placenta — An oval or discoid spongy structure in the uterus during pregnancy, joining mother and fetus and through which the fetus derives its nourishment.

Plasma — The fluid portion of blood in which white blood cells, red blood cells and platelets are suspended.

Pot-belly — Fatty abdomen.

Preservative — A substance such as sugar, salt, vinegar, ethyl alcohol, etc., which is added to medicines or food materials to prevent them from spoiling.

Purine — Purines are the end products of nucleoprotein digestion.

Rancid — Offensive or having disagreable taste from decomposition, especially of the fatty substance.

Rancidy — The quality of being rancid.

Reduction — A type of chemical reaction in which oxygen is removed or hydrogen is added to a substance or in which a substance gains electrons.

Regurgitation — The backward flow of undigested food from the stomach to the mouth.

Residue — Remainder; the contents remaining in the intestinal tract after digestion of food which includes fibres and other unabsorbed products.

Respiration — The exchange of oxygen and carbon dioxide between atmosphere and the body cells, including inspiration and expiration.

Retinol equivalent (R.E.) — A unit used to express vitamin A activity; 1 R.E. = 3.33 I.U.

Rigor mortis — The stiffness that occurs in dead bodies.

Sanitary — Pertaining to cleanliness.

Satiety — Feeling of satisfaction following meals.

Semipermeable membrane — A membrane through which the fluids but not the dissolved substance passes away.

Serum — After clotting of blood, the watery portion is called as serum which is plasma excluding fibrinogen.

Sewage — Waste matter carried through sewers.

Shelf-life — The period for which a food may be kept safely for eating, on a shelf.

Specific gravity — The weight of a substance compared with the weight of an equal valume of water.

Stillbirth — Birth of a dead child.

Syndrome — A group of symptoms and signs that collectively indicate a particular disease, e.g., burning feet syndrome and nephrotic syndrome etc.

1 Tablespoonful = 15 mls.

1 Teaspoonful (tsp) = 5 mls.

Thyroxine — An iodine-containing hormone of the thyroid gland which increases the rate of cell metabolism. It is used in the treatment of hypothyroidism.

Tissue — A collection of similar cells performing a particular function.

Toxin — A poisonous substance which is a form of protein, produced by some plants, animals and pathogenic bacteria.

Urea — It is the chief nitrogenous constituent of urine and the chief nitrogenous end-product of protein metabolism, which is formed in the liver from ammonia derived from amino acids by deamination. Retention of urea in the blood, which is usually excreted in the urine is known as uremia. Normal value of urea in the blood is 30 mgs./100 mls. of blood.

Viscosity — Stickness.

Vulnerable — Capable to be injured or damaged easily.

* * * * *

CHAPTER 2

CONSTITUENTS OF FOOD AND THEIR FUNCTIONS

CLASSIFICATION OF FOOD

There are many ways of classifying the foods :

(1) Classification of foods by origin —

1. Foods of animal origin, e.g., milk, egg, fish, meat etc.
2. Foods of vegetable origin, e.g., vegetables such as soyabean, cereals, pulses, dry fruits etc.

(2) Classification of foods by chemical composition —

1. Proteins
2. Fats
3. Carbohydrates
4. Vitamins
5. Minerals

(3) Classification of foods by prominent function —

1. Body building foods, e.g., milk, eggs, poultry, fish, meat, pulses and dry fruits etc.

2. Energy giving foods, e.g., cereals, sugar and jaggery, roots and tubers (vegetables), fats (ghee) and oils etc.
3. Protective foods, e.g., Vegetables, fruits and milk etc.

(4) Classification of foods by nutritive value —

1. Cereals and millets
2. Pulses
3. Vegetables
4. Nuts and oil seeds
5. Fruits
6. Animal foods
7. Fats and oils
8. Sugar and jaggery
9. Condiments and spices
10. Miscellaneous foods.

NUTRIENTS

Nutrients are the chemical substances required for repair of the tissues, growth and development and proper functioning of the body and maintenance of life. The requirement of nutrients is changed at different ages, during pregnancy and lactation, illness and trauma. There are about 50 different nutrients in the food. Most natural foods contain more than one nutrient. Each nutrient has some specific functions in the body. Nutrients are divided into two main groups :

I. Macronutrients — They include proteins, fats and carbohydrates which are taken in large quantities and form the main bulk of food. They are energy-producing factors which supply the necessary energy to the body in the form of calories and converted to structural components of cells, or stored as fat when they are in excess of their requirement. The proper utilization of these nutrients require appropriate concentration of micronutrients. In Indian diet they supply the total energy in the following proportions.

Proteins	—	7-15%
Fats	—	10-30%
Carbohydrates	—	65-80%

II. Micronutrients — They include vitamins and minerals. They are called micronutrients because they are required in very small quantities which may vary from a fraction of a milligram to several grams. They are required for the proper metabolism and functioning of the cells and tissues of the body.

MACRONUTRIENTS

Proteins

Proteins are the complex organic nitrogenous compounds, composed of carbon, hydrogen, oxygen, nitrogen and sulphur in varying amounts, which are found naturally in plants and animals. Some proteins also contain phosphorus and iron and occasionally other elements. Proteins differ from carbohydrates and fats in that they contain nitrogen in addition to carbon, hydrogen and oxygen. Proteins constitute about 20 percent of the body weight in an adult of which one third is in the muscles, one tenth in the skin, one fifth in the cartilages and bones and the remaining part in the tissues and body fluids. Proteins are the chief constituents of plasma of cells. 7 to 15 % energy is being supplied to the body by proteins. When body is not getting sufficent energy from proteins, first fat reserves of the body are being utilized and later on body uses muscle protein as a source of energy.

Proteins are made up of smaller units called amino acids. They are the end products of protein digestion which are absorbed through the wall of the small intestine. There are 24 amino acids required by the human body of which 9 are called "essential amino acids (EAA)" because the body can not synthesize them in sufficient quantity and hence they are to be obtained from the diet. They are as follows —

1. Leucine
2. Isoleucine
3. Lysine
4. Methionine
5. Phenylalanine
6. Threonine
7. Valine
8. Tryptophan
9. Histidine

The protein intake must satisfy the need for all the essential amino acids because new tissues can not be formed unless all the essential amino acids are present in the diet. Requirement of essential amino acids (EAA) decreases sharply as one advances in age. The quality of the diet is far more critical for the infant than for the adult.

Non-essential amino acids are synthesized within the body. They include arginine, asparaginic acid, serine, glutamic acid, proline and glycine etc.

Both essential and non-essential amino acids are needed for synthesis of tissue proteins. Essential amino acids must be supplied through diet, whereas non-essential amino acids can be synthesized by the body.

A protein is said to be "biologically complete" if it contains all the essential amino acids in sufficient quantity for the human needs. When one or more of the essential amino acids are lacking, the protien is said to be "biologically incomplete."

Animal proteins are superior to vegetable proteins because they are "biologically complete." For example, milk and egg proteins have all amino acids which are most suitable for humans.

Functions of Proteins —

1. Body building in infants and very young children as proteins are required for growth and development of the muscles, organs of

the body, endocrine glands, bone matrix, teeth, skin, hair and nails etc.

2. Repair and maintenance of the body tissues.
3. Maintenance of osmotic pressure.
4. Proteins provide energy (4 Kcals per one gram).
5. Fetal development in pregnancy.
6. Proteins are required for milk formation during lactation period.
7. Synthesis of certain substances as -
   - Antibodies.
   - Plasma proteins.
   - Hemoglobin.
   - Enzymes like trypsin and pepsin.
   - Hormones like insulin and thyroxine.
   - Coagulation factors.
8. Proteins are connected with the immune mechanism of the body, e.g., the cell mediated immune response and the bactericidal activity of leucocytes have been found to be lowered in severe forms of protein-energy malnutrition.

Sources of Proteins

There are two main dietary sources of proteins :

(A) Animal sources — Proteins of animal origin are found in milk, cheese, eggs, fish and meat etc.

Animal proteins contain all the essential amino acids (EAA) in proper quantity, so these are known as class I proteins. Egg proteins are the best because of their high biological value and digestibility.

(B) Vegetable sources — Vegetable proteins are found in cereals, millets, pulses, nuts, oilseeds, vegetables and fruits. There is deficiency of one or two amino acids in vegetable proteins, so vegetable proteins are known as class II proteins. In developing countries like India, cereals and pulses are the main sources of dietary protein because they are cheaper, easily available and consumed in bulk. Some people do not take animal protein only due to religious reasons.

***Table 1.* Protein content of some food-stuffs (gms/100 gms)**

Aminal foods			Vegetable foods		
Milk (Cow)	—	3.5	*Cereals :*		
Milk (Human)	—	1.2	Wheat	—	11.8
Cheese	—	18.3	Rice	—	7.0
Egg (Hen)	—	13.3	Ma ize	—	11.1
Fish	—	21.5	*Millets (Smaller grains) :*		
Meat	—	18.5	Jowar	—	10.4
			Bajra	—	11.6
			Ragi	—	7.3
			Pulses (Legumes) :		
			Urad	—	24.0
			Arhar	—	22.3
			Moong	—	24.0
			Massor	—	25.0
			Gram (Chana)	—	17.1
			Peas (dried)	—	19.7
			Soyabean	—	42.0
			Nuts (dry fruits) :		
			Almond	—	20.8
			Walnut	—	15.6
			Cashewnut	—	21.2
			Groundnut	—	26.7
			Pistachio	—	19.8

Vegetables :		
Potato	—	1.6
Fruits :		
Banana	—	1.0

Supplementary action of proteins — When two or more vegetarian foods are taken together, as wheat which is deficient in the essential amino acid (EAA) lysine is eaten in the form of chapati or roti with a pulse which is deficient in methionine (EAA), they supplement each other and provide a protein comparable to animal protein in respect of essential amino acids. Thus it is possible for a vegetarian to obtain a class I protein from mixed diets of cereals, pulses and vegetables. This is known as the supplementary action of protein.

Assessment of protein nutrition status — State of protein nutrition is assessed by measuring the serum albumin concentration. It should be more than 3.5 gms/100 mls. of blood serum, 3.5 gms/100 of blood serum is considered mild degree of malnutrition, 3.0 gms/100 mls of blood serum indicates severe malnutrition.

Quality of Protein

All proteins are not of the same quality. They differ from each other in many ways —

Digestibility co-efficient — It is the percentage of ingested protein absorbed into blood stream after the process of digestion is complete. One may eat 100 gms. of proteins but all the 100 gms. will not be absorbed. Absorption differs from protein to protein.

Biological value — It is the percentage of nitrogen retained in the body out of the nitrogen absorbed from the diet, for the growth and maintenance of tissues. Some nitrogen is passed in the urine and feces etc.

Net protein utilization (NPU) percentage

$$= \frac{\text{Digestibility coefficient} \times \text{Biological value}}{100}$$

i.e., the net protein utilization (NPU) is the product of digestibility coeffecient and Biological value divided by 100.

Effects of Heat on Protein

Under normal conditions of cooking the digestibility of food protein is generally improved and no damage occurs to the availability of amino acids. In the raw state soyabean, peas etc., contain trypsin inhibitors which lower the digestibility of proteins. Mild heating destroys these inhibitors and improves the protein digestibility and thereby the nutritive value. But in presence of sugar, protein on heating suffers from severe damages as in the process of baking of biscuits.

Daily requirement of protein — Indian Council of Medical Research (ICMR) in 1989 recommended 1.0 gram protein per Kilogram of body weight per day for an Indian adult, assuming a net protein utilization (NPU) percentage 65 for the dietary proteins.

***Table 2.* Recommended daily requirement of proteins**

Age	Daily requirement of proteins
For infants : (01-12 months)	
(a) 0 — 3 months	2.3 gms. per kg. of body weight
(b) 3 — 6 months	1.8 gms. per kg. of body weight
(c) 6 — 9 months	1.65 gms. per kg. of body weight
(d) 9 — 12 months	1.50 gms. per kg. of body weight
For children :	
(a) 1 — 3 yrs.	22 gms. per day.
(b) 4 — 6 yrs.	29 gms. per day.
(c) 7 — 9 yrs.	40 gms. per day.
Adolescents : Males	
10 — 12 yrs.	54 gms. per day.
13 — 15 yrs.	70 gms. per day.
16 — 18 yrs.	78 gms. per day.

Adolescents : Females			
10	—	12 yrs.	57 gms. per day.
13	—	15 yrs.	65 gms. per day.
16	—	18 yrs.	63 gms. per day.

Man (60 kg. body weight)	60 gms. per day.
Woman (50 kg. body weight)	50 gms. per day.
During pregnancy (upto 6 months)	50+15=65 gms. per day.
During lactation (0-6 Months)	50+25=75 gms. per day.

Young children (0-6 yrs.) require proportionately more protein for each kilogram of body weight than adults as they are more vulnerable to malnutrition.

The protein requirements of women are increased during pregnancy by about 15 gms per day and during lactation (0-6 months) by about 25 gms. per day, above their normal requirements.

In addition to the above conditions daily protein requirement is also increased in wasting diseases such as tuberculosis etc., excessive menstruation, hemorrhage after an accident and destruction of tissues due to burns.

Protein Quantity

The way of evaluating foods as the source of protein is to determine that what percent of their energy value is supplied by thier protein content. This is known as Protein-Energy Ratio (PE ratio or percentage)

$$\text{PE percent} = \frac{\text{Energy from protein}}{\text{Total energy in the diet}} \times 100$$

PE% of milk (Cow) is 20, dal 24, rice 8, potato 6, banana 4 and fish 80.

If PE is less than 4%, protein is inadequate and the person will not be able to eat enough to satisfy protein requirements. It is recommended that protein should be for 15-20 per cent of the total daily energy intake.

Deficiency of protein — A decrease in the amount of protein in the blood is called hypoproteinemia. 7-15% energy is being supplied to the body by proteins. When body is not getting sufficient energy from proteins, first fat depots of the body are being utilized and later on body uses muscle protein as a source of energy. Protein deficiency causes Protein-energy Malnutrition (PEM) in children of six months to 3 years of age which is a widespread condition in india.

Excess of protein — An excess of protein in the blood is called hyperproteinemia. If much more proteins are consumed than required, excess of proteins are used as source of energy only and not for body building and tissue repair. But proteins should not be taken in large quantities than carbohydrates as carbohydrates are richer sources of energy (calories).

Conditions caused by deficiency and excess of protein are described in detail in the chapter *"Nutritional disorders."*

Utilization of proteins — There is no any proteolytic (protein splitting) enzyme in the saliva of the oral cavity so the digestion of proteins starts only in the stomach. Pepsin enzyme secreted by the gastric glands in the stomach, and hydrochloric acid of the gastric juice breakdown the protein to peptones and proteoses. In case of milk, milk protein caseinogen is first converted into casein by the action of the enzyme renin present in hydrochloric acid. Casein combines with calcium to form calcium caseinate. Pepsin converts calcium caseinate into peptones. Now major part of protein digestion occurs in the small intestine. The principal proteolytic enzymes are present in the pancreatic juice which is drained into the upper part of the small intestine (duodenum). These enzymes are trypsin and chymotrypsin which convert the peptones derived from original food protein into simple polypeptides. Later on, the enzyme erepsin secreted by the mucous membrane of the small intestine breaks down polypeptides into the amino acids. These dietary (exogenous) or essential amino acids are absorbed into the blood circulation through the blood capillaries of the intestinal mucosa and are carried to the liver by portal vein. Thence the amino acids reach the respective tissues where they are utilized by the body.

Vegetable proteins are digested in less quantity due to cellulose than those of animal origin.

Fats

Fats are also macronutrients essential for the human body. They provide the body maximum energy, 9 kcals per gram of fats, and perform various functions. Like carbohydrates, fats are also composed of carbon, hydrogen and oxygen, but they differ from carbohydrates in that they contain much less oxygen and much more carbon. They are solid at 20°C temp. and are called oils if they are liquid at that temperature. Fats are insoluble in water but soluble in ether etc. Fats on hydrolysis yield glycerol and fatty acids, i.e., glycerol and fatty acids are the end products of fat digestion.

Glycerol — It is a sweet viscous fluid obtained by the saponification of fats.

Fatty acids — Fatty acids and glycerol are formed in the small intestine as a result of fat digestion, which are absorbed through the lacteals or lymphatic vassels present in the intestinal walls, into the lymph and then ultimately are carried into the blood stream. The most important fatty acids are lauric, palmitic, stearic, linoleic, linolenic, arachidonic and oleic acid etc.

Essential fatty acids — These fatty acids are those that can not be synthesized by the human body and are essential for maintaining health. They can be derived only from food. These are present in vegetable oils in large quantities than animal fats. Three fatty acids named linoleic, linolenic and arachidonic acid are essential fatty acids of which linoleic acid is most important as it serves a basis for the production of other essential fatty acids e.g. linolenic acid and arachidonic acid.

Fatty acids are divided into two groups —

1. Saturated fatty acids.
2. Unsaturated fatty acids.

Saturated fatty acids — When vegetable oils are hydrogenated, i.e., saturated with hydrogen under conditions of optimum temperature and pressure in the presence of a catalyst, the liquid oils are converted into semi-solid and solid fat which is known as "Vanaspati Ghee or Vegetable Ghee." This process of addition of hydrogen to vegetable oils is called hydrogenation. During hydrogenation, unsaturated fatty acids are converted into saturated fatty acids which are incapable of absorbing more hydrogen. After hydrogenation the vegetable oils, i.e., vanaspati ghee can be kept for a long time even in hot and humid climate but in vanaspati ghee or vegetable ghee valuable essential fatty acids are decreased drastically, as groundnut oil contains 28% fatty acids while on hydrogenation their amount is reduced to only 2%. Since vanaspati ghee is lacking in fat soluble vitamins, it is fortified with vitamin A and D by Government regulation to the extent of 2500 IU of vitamin A and 175 IU of vitamin D per 100 gms of vanaspati ghee.

Examples of saturated fatty acids are lauric, palmitic and stearic acid which are mostly found in animal fats but they are also found in vegetable oils as groundnut oil and coconut oil etc. In human nutrition decreasing intake of saturated fatty acids lower the cholesterol content of the blood. When fatty acids are of the saturated type, i.e., they have full number of hydrogen atoms and are incapable to absorb more hydrogen, the particular fat in which they are present, is called saturated fat. Examples are ghee, butter and various artificially saturated fats like margarine and vanaspati preparations as Dalda and Rath etc. Saturated fat is generally found in a solid state and has a tendency to get frozen easily. Saturated fats as ghee and butter etc., raise the blood cholesterol level.

Unsaturated fatty acids — Thes fatty acids are not saturated with hydrogen, so are capable of absorbing extra hydrogen. Oleic acid, linoleic acid and linolenic acid etc., are unsaturated fatty acids. These fatty acids are not formed in the body and therefore are provided by the diet. They do not allow the blood cholesterol level to rise.

When the fatty acids are of the unsaturated type, the particular fat in which they are present is called unsaturated fat. Practically speaking, all the natural vegetable oils and the oils derived from marine fish are of the unsaturated type.

Unsaturated fatty acids are further divided into monounsaturated fatty acids and polyunsaturated fatty acids. The unsaturated fatty acid is called 'monounsaturated fatty acid' when the unsaturation is limited to one 'double bond', e.g., oleic acid. When there are two or more double bonds in the chemical structure of fatty acid, it is called "polyunsaturated fatty acid", e.g., linolenic acid, linoleic acid and arachidonic acid. Linolenic acid and linoleic acid are essential fatty acids. Unsaturated fatty acids are generally found in vegetable oils and marine fish oils.

***Table 3*. Fatty acid content of different fats (Percent)**

Fats	Saturated fatty acids	Monounsaturated fatty acids	Polyunsaturated fatty acids
Groundnut oil	19	50	31
Coconut oil	92	6	2
Palm oil	46	44	10
Soyabean oil	14	24	62
Corn oil	8	27	65
Cotton seed oil	25	25	50
Sunflower seed oil	8	27	65
Butter	60	37	3
Margarine	25	25	50

Dietary sources of essential fatty acids

Essential fatty acids	Dietary source	Percent
Linoleic acid	Groundnut oil	39
	Mustard oil	15
	Palm oil	9
	Coconut oil	2
	Sesame oil	40
	Soyabean oil	51
	Sunflower oil	56
	Corn oil	57
Linolenic acid	Soyabean oil	7
	Green leaves	Varied
Arachidonic acid	Milk	0.4—0.6
	Eggs, meat	0.3—0.5

Sources of Fats

The dietary sources of fats are classified as follows —

(A) Animal fats.

(B) Vegetable fats.

(C) Other sources.

A. Animal fats —They are milk, cheese, ghee, butter, eggs, fish and meat. Animal fats are mostly saturated fats and they are poor sources of essential fatty acids but are good sources of Vitamin A & D.

B. Vegetable fats — They are vegetable oils such as mustard oil, groundnut oil, sesame oil and coconut oil etc.

Animal and vegetable fats are known as visible fats because they are visible to the naked eyes, can be separated from their natural sources, e.g., ghee or butter from milk and it is very easy to estimate their intake in the diet.

C. Other sources — Small quantities of fat are found in most other foods such as cereals, pulses, nuts etc. Such fats are hidden and are not visible to the naked eyes and it is difficult to estimate their intake in the daily diet. These are known as invisible fats.

Examples : Rice — 3%
Wheat — 3%
Jowar — 4%
Bajra — 6.5%

In India large consumption of cereals and pulses etc., provides considerable amounts of "Invisible fat." So the daily consumption of invisible fats exceeds the visible fats in india.

***Table 4.* Important sources of Fat (percent)**

Cow milk	—	3.5%	Cashewnut	—	46%
Ghee	—	100 %	Soyabean	—	19.5%
Butter	—	81%	Egg	—	13.3%
Almond	—	58.9%	Meat	—	13.3%
Groundnut	—	40%	Fish	—	3.2%

Refining — Refining is the process by which the quality and taste of the oils are improved by treating them with the steam and alkali etc.

Functions of Fats

1. The main function of fats is to supply energy. Fats are high energy foods. Every gram of fat provides 9 Calories of energy which is twice more than that of carbohydrates and proteins.
2. Fats are carriers of fat-soluble vitamins A,D,E and K.
3. Fats in the body give support to the internal organs such as heart, kidneys and intestines etc.
4. Fats provide taste to the food.
5. Fat layer below the skin acts as insulator, thus reducing the heat loss from the body surface in cold weather maintains the body temperature.
6. Fats spare proteins from being used for energy as they supply energy.

7. Fats, especially vegetable fats are rich sources of essential fatty acids which are needed by the body for the growth, for structural integrity of the cell membrane and decreased platelet adhesiveness.
8. Diet rich in essential fatty acids (EEA) reduce the serum cholesterol and low-density lipoproteins.
9. Polyunsaturated fatty acids are precursors of prostaglandins, i.e., local hormones which play a part in controlling many of the physiological functions of the body such as vascular homeostasis, acid secretion in the stomach, gastro-intestinal mobility, physiology of the lungs, kidney function and reproduction.
10. Cholesterol (a type of fat) is a precursor of steroid hormones, a component of the nervous tissue and a normal constituent of bile. Cholesterol is important in metabolism.

Characteristics of Fat

Hydrogenation — In the presence of a catalyst a liquid unsaturated fat is converted into a solid saturated fat by the addition of hydrogen to unsaturated fat.

Emulsification — Fats are capable of forming emulsions with liquids, i.e., the large fat globules are broken down into smaller, uniformly distributed particles in the intestine, largely accomplished through the action of bile acids, which lower the surface tension.

Saponification — Conversion of fat into soap, the hydrolysis or splitting of fat by an alkali yields glycerol and fatty acids, i.e., soap is formed.

Rancidity — When fats are exposed to excess of atmospheric oxygen at room temperature, it results in change of odor and flavor, which is termed as rancidity.

Effect of heat on fats — Excessive heating of fats leads to the break down of glycerol producing a pungent compound known as acrolin which is irritating to the intestinal mucosa.

Saturated fats like ghee, butter and artificially saturated vanaspati ghee etc. raise the blood cholesterol level while on the other hand unsaturated fats like mustard oil, groundnut oil or sesame oil etc., lower the blood cholesterol level.

Daily requirement of fats —The Indian Council of Medical Research (ICMR) in 1989 has recommended a daily intake of not more than 20% of the total energy intake through fats. At least 50% of fat intake should consist of vegetable oils rich in essential fatty acids. 15 gms. of the vegetable oils should be in the diet.

***Table 5*. Recommended intake of dietary fat**

Group	Particulars	Body weight *kg.*	Net energy *Kcals/day*	Fat *gms/day*
Man	Sedentary work		2425	
	Moderate work	60	2875	20
	Heavy work		3800	
Women	Sedentary work		1875	
	Moderate work	50	2225	20
	Heavy work		2925	
	Pregnant women	50	+300	30
	During Lactation			
	0—6 months		+550	
	6—12 months	50	+400	45
Children	1—3 yrs.	12.2	1240	
	4—6 yrs.	19.0	1690	25
	7—9 yrs.	26.9	1950	
Boys	10—12 yrs.	35.4	2190	
Girls	10—12 yrs.	31.5	1970	22
Boys	13 —15 yrs.	47.8	2450	
Girls	13—15 yrs.	46.7	2060	22
Boys	16—18 yrs.	57.1	2640	
Girls	16— 18 yrs.	49.9	2060	22

Utilization of fats in the body — When someone takes food, it enters the stomach where the enzyme gastric lipase causes hydrolysis of fat of the food to some extent (hydrolysis is the process of splitting fat into smaller particles by uniting with water). Then the food enters the duodenum where the pancreatic juice containing lipase is drained and succus entericus of the mucosa of small intestine also secretes lipase. So the food in the duodenum is more hydrolysed and it is also emulsified by bile secretion. By disintegration through hydrolysis by the enzyme lipase and emulsification by bile, the fat is broken down into glycerol and fatty acids in the duodenum, the 1st part of the small intestine.

Glycerol and fatty acids are absorbed through the villi present in the walls of small intestine and enter the lacteals, i.e., fine lymph vessels present inside the villi and mix up with their lymph. Glycerol and fatty acids mixing with the lymph are carried to the cisterna chyli (the origin of thoracic duct) by many larger lymph vessels whence these are ultimately carried to the blood stream by thoracic duct and reach the liver by portal vein, where some changes occur in them. Glycerol and fatty acids circulating in the blood reach every cell of the body where they are utilized to give heat and energy. Some of the glycerol and fatty acids are stored in the form of fat depots which contain vitamin A & D.

Carbohydrates

The third major component of food is carbohydrate, which is the main source of energy, providing 4 Kcals. per gram of carbohydrate. It is also essential for the oxidation of fats and for the synthesis of certain non-essential amino acids. Carbohydrates are compounds which contain carbon, hydrogen and oxygen. Hydrogen and oxygen are present in the same proportion as in water, i.e., in the ratio of 2:1. Carbohydrates are the main source of energy for our body. About 70% of total energy requirement is supplied by carbohydrates.

Carbohydrates are classified as follows —

I. Monosachharides : Glucose, Fructose, Galactose.

II. Disaccharides : Sucrose (Cane-sugar), Lactose, Maltose.

III. Polysachharides : Starch, Glycogen, Cellulose, Pectin.

Monosachharides — They contain single sugar unit. They are the simplest form of carbohydrates which can not be hydrolysed to more simpler forms. They are derived from the digestion of polysachharides and disachharides. According to the number of carbon atoms present in their chemical structure, monosachharides are grouped into biose (2-carbon), triose (3-carbon), tetrose (4-carbon), pentose (5-carbon), and hexose (6-carbon). Carbohydrates are absorbed from the intestine only in the form of monosachharides. They are glucose, fructose and galactose. Glucose and fructose may be taken as such, i.e., these are not required to be digested, they are directly absorbed from the intestine, or they may be derived from other carbohydrates.

Glucose — Glucose is the end product of carbohydrate digestion and is the chief source of energy for the body. It is white, crystalline powder easily soluble in water with sweet taste. It is readily absorbed from the stomach. Excess of glucose is converted into glycogen which is stored in the liver and muscles for use when needed, and when it is much more, it is converted into fat which is stored as adipose tissue. Normal blood sugar (glucose) level (fasting) is 80 to 110 mg. per 100 mls. of blood which is maintained by insulin. In the deficiency of insulin less glucose is converted into glycogen so glucose level is raised in the blood and becomes above normal, the condition is called hyperglycemia. When the glucose level becomes above renal threshold, glucose appears in the urine, the condition is known as glycosuria which is a symptom of the diabetes mellitus. In excess of insulin the more glucose is converted into glycogen, so the blood glucose level falls below normal, the condition is known as hypoglycemia.

Fructose — It is known as fruit-sugar or levulose. It is sweeter than glucose. It is also obtained by the hydrolysis of sucrose. It is hexose, i.e., having 6 atoms of carbon. It is found in fruit juices and honey etc. It is metabolized to provide a source of energy or may be stored in the body after being converted into glycogen.

Galactose — It is a simple hexose sugar. It is not found free in nature but is formed along with the glucose in the hydrolysis of lactose. It is a component of cerebrosides present in the brain and nervous tissue. Hence, it is nutritionally important. It is readily absorbed in the digestive tract; in the liver it is converted into glucose and may be stored as glycogen.

Disachharides — They are composed of two monosachharides.

Sucrose (Cane-sugar) — It is found in sugar-cane and beet root. So it is manufactured on a large scale from sugar-cane or beet root. It is formed by the condensation of one molecule of glucose and one molecule of fructose. It is easily hydrolyzed to glucose and fructose by the enzyme sucrase present in the intestinal juice.

Monosachharides resulting from the digestion of sucrose are absorbed by the small intestine and carried to the liver, where they may be converted into glycogen and stored as such if they are not required immediately for energy.

Lactose — A disachharide that is present in milk of all mammals. It yields glucose and galactose on hydrolysis by the enzyme lactase present in the intestinal juice. Lactose is formed by condensation of one molecule of glucose and one molecule of galactose. Bacteria can convert lactose into lactic acid and butyric acids, as in souring of milk. The milk of mammals cantains 4% to 7% lactose. Its presence in the urine indicates the obstruction to the flow of milk after cessation of nursing.

Maltose — A disaccharide present in malt, malt products and sprouting seeds. It is formed when starch present in the food in digested, i.e., hydrolysed by salivary and pancreatic enzyme amylase, and is converted into glucose by the enzyme maltase. Maltose is formed in the cereal grains during germination by the hydrolysis of starch.

Polysachharides — They are complex carbohydrates of high molecular weight, usually insoluble in water, made up of condensation of several molecules of monosachharides which are readily absorbed and assimilated. Polysaccharides constitute the main bulk of our daily food.

Starch — Starch is a polysachharide formed in nature by condensation of a large number of glucose molecules. It is formed in cereals as wheat, rice, maize, barley etc., pulses, underground vegetables such as potato, sweet potato and beet root etc. and fruits like banana, apple, guava and mango etc. It is insoluble in water. It is of high molecular weight and yields monosachharides on complete hydrolysis, which are readily absorbed. When some fruits ripen, the starch is chaged to sugar, while some vegetables as peas change sugar into starch as their seeds develop.

Glycogen — It is called *"animal starch"*, a whitish powder that can be formed from animal liver and muscles and other animal tissues. It is found in the liver and muscles. When there is no requirement of the simple sugar (glucose) present in solution in the body, it is deposited in the liver and muscles as animal starch or glycogen. Glycogen is again converted into glucose when glucose is needed as the body becomes active. Glycogen (Carbohydrate reserve) of an adult is about 500 gms. It is rapidly exhausted when a man is fasting.

Cellulose — It is an indigestible component of carbohydrate with scarcely any nutritive value, contributes to dietary fibre.

Fibres — Dietary fibres are not digested by the digestive juice in the gastro-intestinal tract and are left unchanged after digestion while all the other constituents of food as protein, fat, starch and sugars are digested and absorbed. Cell-walls of the plants are composed of cellulose (fibres) so fibres are found in fruits, vegetables particularly leafy vegetables and grains in significant quantities. Fibres provide non-caloric diet, as they provide no energy.

Action of Fibres

1. When fibres are taken with the food, they absorb water and increase the bulk of stool and thereby increasing peristaltic movements of the intestines cause evacuation properly, i.e., they relieve constipation.
2. Fibres also reduce the body weight and so help in causing slimness.
3. Certain types of fibres lower the blood cholesterol level.
4. Diets containing much fibres provide some protection against coronary heart disease by decreasing intake of protein, fat and simple carbohydrate. Some fibres tend to bind cholesterol and reduce its absorption from the intestinal tract.
5. Diet containing fibres may protect against cancer of the intestine.

Daily requirement of fibres — 10 to 12 grams.

Pectin — A purified carbohydrate obtained from peel of citrus fruits, or from the pulp of apple. Cellulose and pectin are not assimilated by human being but add bulk of the stool.

Any excess of carbohydrate is converted into fat which is stored as fat depots or adipose tissue. In case of leanness glycogen is broken down to glucose which is oxidized and energy is produced which is used by the body.

Functions of carbohydrates

1. The main function of carbohydrate is to give energy. Each gram of it provides 4 kcals of energy when glucose is oxidized.
2. Carbohydrates as sugar adds flavor and taste to the diet.
3. Cellulose and pectin stimulate the peristaltic movements of the intestines causing evacuation and relieves constipation.

4. Carbohydrates also help in digestion and absorption of food. Digestive action of carbohydrate takes place in the small intestine.
5. Carbohydrates with the help of lactose help in growth of the desirable bacteria in the intestine which are useful in the synthesis of vitamin B Complex.
6. Glucose in the body helps in synthesis of amino acids.
7. Lactose increases the absorption and utilization of calcium.
8. Carbohydrates are required for the formation of nucleic acid, galactoside of the nervous tissues and matrix of the connective tissue.
9. Protein sparing action — The body will use carbohydrate as a source of energy when it is adequately supplied in the diet sparing protein for tissue building purposes.

Daily requirement of carbohydrates — A normal adult requires to take about 400 grams per day.

Utilization of carbohydrates in the body — The enzyme ptyalin in the saliva of mouth secreted by the salivary glands partly digest the carbohydrates by which polysachharide is converted into disachharide. Hydrochloric acid in the stomach causes some hydrolysis of the carbohydrate food resulting in the partial disintegration of disachharide. However, the major part of carbohydrate digestion and its final absorption take place inside the small intestine. The cells of the mucous membrane of the small intestine secrete the enzyme 'sucrase' for sucrose, 'lactase' for lactose and 'maltase' for maltose. The pancreatic juice containing the enzyme amylase is drained into the duodenum at the time of digestion. Amylase is the principal carbohydrate splitting enzyme in the body. Thus, the carbohydrate food ingested, whether as polysachharide, disachharide or even monosachharide is ultimately broken down into simple monosachharides through the successive stages of digestion. Only as monosachharide derived from the complex carbohydrate food or taken as such, the carbohydrate is absorbed into the blood circulation through the intestinal mucous membrane and subsequently reach the liver via the portal veins where its metabolism occurs.

The principal source of energy is glucose. The amount of glucose in excess of the immediate need of the body and for the maintenance of normal blood sugar (glucose) level, is converted into a polysachharide called glycogen which is stored in the liver and muscles. The conversion of glucose into glycogen is called glycogenesis. The glycogen can be reconverted into glucose on body's demand, to flow into the general blood circulation.The process of conversion of glycogen into glucose is called glycogenolysis.

Conditions caused by deficiency and excess of protien, fats and carbohydrates are described in the chapter of "*Nutritional disorders.*"

MICRONUTRIENTS

Vitamins

A vitamin belongs to a group of organic compounds found in many foods which are essential in very small quantities for the normal function and maintenance of good health of the body, though they do not yield energy, nor they build the body. They fall in the category of micronutrients. Vitamins are of 6 types, i.e., vitamins A, B, C, D, E and K. Each vitamin has a specific function to perform and deficiency of any particular vitamin may lead to specific deficiency diseases.

For normal functioning of the body and good health usually a well balanced diet contains all the vitamins in adequate quantities to supply to a healthy person, but even then in growing children, pregnant women, lactating mothers, general debility and convalescence period of a chronic disease more vitamins are required.

Vitamins are divided into two groups :

(A) Fat-soluble vitamins - Vitamins A, D, E, and K.

(B) Water-soluble vitamins - Vitamins B and C.

FAT-SOLUBLE VITAMINS

Vitamin A

Vitamin A is also known as growth-promoting factor because it is essential for the growth of the body, and anti-infective vitamin because it protects the body from infection. Vitamin A covers both a pre-formed vitamin — retinol, and a precursor or provitamin — beta-carotene. About 30% of the beta-carotene is converted into retinol in the intestinal mucosa. This action is poorly accomplished in malnourished children and those suffering from diarrhea. The absorption of both retinol and beta-carotene is facilitated by bile salts. Vitamin A is rapidly destroyed on exposure to high temperature in the presence of air. Vitamin E prevents the destruction of Vitamin A in the body. Vitamin A is stored in the liver as retinol.

About 6 mcg of beta-carotene = 1 mcg of retinol.

The older 1 International Unit (IU) of Vitamin A = 0.3 mcg of retinol.

Sources of vitamin A — Vitamin A is found in animal food as well as in plant foods. In animal foods vitamin A is found as pre-formed vitamin A (retinol) and in plant foods as pro-vitamin i.e., precursor of vitamin A (beta-carotene)

Animal sources of vitamin A (retinol) — Animal sources of vitamin A are milk, cheese, butter, ghee, egg-yolk, fish liver oils, liver and meat etc. Fish liver oils are the richest source of retinol. One teaspoonful of cod liver oil or shark liver oil supplies about 6000 IU of vitamin A.

Plant sources of vitamin A — Deep-green leafy vegetables, the darker the green leaves, the higher is the carotene content. Spinach, amaranth, coriander, mint, cabbage, fenugreek, pumpkin, bottle gourd, yellow or red vegetables as carrots and beet, tomatoes, fruits like ripe papaya and ripe mango etc. are the rich sources of vitamin A.

Fortified foods — Foods fortified with vitamin A as vanaspati ghee, margarine and milk etc., can be an important source of vitamin A.

Table 6. **Retinol content of some selected foods**

	mcg/100 gms
Carrot	1167
Spinach	607
Amaranth	515
Green leaves	300
Tomato	84
Ripe papaya	118
Ripe mango	313
Milk (Cow)	38
Cheese	350
Butter	825
Egg	140
Margarine	900
Cod liver oil	18,000
Halibut liver oil	900,000
Liver, ox	16,500
Fish	40

Functions of vitamin A

1. Vitamin A is necessary for maintaining the integrity and the normal functioning of the epithelial tissue of the skin and eyes as well as of the lining of the intestinal, respiratory and urinary tracts.
2. It is essential for the growth of the body, especially of the bones.
3. Vitamin A is an anti-infective vitamin, i.e., it protects the body from infection.

4. Vitamin A is necessary for normal vision by contributing to the production of visual purple (rhodopsin) in the retinal rods which are needed for vision in dim light.
5. It plays a role in immunological defence mechanism of the body.
6. Beta-carotene is very important antioxidant vitamin which prevents atherosclerosis and consequently coronary heart disease.
7. Vitamin A is essential to maintain normal reproductive function in males.
8. It is believed to prevent the aging process in the skin.

Daily requirement of vitamin A—Daily requirement of vitamin A for different groups of people in term of retinol and b-carotene is given in the following table.

***Table 7.* Daily requirement of vitamin A recommended by ICMR**

Group		Retinol *(mcg.)*	β-carotene *(mcg.)*
Adult	Man	600	2400
	Woman	600	2400
	Pregnancy	600	2400
	Lactation	950	3800
Infants	0-12 months	350	1200
Children	1-6 years	400	1600
	7-12 years	600	2400
Adolescence	13-19 years	600	2400

Being a fat-soluble vitamin, it can be stored in the body. Approximately 90% i.e., about 100,000 mcg. of vitamin A is stored in the liver, which may last for 6 to 9 months. Consumption of excess of vitamin A causes its toxicity which may disappear on withdrawal of vitamin A intake.

Fifty percent of vitamin A is lost during storage and cooking, a loss of 15 to 20% of carotene was seen in vegetables stored at room temperature for 24 hrs. only.

Conditions caused by deficiency and excess of vitamin A are described in the chapter of "*Nutritional disorders.*"

Vitamin D

Vitamin D is also known as antirachitic vitamin as it protects the children from rickets. Vitamin D group includes Calciferol (vitamin D_2), Cholecalciferol (vitamin D_3), irradiated 22-dihydroergosterol (vitamin D_4) and irradiated dehydrositosterol. The nutritionally important are calciferol (vitamin D_2) and cholecalciferol (vitamin D_3). Calciferol (vitamin D_2) is formed in the plants when ergosterol found in plants is exposed to ultraviolet light. Cholecalciferol (vitamin D_3) is formed in the deeper layer of the epidermins of the skin from the organic chemical 7-dehydrocholesterol (a sterol found in the skin) by the irradiation caused by ultraviolet rays of sunlight, when skin is exposed to sunlight. It is also found in animal fats and fish liver oils, Vitamin D is stored largely in the fat depots. In fact, dietary vitamin D_3 (cholecalciferol) is not required at all if the sunlight is adequately available. It can be formed in the body in sufficient quantities by simple exposure to sunlight, even for 5 minutes per day. Those with fair skin are able to produce more vitamin D, since more of the sun's ultraviolet rays can penetrate the fair skin, i.e., 50 to 70% in comparison to 5 to 30% in dark skins.

Actually vitamin D is considered as a hormone and not a vitamin. Because like a hormone it is synthesized by the tissue cells of an organ (i.e., skin) and acts on distant target organ like small intestine and bones, being carried by the blood.

Vitamin D is measured in terms of international unit (IU). One international unit (IU) of vitamin D = 0.025 μg (mcg) of calciferol, i.e., to convert international units into micrograms (mcg or μg), divide them by 40.

Sources of vitamin D Vitamin D is derived from both sunlight and foods.

Sunlight— Vitamin D is synthesized by the body by the action of ultraviolet rays of sunlight on 7-dehydrocholesterol, present in large quantity in the skin. Air pollution and black skin can filter off the ultravoilet rays of the sun. Black skin can filter off 95% of the ultraviolet rays, so vitamin D is not synthesized sufficiently in the skin of Negroes.

Foods— Vitamin D is found only in foods of animal origin and not in foods of vegetable origin, e.g., milk, butter, egg, liver, fish fat and fish liver oils etc. Fish liver oils, although not considered to be food are the richest sources of vitamin D. Some foods like milk, margarine, vanaspati ghee and infants' foods etc., are artificially fortified with vitamin D.

***Table 8*. Vitamin D content of certain foods in mcg an IU per 100 gms**

Milk, whole	—	.1 mcg or 4 IU
Butter	—	.5-1.5 mcg or 20-60 IU
Eggs	—	1.25-1.5 mcg or 50-60 IU
Fish fat	—	5-30 mcg or 200-1200 IU
Shark liver oil	—	30-100 mcg or 1200-4000 IU
Cod liver oil	—	200-500 mcg or 8000-20,000 IU
Halibut liver oil	—	500-10,000 mcg or 20,000-400,000 IU

Vitamin D is stored in the body in fatty tissues and in the liver.

Functions of vitamin D

Vitamin D helps in the absorption of dietary calcium and phosphorus from the intestine and maintains their concentration in the blood, hence it is required for the normal calcification and development of bones and teeth. It increases the reabsorption of calcium and phosphate from the renal tubules and makes them available at the site of new bone formation as calcium phosphate. Parathyroid glands through the hormone 'parathormone' regulates the calcium and phosphorus metabolism. It permits the normal growth of the body.

Daily requirement of vitamin D — Vitamin D is normally synthesized in the skin in the sunlight, so when adequate sunlight exposure is available, no daily requirement of vitamin D is being recommended by ICMR. If no sunlight is available or there is inadequate sunlight, vitamin D may be required as follows —

Daily requirements of vitamin D are

Infants and children	—	5.0 mcg. (200 IU)
Adults	—	2.5 mcg. (100 IU)
Pregnancy and lactation	—	10 mcg. (400 IU)

Deficiency of vitamin D, mainly causes rickets in children and osteomalacia in women. For conditions caused by deficiency and excess of vitamin D. see chapter "*Nutritional disorders.*"

Vitamin E

This vitamin is also known as tocopherol, the most potent and active type being alpha-tocopherol which is commercially synthesized. It is also known as anti-sterility vitamin because it prevents and cures the sterility in men. Vitamin E requires the presence of fats and bile salts for its absorption into the intestinal wall. It is not destroyed on heating and nor in acids. Decomposition of vitamin E occurs in ultraviolet rays. It is expressed in terms of international units. The usual plasma level of vitamin E in adults is between 0.8 and 1.4 mg. per 100 mls.

Sources of vitamin E

It is widely distributed in foods, the richest sources of vitamin E are vegetable oils. It is also found in fish liver oils. It is derived from germinating grain or gram, dark green leafy vegetables, legumes, sunflower seed, soyabean, cotton seed, corn, nuts, milk, butter and egg-yolk etc. Foods of amimal origin are low in vitamin E.

Functions of vitamin E

(1) It promotes the functions of the muscles and is necessary for muscular development.

(2) It has vasodilator action so it is used in angina pectoris, Buerger's disease or intermittent claudication and Raynaud's disease etc.

(3) It is necessary for normal reproduction. It prevents abortion and cures sterility in men so it is also known as anti-sterility vitamin.

(4) It prevents or delays ageing.

(5) It prevents coronary heart disease from atherosclerosis.

(6) It prevents the development of cancer.

(7) It protects the red blood cells from hemolysis.

(8) Vitamin E prevents the oxidation of the unsaturated fatty acids and acts as an antioxidant.

(9) It helps in maintaining the stability and integrity of cell membranes.

(10) It improves immune response.

Vitamin E is stored in liver, muscle and body fat.

Daily requirement — Daily requirement of vitamin E is 5 to 15 IU or 0.8 mg. per gram of essential fatty acids consumed as suggested by ICMR. or daily allowance for men is 10mg. and for women is 8 mg. Large daily dose of 100 to 400 IU has been advised for the treatment of muscular diseases, abortion, sterility etc. Due to its vasodilator action it is used in angina pectoris, intermittent claudication or Buerger's disease and Raynaud's disease etc., in higher doses, i.e., 400 IU to 800 IU.

For conditions caused by deficiency and excess of Vitamin E see chapter "*Nutritional disorders.*"

Vitamin K

Vitamin K is also known as anti-hemorrhagic factor because it helps in checking the bleeding from the body. There are mainly two types of vitamin K. One is vitamin K_1 or phytomenadione and the other is K_2 or menadione. Water-soluble vitamin K analogues are manufactured commercially. Vitamin K is stored in the liver.

Natural sources — Vitamin K_1 is found in abundance in dark green leafy vegetables, spinach, cabbage, cauliflower, tomatoes, soyabean, some fruits, milk, cow's milk is the richest source (60 mcg/L) than human milk (15 mcg/L), egg, fish, liver and meat etc. Vitamin K_2 is synthesized in the large intestine by the action of normal intestinal bacteria. Administration of an oral antibiotic for more than a week may destroy the normal intestinal bacterial flora (A source of vitamin K_2) and so may cause a deficiency of vitamin K.

Function — Vitamin K helps in coagulation of blood in the body, being associated with the formation of prothrombin in the liver, whcih is essential for the clotting of blood. Bleeding occurs from any site in the body in its deficiency and so it is used as a coagulant of blood or to stop the bleeding.

Daily requirement — No recommendation has been made for daily requirement by ICMR as ordinarily vitamin K deficiency does not occur, or a normal adult requires 2 to 3 mg. of vitamin K daily or 0.03 mg. per kg. of body weight is recommended for an adult.

Like other fat-soluble vitamins, vitamin K can be destroyed by freezing, by mineral oils and rancid fats. It is resistant to heat and cooking process.

For conditions caused by deficiency and excess of vitamin K, see Chapter *"Nutritional disorders."*

WATER-SOLUBLE VITAMINS

Vitamin B Complex

Vitamin B Complex is a group of water-soluble vitamins which are destroyed by excessive heating for 2 to 4 hours. It includes the following vitamins (factors). Each member vitamin or factor has a separate function to perform. All the B vitamins are inter-related.

1. Vitamin B_1 or thiamine hydrochloride
2. Vitamin B_2 or riboflavine

3. Vitamin B_6 or pyridoxine hydrochloride
4. Niacin or nicotinic acid
5. Vitamin B_{12} or cyanocobalamin
6. Folic acid
7. Pantothenic acid
8. Choline
9. Inositol
10. Biotin
11. Para-aminobenzoic acid.

1. Vitamin B_1 or thiamine hydrochloride

It is water-soluble and heat-labile particularly in alkaline medium. Vitamin B_1 is not stored in the body to any appreciable extent, only 25-30 mgs. of vitamin B_1 are found in the body of a normal adult, hence its deficiency develops within a few weeks. It is derived from plant and animal foods but a small amount may be synthesized in the digestive tract.

Sources — Vitamin B_1 is found in most of the plant and animal foods. Important sources are —main sources of vitamin B_1 in the diet of Indian people are cereals as rice and wheat which contribute 60-85% of the total supply. Rice-bran and grain-husk contain more vitamin B_1 than polished milled rice and wheat flour. In addition to cereals, pulses, vegetables, legumes, fruits, oilseeds, nuts especially groundnuts, milk, yeast, egg, fish and meat etc. are the sources of vitamin B_1. Milk is an important source of vitamin B_1 for infants.

Functions of vitamin B_1 (Thiamine hydrochloride)

(1) Vitamin B_1 is essential for the utilization or metabolism of carbohydrate. The more carbohydrate is taken, the more vitamin B_1 is required.

(2) It is essential for the maintenance of good appetite and normal digestion.

(3) It is essential for the normal function and maintenance of health of the nerves.

(4) It has a specific role in the functions of the brain.

(5) It protects the body from cardiac and nervous diseases.

(6) It affects the growth.

Table 9. **Dietary sources of vitamin B_1 (Thiamine hydrochloride)**

Foods of vegetable origin *mg./100 gms.*		Foods of animal origin *mg./100 gms*	
Wheat whole	0.45	Milk, cow's	0.05
Rice, raw home pounded	0.21	Egg, hen's	0.10
Rice, milled	0.06	Mutton	0.18
Chane ki dal	0.48	Liver, sheep	0.36
Groundnut	0.90		
Almonds	0.24		

Vitamin B_1 or thiamine is destroyed in the following conditions—

1. Vitamin B_1 is lost from the rice during the process of milling.
2. Being water-soluble vitamin, further losses of vitamin B_1 take place during washing and cooking of rice.
3. Much of the thiamine in vegetables and fruits is generally lost during their storage for a long time.
4. Thiamine is also destroyed in toasting bread and in cereals cooked with baking soda.

Daily requirement—Daily requirement of vitamin B_1 or thiamine for an adult is 1.2 to 2 mg. or 0.5 mg. per 1000 Kcals of energy intake. The body contains about 30 mg. of vitamin B_1 and if more than this is given, it is merely lost in the urine. In infants 20 mg. of thiamine per 100 mls of milk is recommended. For details see table—

Table 10. **Daily requirement of vitamin B_1 (Thiamine hydrochloride)**

Group	Particulars	Body weight	Vitamin B_1 (mg/day)
Man	Sedentary work		1.2
	Moderate work	60 kgs.	1.4
	Heavy work		1.6
Woman	Sedentary work		0.9
	Moderate work	50 kgs.	1.1
	Heavy work		1.2
	Pregnant woman	50 kgs.	+0.2
	Lactating mother		
	0—6 months		+0.3
	6—12 months	50 kgs.	+0.2
Infants	0—6 months	5.4 kgs	55 μg/kg
	6—12 months	8.6 kgs	50 μg/kg
Children	1—3 years	12.2 kgs.	0.6
	4—6 years	19.0 kgs.	0.9
	7—9 years	26.9 kgs	1.0
Boys	10—12 years	35.4 kgs.	1.1
Girls	10—12 years	31.5 kgs.	1.0
Boys	13—15 years	47.8 kgs.	1.2
Girls	13—15 years	46.7 kgs.	1.0
Boys	16—18 years	57.1 kgs.	1.3
Girls	16—18 years	49.9 kgs.	1.0

2. Vitamin B_2 or riboflavine

It is yellow colored pigment widely distributed in plant foods and in small amounts in animal foods. It is stable to heat and acid solution but is decomposed on exposure to light.

Natural sources—Vitamin B_2 or riboflavine is found in abundance in green leafy vegetables, milk, and milk products, groundnut, yeast, egg, poultry, fish, meat and liver etc. Cereals and pulses are relatively poor sources of vitamin B_2 but because of the bulk in which they are consumed, they contribute to a lot of riboflavine to Indian diets. Germination increases the riboflavine content of cereals and pulses. It is also synthesized by bacteria in the body.

Table 11. **Dietary sources of vitamin B_2 (riboflavine)**

Foods of vegetative origin	mg./100 gms
Leafy vegetables	0.15-0.30
Whole cereals	0.10-0.16
Milled cereals	0.03-0.08
Pulses	0.21-0.32
Foods of animal origin	**mg./100 gms**
Milk, Cow's	0.19
Egg, hen's	0.40
Liver, sheep	1.70
Meat	0.14

Functions of vitamin B_2 (Riboflavine)

(1) Riboflavine plays an important role in many enzyme systems involved in the metabolism of proteins, fats and carbohydrates.

(2) It is essential for growth.

(3) It is associated with tissue repair.

(4) It plays a role in cellular oxidation.

Daily requirement—Daily requirement of riboflavine is 0.6 mg./ 1000 Kcal of energy intake for all or it varies from 0.7 mg. for an infant to 1.7 mg. for an adult per day which is increased during pregnancy and lactation.

For treatment purposes 5 mg. can be given two to three times a day for a long period.

Table 12. **Daily requirement of vitamin B_2 or riboflavine**

Group	Particulars	Body weight *in kg.*	Riboflavine *mg./day*
Man	Sedentary work		1.4
	Moderate work	60	1.6

	Heavy work		1.9
Woman	Sedentary work		1.1
	Moderate work	50	1.3
	Heavy work		1.5
	Pregnant woman	50	+0.2
	Lactating mother		
	0 - 6 months		+4
	6 - 12 months	50	+0.2
Infants	0 - 6 months	5.4	65 μg/kg./day
	6 -12 months	8.6	60 μg/kg./day
Children	1- 3 years	12.2	0.7
	4 - 6 years	19.00	1.0
	7 - 9 years	26.9	1.2
Boys	10 - 12 years	35.4	1.3
Girls	10 - 12 years	31.5	1.2
Boys	13 - 15 years	47.8	1.5
Girls	13 - 15 years	46.7	1.2
Boys	16 - 18 years	57.1	1.6
Girls	16 - 18 years	49.9	1.2

3. Vitamin B_6 or pyridoxine hydrochloride

Vitamin B_6 exists in three forms : pyridoxine, pyridoxal and pyridoxamine having similar functions in the human body. It is soluble in water and distributed throughout plant and animal kingdom. In the process of cooking or boiling much of the vitamin B_6 in the milk or meat is lost. The loss of this vitamin from vegetables during cooking is insignificant. Its deficiency occurs very rarely as balanced diets usually contain pyridoxine hydrochloride in sufficient quantities.

Natural sources — Vitamin B_6 is found in milk, cheese, egg-yolk, fish, liver, meat cereals, pulses, ground nuts, yeast, soyabean, legumes, fruits and vegetables.

Functions of vitamin B_6 (Pyridoxine hydrochloride)

(1) Vitamin B_6 plays an important role in the metabolism of amino acids, fats and carbohydrates.

(2) It is essential for maintaining the nerves in normal conditions.

Curative effects of Vitamin B_6 — It has beneficial effects in the following conditions.

1. Morning sickness, i.e., nausea and vomiting in pregnancy.
2. Nausea and vomiting after anesthesia.
3. Vitamin B_6 deficiency syndrome produced by the drug isoniazide (INH) used for the treatment of tuberculosis.
4. Radiation sickness.
5. Nervous disorders in the new born infants.
6. Tremors and convulsions.
7. Microcytic anemia.

Daily requirement — Daily requirements of vitamin B_6 for adults vary directly with protein intake, if diet contains 100 gms of protein, the requirement of vitamin B_6 is 1.25 mg. Generally adults require 2 mgs. per day, during pregnancy and lactation more vitamin B_6 i.e. 2.5 mgs. per day are required.

***Table 13*. Daily requirement of vitamin B_6 or pyridoxine hydrochloride**

Group	Particulars	Body weight (kg)	Vitamin B_6 (mg/day)
Man	Sedentary work		
	Moderate work	60	2.0
	Heavy work		
Woman	Sedentary work		
	Moderate work	50	2.0
	Heavy work		

	Pregnant woman	50	2.5
	Lactating mother		
	0 – 6 months		
	6 – 12 months	50	2.5
Infants	0 – 6 months	5.4	0.1
	6 – 12 months	8.6	0.4
Children	1 – 3 years	12.2	
	4 – 6 years	19.0	0.9
	7 – 9 years	26.9	1.6
Boys	10 – 12 years	35.4	
Girls	10 – 12 years	31.5	1.6
Boys	13 – 15 years	47.8	
Girls	13 – 15 years	46.7	2.0
Boys	16 – 18 years	57.1	
Girls	16 – 18 years	49.9	2.0

4. Niacin or Nicotinic acid

Niacin or nicotinic acid is an important factor of vitamin B complex. Its deficiency causes pellagra, so it is also known as pellagra-preventing factor and is used in the treatment of pellagra. An essential amino acid, tryptophan acts as its precursor in the human body. It is heat stable.

Natural sources — Niacin or nicotinic acid is formed from the essential amino acid tryptophan. 1 mg. of niacin is formed from 60 mg. of dietary tryptophan. So the diet containing liberal amounts of tryptophan will provide enough niacin. Cereals (whole wheat, rice), pulses, groundnut, fish, poultry, liver and meat are good sources of niacin and/or tryptophan. Milk is a poor source of niacin but its proteins are rich in tryptophan which is converted in the body into niacin.

Functions of niacin or nicotinic acid

(1) Niacin or nicotinic acid is essential for the metabolism of proteins, fats and carbohydrates, through enzymatic action.

(2) Niacin is also essential for the normal functioning of the skin, so the skin diseases do not occur when it is present in the diet in

sufficient quantity. Its deficiency causes a skin disease pellagra, so it is used in the treatment of pellagra.

(3) It is essential for the normal functioning of the intestines.

(4) It is also essential for the normal functioning of the nervous system.

(5) It has vasodilator action so it is used in the treatment of angina pectoris and Buerger's disease or thromboangitis obliterans etc.

(6) It lowers the blood cholesterol level.

Daily requirement — Recommended daily allowance is 6.6 mg. per 1000 Kcals of energy intake. For details see the following table

Table 14. **Daily requirement of Niacin or nicotinic acid**

Group	Particulars	Body weight (kgs)	Niacin (mg/day)
Man	Sedentary work		16
	Moderate work	60	18
	Heavy work		21
Woman	Sedentary work		12
	Moderate work	50	14
	Heavy work		16
	Pregnant woman	50	+2
	Lactating mother		
	0 – 6 months		
	6 – 12 months	50	+3
Infants	0 – 6 months	5.4	710 µg/kg body
	6 – 12 months	8.6	650 µg/kg body
Children	1 - 3 years	12.2	8
	4 – 6 years	19.0	11
	7 – 9 years	26.9	13
Boys	10 – 2 years	35.4	15
Girls	10 – 12 years	31.5	13

Boys	13 – 15 years	47.8	16
Girls	13 – 15 years	46.7	14
Boys	16 – 18 years	57.1	17
Girls	16 – 18 years	49.9	14

Niacin or nicotinic acid may be given in higher dose up to 200 mg. daily in divided doses on occurrence of its deficiency disease.

5. Vitamin B_{12} or Cyanocobalamin

Vitamin B_{12} or cyanocobalamin is essential for hemopoiesis, i.e., development of red blood cells in the red bone marrow, so it is also called as "hematinic principle" or "anti-anemic factor". It is the extrinsic factor (that comes from outside along with the food) which is absorbed from the terminal portion of the ileum and requires a substance present in the gastric juice secreted by the stomach walls, the intrinsic factor (being inside the body), for its absorption.

Sources — Vitamin B_{12} is found in foods of animal origin. It is found in milk, cheese, eggs, fish, liver and meat etc., and is also synthesized by bacteria in the intestine. It is not found in foods of vegetable origin.

Liver is the main storage site of vitamin B_{12}. About 2 mgs. of vitamin B_{12} are stored in the liver, and another 2 mg. elsewhere in the body. These stores are sufficient to tide over any deficiency for one to three years. Because of these reserves deficiency of vitamin B_{12} rarely occurs.

Functions of vitamin B_{12} (Cyanocobalamin)

(1) Vitamin B_{12} or cyanocobalamin is essential for hemopoiesis, i.e., the formation of mature red blood cells in the red bone marrow, so it is called 'hematinic principle' or 'anti-anemic factor'.

(2) It is required for the formation of DNA

(3) It is essential for the formation of fatty substance myelin protecting the nervous tissues.

Daily requirement of Vitamin B_{12} recommended by ICMR (1981)

(a) Normal adults	1 mcg./day
(b) Pregnancy	1.5 mcg./day
(c) Lactation	1.5 mcg./day
(d) Infants and children	0.2 mcg./day

Deficiency — Deficiency of vitamin B_{12} takes at least 3 years to appear as there are large stores of vitamin B_{12} in the liver. Deficiency occurs because —

1. Diet may be poor or pure vegetarian. It occurs mostly in strict vegetarians who do not even drink milk.
2. There may be deficiency of intrinsic factor due to gastric atrophy.
3. There may be disease of the terminal ileum reducing or eliminating the site of absorption of vitamin B_{12}, e.g., Crohn's disease.

Deficiency of vitamin B_{12} causes pernicious anemia, subacute combined degeneration of the spinal cord, hyperglycemia and anorexia.

Uses — Vitamin B_{12} is used in the treatment of pernicious anemia, subacute combined degeneration of the spinal cord and for the formation of red blood cells in the red bone marrow.

6. Folic Acid

Folic acid is one of the most important vitamins essential for the human being. It is also known and folacin.

Folic acid occurs in food in two forms : The free folates and bound folates. The total folates represent both the groups. Free folate is rapidly absorbed, primarily from the proximal part of the small intestine. The availability of bound folate is uncertain. It is heat labile, i.e., it is destroyed on heating.

Sources — Folic acid is present in a wide variety of foods. Fresh green leafy vegetables, fruits and liver are rich sources of folic acid. Milk, egg and meat are poor sources of folic acid. Cereals are also poor in folic acid content. Pulses contain folic acid more than the cereals.

***Table 15*. Dietary sources of folic acid**

Food	mcg./100 gms.
Green leafy vegetables	30
Soyabean	30
Peas	24
Apple	6
Milk	1.5
Groundnut	16
Egg	10
Liver	150
Fish	15
Meat	14

Functions of Folic Acid

(1) Folic acid is essential for the erythropoiesis or formation of red blood cells.

(2) Folic acid plays a role in the synthesis of nucleic acid including the DNA (which constitute the chromosome)

(3) It is essential for normal functioning of the brain.

Daily requirement of folic acid — Daily requirement of folic acid is greatest during pregnancy. During pregnancy it increases the birth weight of infants and decreases the incidence of low birth weight babies.

Table 16. **Daily requirement of folic acid**

Group	Particulars	Body weight in kgs.	Folic acid mcg./day
Man	Sedentary work		
	Moderate work	60	100
	Heavy work		
Woman	Sedentary work		
	Moderate work	50	100
	Heavy work		
	Pregnant woman	50	400
	Lactating Mother		
	0 -6 months		
	6 -12 months	50	150
Infants	0 -6 months	5.4	
	6 -12 months	8.6	25
Children	1 -3 years	12.2	30
	4 - 6 years	19.0	40
	7 - 9 years	26.9	60
Boys	10 -12 years	35.4	
Girls	10 -12 years	31.5	70
Boys	13 -15 years	47.8	
Girls	13 -15 years	46.7	100
Boys	16 -18 years	57.1	
Girls	16 -18 years	49.9	100

Deficiency — Body store of folic acid is 5 to 10 mg. only so its deficiency may develop quickly. It is heat labile, so over cooking of the food destroys it. Deficiency may occur simply from a poor diet, and is usually found in pregnancy and lactation where its requirements are increased. Folic acid deficiency may occur in alcoholics also.

7. Pantothenic Acid

Pantothenic acid is related to the function of adrenal cortex. It plays a role in the biosynthesis of corticosteroids. It is heat labile and is destroyed on cooking the food. It is decomposed by alkali. Human blood normally contains 18 to 35 mg. of pantothenic acid per 100 mls of blood, mostly present in the cells as co-enzyme. Deficiency of pantothenic acid in man is rare due to its availability in all the food-stuffs.

Sources — Pantothenic acid is found in fresh vegetables, fruits, wheat flour, yeast, milk, egg-yolk, liver and meat etc., and commercially available as calcium pantothenate.

Functions of Pantothenic Acid

(1) It is necessary for the metabolic processes (particularly for the carbohydrate metabolism).

(2) It helps in the production of corticosteroid hormones from the adrenal cortex

(3) It helps in the synthesis of acetylcholine.

(4) It is important for growth.

***Table 17.* Daily requirement of pantothenic acid**

	mg./day
Infants	1.5 to 2.5
Children	5 to 8
Adolescents	5 to 9
Adults	10
Pregnant and Lactating women	5 to 10

Deficiency of pantothenic acid is rare as it is found in all the common foods.

8. Choline

Choline is a component of phospholipids which are essential constituents of the cells in the body, so all the living cells in the body contain choline. It is a lipotropic factor and plays a role in the transport of fat from the liver.

Sources — Choline is found in vegetables, legumes, fruits, cereals, milk, yeast, egg-yolk and meat etc.

Functions of Choline

(1) Choline is lipotropic factor and plays a role in the transport of fat from the liver.

(2) It helps in the removal of adipose tissues.

(3) Choline enhances the oxidation of fatty acids and cholesterol in the blood and so prevents the accumulation of fat and cholesterol in the blood.

(4) It helps in the synthesis of the neurotransmitter acetylcholine and so it is essential for the transfer of nerve impulses.

Daily requirement — Daily requirement of choline is not known. However, 10 mg. of choline per day may be taken depending upon the intake of unsaturated fats and alcohol.

Deficiency — Deficiency of choline causes enlargement of the liver due to fatty degeneration. Fatty liver and alcoholic cirrhosis of liver improve with choline.

9. Inositol

Inositol in chemical structure is an alcohol and related to the glucose, i.e., a monosaccharide. It is a lipotropic factor and present in the phospholipids of the plasma lipoproteins and cell membrane. Inositol associated with choline is found in the liver, kidney, heart muscle, in the brain and eyes. Certain amount of it is lost during food processing. Its deficiency in man is rare.

Sources — Inositol is found in green leaves, orange, lemon, wheat germ, yeast and lecithin etc.

Functions of Inositol

(1) Inositol plays a role in the transport of fat from the liver and thereby prevents the accumulation of fat in the liver. Hence it is often used as a medicine for improving the function of liver cells and/or for the correction of fatty change in the liver. It is available as one of the ingredients of multivitamin preparations.

(2) It has a sedative effect so it causes relief in insomnia and anxiety.

Daily requirement — 10 mg.

Deficiency — Deficiency of inositol causes alopecia or loss of hair or falling of hair and so inositol is used in the treatment of alopecia. Deficiency of inositol also causes stunted growth.

10. Biotin

Biotin was called previously as vitamin 'H'. It was also called anti-egg white injury factor (avidin). The active principle present in egg-white and responsible for producing 'egg white injury' is a protein called avidin. It is required by the body in very small quantities, i.e.,1 mcg. daily and since it is found in all common foods, its deficiency rarely occurs. Biotin is very stable to heat, light and acids, Use of antibiotics destroys biotin. Raw egg-white prevents its absorption. Intestinal bacteria are able to synthesize some biotin.

Sources of biotin — It in found in all common foods, so its deficiency in man is rare. Cereals, dairy products and meat etc. are poor sources, while pulses, nuts and vegetables like cauliflower etc., are rich sources.

Functions of Biotin

(1) Biotin helps to maintain the skin and nervous system in healthy condition.

(2) Biotin takes important part in the metabolism and is essential for the synthesis of tatty acids in the body.

(3) It assists in the synthesis of hemoglobin.

(4) It also assists in the manufacture of glycogen which is a form of storing energy in the liver.

Daily requirement of biotin — 50 to 60 mcg. for adults, 20 to 40 mcg. for children and 10 to 15 mcg. for infants.

Deficiency — Cow's milk contains approximately 50 mcg. biotin per litre while human milk contains only 4 mcg. per litre. Deficiency of biotin occurs in infants fed on breast milk and suffering from diarrhea.

The substance known as avidin in raw egg-white is a glycoprotein that binds biotin and thereby prevents its absorption from the digestive tract and hence deficiency of biotin occurs in an adult who consumed daily 4 to 12 raw eggs and 1 to 4 quarts of wine.

11. Para - aminobenzoic acid (PABA)

Para-aminobenzoic acid is essential for the synthesis of folic acid in the body. The main function of para-aminobenzoic acid is in the prevention and correction of harmful effects of ultraviolet rays of the sun. It prevents premature greying of hairs. It is often used as oral tablets and liquid preparations along with other B-Complex vitamins. It is used locally in the treatment of sunburn, dark patches on the skin due to excessive pigmentation and possible skin cancer, alone or in combination with some other medicines, in the form of lotions or creams. Most of the sun-screen lotions now-a-days contain para-aminobenzoic acid as an important ingredient for the protection against the harmful effects of ultraviolet rays of the sun. As such it is considered as an important sun protection factor (SPF).

Vitamin C or Ascorbic Acid

Vitamin C is also known as 'anti-scorbutic vitamin' because its deficiency causes scurvy and it acts against scurvy. Vitamin C is a water-soluble vitamin and being water-soluble it cannot be stored in the body. It is heat-labile and is the most sensitive of all the vitamins to heat, i.e., it is readily destroyed on heating. Smoking destroys vitamin C, each cigarette smoked uses up to 25 mg. of vitamin C, i.e., equivalent to an orange. It is comparatively stable in acid medium. Any kind of stress, i.e., mental stress and physical stress such as extremes of temperatures, fatigue or illness also depletes vitamin C. The body of a normal adult contains about 5 gms of vitamin C.

Sources — Vitamin C is found in amla, lemon or lime juice, tomatoes, green leafy vegetables as spinach, cabbage, amaranth etc., root vegetables as radish and turnip etc., and tubers as potatoes and onion etc. Fruits as guava, orange, mango ripe, papaya ripe, apple and pine apple also contain vitamin C. Germinating pulses, as chana dal contains vitamin C. Milk, fish and meat contain very small amounts of vitamin C, though mother's milk contains a good amount of vitamin C. Amla or the Indian goose berry is one of the richest sources of vitamin C both in the fresh as well as in the dry condition, guava comes next.

***Table 18.* Dietary sources of vitamin C (mgs./100 gms of food)**

	Food	mgs./100 gms.
Fruits		
	Amla	700
	Guava	300
	Lime juice	63
	Orange	68
	Mango, ripe	24
	Apple	2-8
	Pine apple	63
	Papaya ripe	46
	Cashew fruit	60
Vegetables		
	Cabbage	124
	Amaranth (Cholai)	99
	Spinach	28
	Cauliflower	56
	Tomatoes	27
	Radish	15
	Potatoes	17
	Brinjal	12
	Capsicum	180
	Onion	11
Germinating pulses		
	Chana dal	16

Animal foods — Milk, fish, and meat etc. contain very small amounts of vitamin C.

Functions of Vitamin C or Ascorbic Acid

(1) Vitamin C is essential for the formation of collagen (a strong, fibrous insoluble protein present in the connective tissues) which provides a supporting matrix (basic substance) for the blood vessels, connective tissues, bones and cartilages. That explains why in vitamin C deficiency this support fails with the result that local hemorrhages occur and the bones are fractured easily.

(2) It increases the resistance of the body to fight with the infection and hence protects the body from common cold, cough, pneumonia and tuberculosis etc.

(3) It helps in wound healing.

(4) Vitamin C has a significant role in carbohydrate metabolism.

(5) It has an important role in the absorption and metabolism of iron.

(6) It is an antioxidant and so prevents or delays ageing process.

(7) It prevents atherosclerosis.

(8) It prevents the vulnerability to coronary heart disease.

(9) Vitamin C prevents the occurrence of cancerous changes in the tissue cells.

(10) It is necessary for the maturity of RBC and WBC.

Daily requirement— Daily requirement of vitamin C is 40 mgs./day for an adult, and pregnant and lactating women require 80 mgs./day, infants 25 mgs./day and older children require the same as that of ordinary adults, i.e., 40 mgs./day. In diarrhea and achlorhydria etc., its absorption is decreased. In such cases vitamin C requirement is 80 mgs./day. The requirement is to be supplied daily, if excess is ingested it is simply excreted in the urine.

Deficiency of vitamin C causes scurvy

Note—For conditions caused by deficiency and excess of water-soluble vitamins B Complex and C, see chapter "Nutritional disorders".

MINERALS

Minerals are inorganic, homogenous solid substances obtained from the earth. They are also found in the human body and are taken with the food in the form of mineral salts in much smaller quantities than the macronutrients or energy-producing food factors and belong to the group of 'micronutrients' along with the vitamins. These are required for growth, repair and regulation of all the vital functions of the body.

These essential minerals are divided into two groups.

(A) Major minerals—These are required in large quantities, as of 100 mgs. or more per day in our diet. There are eight major minerals.

1. Calcium (Ca)
2. Phosphorus (P)
3. Sodium (Na)
4. Chlorine (Cl)
5. Potassium (K)
6. Magnesium (Mg)
7. Sulphur (S)
8. Strontium (Sr)

(B) Minor minerals or trace elements—These are required in very small quantities, not exceeding a few milligrams per day. The minor minerals or trace elements take part in enzymatic metabolic reactions in the body. However, the exact role and daily requirement of all the essential trace elements are not well understood except those of Iron and Iodine. The minor minerals or trace elements that have some definite roles in human nutrition are eight in number as follows :

1. Iron (Fe)
2. Iodine (I)
3. Copper (Cu)
4. Fluorine (F)
5. Manganese (Mn)
6. Zinc (Zn)
7. Cobalt (Co)
8. Selenium (Se)

(A) Major Minerals

These are associated with clearly recognizable clinical conditions in man. These are as follows :

1. Calcium (Ca)

Calcium is a silver white metallic element of which Ca is the symbol. It is a major mineral element of the body and it constitutes 1.5 to 2.00 percent of the body weight of an adult. An average adult body contains about 1200 gms. of calcium of which 98% is found in the bones as calcium phosphate and remaining in the soft tissues. Normal blood calcium level is 9 to 11 mgs. per 100 mls. of blood. When blood calcium level is below normal, the condition is called hypocalcemia, when it is above normal, the condition is called hypercalcemia.

Sources — 1—Milk : One litre of cow's milk provides about 1200mgs. of calcium and human milk about 300 mgs. 2—Milk products as cheese, curd, skimmed milk and butter etc. 3—Eggs. 4—Fish, 5—Vegetables: Green leafy vegetables as spinach and amaranth etc., and other vegetables as radish, carrots, beet root, lady's finger and onion etc. 6—Cereals. 7—Millets. 8—Pulses. 9—Almond. 10.—Drinking water provides up to 200 mgs. of calcium per day.

Functions of Calcium

(1) Calcium is necessary for the formation and hardness of bones and teeth.

(2) It is of great importance in blood coagulation.

(3) It plays a role in muscle contraction and relaxation and maintains its activity.

(4) It controls cardiac action.

(5) It regulates the capillary permeability.

(6) It keeps the cell membranes intact.

(7) It regulates the formation and breakdown of acetylcholine, the substance necessary for the transmission of impulses from one nerve fibre to the other and hence maintains the normal state of neuro-muscular excitability.

(8) It assists in the absorption of vitamin B_{12} through the intestinal wall.

(9) Fat-splitting pancreatic enzyme is activated by calcium.

Salts of Calcium of Medical Importance

Calcium carbonate—A fine, white, tasteless and odorless powder found in the chalk and is used as an antacid.

Calcium chloride — It has saline taste and is used to raise the calcium content of the blood in case of hypocalcemia, and as an antidote in magnesium poisoning.

Calcium gluconate—A granular white powder without odor and taste of which the actions are the same as that of calcium chloride.

Calcium lactate — It is a white odorless and tasteless powder used orally or parenterally as an alternative to calcium gluconate. It is used in chronic plumbism.

Calcium oxalate — It is present in the urine in crystalline form and is a constituent of some renal calculi.

Calcium pantothenate — It is one of the factors of vitamin B complex which is generally used for burning feet syndrome.

Calcium phosphate — It is a white powder which is used as an antacid in the treatment of hyperacidity.

Calcium sulfate — A white powder that absorbs water and is used in making plaster of paris.

Daily requirement — Requirement of calcium for an adult of average body is 400 mgs, pregnant and lactating women 1 to 1.5 gm., Infants 500 mg., children of 1 to 9 years 400 mg., boys and girls of 10 to 15 years of age 600 mg. and 16-18 years 500 mg. per day. Pregnant and lactating women require more calcium because during pregnancy and infancy bones of the infants are formed.

Deficiency of calcium causes osteoporosis in adults, rickets in children and osteomalacia in women, especially during pregnancy. Excess of calcium causes hypertension, overgrowth of the bones and it is excreted in the urine as calcium phosphate which is deposited on the earth like white lime, at the end of urination.

2. Phosphorus (P)

Phosphorus is a nonmetallic chemical element of which P is the symbol. It is essential for the formation and development of bones and teeth and is found in them as calcium phosphate and it is found as sodium phosphate and potassium phosphate in all living cells and body fluids.

Normal serum level of phosphorus is 2.5 to 4.5 mgs. per 100 mls. in adult and 4.0 to 5.0 mgs./100 mls in children. In rickets, phosphorus level is lower than 3 mgs./100 mls. Serum concentration of phosphorus and calcium have reciprocal relationship, i.e., if one increases, the other decreases. In hyperphosphatemia, the patient suffers from hypocalcemia, and vice-versa. The average adult body contains 600-900 gms. of phosphorus in various forms. 70% to 80% of phosphorus is found as calcium phosphate in the bones and teeth.

Phosphorus in elemental form is extremely poisonous, it causes intense inflammation. Vitamin D is essential for the absorption and metabolism of phosphorus . Excess of phosphorus is excreted by the kidneys in the urine and by intestines in the feces, about 60% being excreted in the urine as phosphates.

Sources — Fishes are the richest source of phosphorus. In addition to that it is found in vegetables as spinach, cabbage, radish, carrots, soyabean and potatoes etc., fruits as apple etc., cereals (wheat, rice and maize), nuts as groundnuts and almond etc., and animal foods as milk. cheese, egg-yolk and meat etc.

Functions of Phosphorus

(1) Phosphorus is necessary for the formation and hardness of bones and teeth in combination with calcium and vitamin D.

(2) It is essential for all metabolisms, especially for carbohydrate metabolism.

(3) It has a special importance in making the health of the nervous system and it makes the brain stronger.

(4) It is an essential part of the body cells and is found in each cell of the body.

(5) It is an essential constituent of cell nucleic acids as DNA or RNA.

Daily requirement — Phosphorus present in the cereals are available to a lesser extent as it is present in the combination with phytin as phytic acid, than that present in milk, eggs, fish and meat. So phosphorus requirement of persons consuming mainly cereal based diets, will be greater than those consuming large quantities of milk, eggs, fish and meat. Calcium (Ca) and Phosphorus (P) Ratio (Ca:P) should be 1:1 for an adult, 1:1.5 for infants and children in the age group of 1 to 3 years because of the increased demand for the very rapid growth of the bones. Adult men and women require 400 mg. of both calcium and phosphorus. Pregnant and lactating women should be provided 1000 mg. (1 Gm) of calcium and phosphorus both. Infants and children upto 3 years of age require calcium 500 mg. and phosphorus 750 mg. per day. Older children, 3 to 9 years of age require 400 mg. of both calcium and phosphorus, boys and girls in the age group of 10-15 years require 600 mg. of both and 16 to 18 years require 500 mg. calcium and phosphorus both.

Deficiency — Phosphorus is widely distributed in all food-stuffs. Phosphorus present in milk and animal foods is available to a greater extent than that present in cereals and pulses. A person absorbs most of the ingested phosphorus. So usually deficiency of phosphorus does not occur, if deficiency of phosphorus occurs, it occurs with that of calcium. Phosphorus deficiency may occur from prolonged and excessive intake of aluminium hydroxide, an antacid used in hyperacidity. Deficiency of phosphorus in the diet may also occur on refining and processing the foods.

Abnormally decreased amount of phosphorus in the blood (2 mg./100 mls or less) is called hypophosphatemia which is associated with hypercalcemia. Abnormally increased amount of phosphorus in the blood is called hyperphosphatemia which is associated with hypocalcemia.

Calcium (Ca) and Phosphorus (P)

Calcium (Ca) and phosphorus are two very important minerals required for the human body. These two major minerals are considered together because their requirements, intestinal absorption and metabolism are interlinked. Both are under control of the parathyroid hormone parathormone and vitamin D. while calcium is directly controlled, phosphorus is indirectly controlled.

3. Sodium (Na)

Sodium is a soft metallic element of which Na is the symbol. A normal human adult body contains about 100 gms. of sodium ion (Na^+) which is the chief constituent of the extracellular fluids (plasma, tissue fluid and lymph) in the body. It is readily oxidized in the air or water.

Sodium is lost from the body through urine and sweat. Normally, the sodium excreted equals the quantity of sodium ingested. Sodium is ingested as it occurs in food or as common salt added to foods during cooking to increase the palatability of food. Ingested sodium is rapidly absorbed from the gastrointestinal tract, distributed throughout the extracellular fluid and finally excreted in the urine. If a person consumes excess of sodium, it is excreted in the urine and is not stored in the body.

Salts of sodium are found in the body and are extensively used in medicine. Its most important salts used in medicine are as follows—

Sodium acetate — It is used to alkalize the urine and is used in kidney dialysis solutions. It is also used as expectorant and diuretic.

Sodium bicarbonate ($NaHCO_3$) — It is a white odorless powder, used as an antacid orally in hyperacidity and intravenously in acidosis and to alkalize the urine. It is also used in solution form externally for washing the mouth, nose and vagina, and as a dressing for minor burns. It is also used as baking powder, so it is also known as baking soda.

Sodium carbonate (Na_2CO_3) — It is a white crystalline powder which is used as a lotion or alkaline bath in the treatment of skin diseases, so it is also known as washing soda.

Sodium chloride (NaCl) — Sodium (Na) and chlorine (Cl) are two important elemental substances essential for the human life and are found in all body fluids. These two are generally present in nature as the sodium chloride salt in which form they are taken with the diet. It is white crystalline compound and is the chief constituent of blood and other body fluids. It is the common salt which is added to the food during cooking and added to food to make it tasty.

Sources of Sodium Chloride

(1) Sodium chloride or common salt is formed from sea water and is available in the market.

(2) It is found naturally in many foods as vegetables like spinach, cauliflower, turnip, onion and methi etc., animal foods as eggs,

fishes and meat etc., and kismis. Foods of animal source are richer in sodium chloride.

Functions of Sodium Chloride or Common Salt

(1) The sodium and chlorine ions are important in maintaining the proper electrolyte balance in body fluids .

(2) Sodium chloride maintains the pH of blood within normal limits or it regulates acid-base balance.

(3) Sodium chloride is used in the preparation of normal saline solution (.9% aqueous solution) which is isotonic and physiological solution, and is used intravenously or by transfusion in the treatment of dehydration.

(4) Common salt or sodium chloride makes the food tasty.

(5) It helps in maintaining the activity of all the organs.

(6) It is also used as emetic.

(7) It removes the constipation.

(8) It is concerned with the conduction of nerve impulses.

(9) It regulates the osmotic pressure of plasma and tissue fluids.

(10) It is concerned with muscular contraction.

(11) It controls the contraction of heart muscle and origination, conduction and maintenance of heart beat.

(12) It helps in absorption of monosaccharides and amino acids from the small intestine.

Daily requirement—Daily requirement of common salt depends upon climate, occupation and physical activity. People working in hot climate as in factories where one has to do work before furnace etc., and the people doing hard labor and working in mines etc., require more common salt. A normal healthy adult requires 10-15 gms. salt per day.

Deficiency — Deficiency of salt causes dehydration, vomiting, and muscular cramps in the hands and legs. Blood pressure is lowered and coma occurs in serious condition.

Excess — In excess of common salt B.P. is raised and edema occurs first on the feet and ankle and then on the whole body.

Restriction of common salt — Salt is restricted in the diet in the following conditions —

- Congestive heart failure in which restriction of salt in the diet causes reduction of edema.
- Renal disease — Restriction of salt acts by reducing the edema.
- Salt is restricted in any other condition where there is fluid retention in the body with edema.
- Cirrhosis liver — Salt restriction prevents accumulation of fluid in abdomen.
- Toxemia of pregnancy — To prevent fluid retention.
- High blood pressure.

Strictly low salt diet should contain 200-300 mgs. sodium chloride and the patient to be on a low salt diet should avoid all salted and canned vegetables, prickles,salted cheese, butter, salted nuts, canned fishes and meat etc.

Moderately low salt diet contains 400-500 mgs. of sodium chloride.

Sodium citrate — It is a white granular powder which is used as an anticoagulant for blood.

Sodium fluoride (NaF) — It is a white crystalline powder which is added to drinking water and used as a 2% solution for application on the teeth for prevention of dental caries.

Sodium iodide (NaI) — It is a colourless crystalline solid that is used as an expectorant.

Sodium lactate — It is a systemic and urinary alkalizer.

Sodium nitrite ($NaNO_2$)—It is an antihypertensive and powerful vasodilator so it is generally used in angina pectoris to lower the blood pressure and dilate the coronary artery.

Sodium salicylate — It is an analgesic, antipyretic and antirheumatic.

4. Chlorine (Cl)

Chlorine is a greenish, highly irritating, very poisonous gaseous element. It is destructive to the mucous membrane of the respiratory passages and excessive inhalation may cause death. It is an active bleaching agent and germicide owing to its oxidizing property. It is used extensively to disinfect the water supplies and treat sewage.

Contaminated water is filtered and chlorine solution is added to disinfect it. Chlorine solution is prepared from bleaching powder. To prepare chlorine solution 200 gms. of bleaching powder, which provides 25% of chlorine, is mixed with one litre of water and thus 5% chlorine solution is prepared. To disinfect the water chlorine solution is mixed with it at the rate of one drop per litre of water, which contains about 2.5 mg. chlorine. Chlorine solution is placed in closed vessel in dark, cold and dry place.

Chlorine tablets are also available in the market. One litre of water is readily disinfected when one tablet of chlorine is mixed with it.

Chlorine (Cl) is generally present in nature with the sodium (Na) as sodium chloride salt in which form both are taken with the food or otherwise. Because sodium and chloride have almost equal and opposite but very significant roles as electrolytes in the body fluids, the two are being considered together. Sodium constitutes the most important cation and chloride constitutes the most important anion of the body fluids. These are most abundantly present in the extracellular body fluids including the blood. Water and electrolyte balance in the body is very important to maintain the health. Electrolyte balance in the blood maintains the pH (chemical reaction) of the blood at 7.4. There are many causes which create disturbances in acid-base balance (pH) of the blood which are manifested as the clinical features of many diseases.

Sodium is the main 'cation' of the extracellular body fluids including the blood. Chloride is the main 'anion' of extracellular fluids and the blood. Sodium chloride is present in all foods of both vegetable and animal source though the foods of animal source are usually richer. That is why the diet should be constituted exclusively of fresh vegetables when low-salt diet is needed. Normal mixed diet contains varying amount of salt and the people of tropical countries in general consume more salt than those in temperate regions. And the vegetarians consume less amount of salt than the non-vegetarians. The salt naturally present in the mixed daily diet is approximately 3 gms. Recommended daily intake of salt in cold climate is 4.5 gms. For the tropical countries (because of the significant loss in sweating) the recommended daily intake of salt is 5 to 10 gms. Habitual high intake of salt causes hypertension (high blood pressure). It is to be restricted in hypertension and any condition in which there is fluid retention in the body with edema. However, excessive sweating as a result of exposure to the heat of sun or working near the furnace of factories will result in considerable loss of water and sodium chloride. In such cases, heavy amount of water with an appropriate amount of common salt is to be taken.

***Table 19*. Daily requirement of sodium chloride (common salt) for tropical countries (gms. per day)**

Adults	Light work	10-15 gms.
	Hard work	15-20 gms.
	Very hard work	25-30 gms.
Children and Adolescents		
Boys and girls		10-25 gms.
Women	Pregnancy first half	10 gms.
	Pregnancy second half	5 gms.
	Lactation	15 gms.

5. Potassium (K)

Potassium is a mineral element found in combination with other elements in the body and constitutes .35% of body weight. The adult human body contains about 250 grams of potassium. Its symbol is K. The normal serum potassium level is 3.5 to 5 mEq/L. Potassium in the form of a salt potassium chloride (KCl) is found mostly (90%) in the intracellular fluid, which is necessary for many chemical reactions occurring in the cells. Only a small amount of potassium is present in extracellular fluid. Large blood cells contain a large amount of potassium ion.

Sources — Potassium is found in almost all the food-stuffs, especially in foods containing protein, so usually its deficiency does not occur. Excellent sources of potassium are cereals, pulses, dried peas and beans, fresh vegetables as tomatoes, carrot, beetroot, spinach, coriander leaves and lemon etc., fresh or dried fruits as amla, orange, guava, banana, apple and papaya etc., nuts, molasses and animal foods as milk, fresh fish and poultry etc.

Table 20. **Potassium content of foods (mgs./100 gms.)**

Food	mgs./100 gms.
Wheat	315
Maize	290
Ragi	408
Bajra	402
Arhar ki dal (red gram dal)	1104
Moong (Green gram)	843
Moong ki dal (Green gram dal)	1150
Urad (Black gram)	650
Urad ki dal (Black gram dal)	800
Dried peas	1000
Dried beans	1000

Tomatoes	146
Carrot	482
Beet root	300
Spinach	570
Coriander leaves	453
Lemon	270
Amla	225
Orange	150
Guava	91
Banana	88
Apple	75
Papaya	69

Functions of Potassium

(1) Potassium regulates the pH (acid-base balance) of the cell contents.

(2) It regulates the osmotic pressure of the cell contents.

(3) It plays an important role in the conduction of nerve impulses.

(4) It is essential for normal excitability of the muscles, especially cardiac muscle.

(5) It is essential for growth and building of tissues.

(6) It is essential for synthesis of glycogen.

Most Important Salts of Potassium Used in Medicine

1. Potassium alum — It is aluminum potassium sulphate which is strongly astringent and used locally to check the bleeding.

2. Potassium bicarbonate ($KHCO_3$) — White crystals or powder, used to neutralize acid of the stomach and to treat acid-base imbalance.

3. Potassium bromide (KBr) — White crystals or powder, used as a sedative.

4. Potassium carbonate (K_2CO_3) — Potash. A white crystalline powder used in pharmaceutical and chemical preparations.

5. Potassium chloride (KCl) — It is used in the treatment of potassium deficiencies and digitalis intoxication.

6. Potassium citrate — It is used as an alkalizer.

7. Potassium hydroxide (KOH) — Caustic potash. It is a grey-white compound used in the preparation of soap and as a chemical reagent.

8. Potassium iodide (KI) — It is a colorless or white crystals having a faint odor of iodine, used as an expectorant.

9. Potassium permanganate ($KMnO_4$) — Crystals of dark purple color used locally to check the bleeding and as an antiseptic.

10. Potassium tartrate — A mild purgative and diuretic.

Daily requirement — A normal healthy adult requires 2 to 5 gms. of potassium per day and because it is found in almost all the food-stuffs, especially in those which contain protein, its deficiency usually does not occur. Balanced mixed diet adequately fulfils the requirement.

Deficiency — Deficient intake of potassium causes hypokalemia or the lowered blood potassium level is called hypokalemia.

Excess — Excessive intake of potassium causes hyperkalemia or the higher blood potassium level is called hyperkalemia.

6. Magnesium (Mg)

Magnesium is a white essential mineral which is a constituent of bones and is present in all the living cells of the body, especially in bones and teeth. It is found in bones and teeth in combination with phosphate. It is also found in extracellular fluid. Human body contains about 25 gms. of magnesium of which about half is found in the skeleton and about 1/5 th in the soft tissues and the rest in teeth etc. Magnesium present in the blood is 2 to 3 mgs./100 mls of blood serum or 1.56 mg./ 100 mls. whole blood. Mg is the symbol of magnesium.

Sources — Magnesium is found in cereals, green vegetables, fruits and animal foods as milk, cheese and eggs etc. Banana is the richest source of magnesium.

Functions of Magnesium

(1) Magnesium is essential for all the living cells.

(2) Magnesium along with calcium, sodium and potassium is needed for the transmission of nerve impulses and the consequent muscle contraction.

(3) It is essential for the normal metabolism of calcium and potassium.

(4) It is essential for the proper functioning, especially of the brain, spinal cord and all the nerves.

(5) It is involved in protein synthesis.

Most Important Salts of Magnesium Used in Medicine

1. Magnesium carbonate ($MgCO_3$) — A white, odorless powder used orally in hyperacidity to neutralize the acid in the stomach.

2. Magnesium chloride ($MgCl_2$) — It is used in the treatment of electrolyte disturbances and in dialysis solutions.

3. Magnesium gluconate — It is a medicine used to replace magnesium in the body.

4. Magnesium hydroxide [$Mg(OH)_2$] — It is a white powder which is called milk of magnesia in aqueous suspension. It is used as a laxative and as an antacid.

5. Magnesium oxide (MgO) — Light magnesia. It is used as a laxative, an antacid and in the treatment of nervous disorders and convulsions.

6. Magnesium salicylate — It is an antipyretic and analgesic.

7. Magnesium sulfate ($MgSO_4$) — Epsom salt. It is in the form of small colorless crystals, which is used as a purgative, an anticonvulsant and topically as an anti-inflammatory agent. It is used intravenously in the management of pregnancy - induced hypertension and to stop preterm labor.

Daily requirement — A normal adult requires 200 to 300 mg. of magnesium per day. Pregnant and lactating women require half of the calcium requirement i.e., 500 mg. to 750 mg. of magnesium per day. Older children require 150-200 mgs./day and infants and pre-school children 100-150 mgs./day.

Deficiency — Usually the deficiency of magnesium does not occur, as it is found in almost all the food-stuffs. Deficiency of magnesium occurs in the patients of chronic diarrhea, cirrhosis of liver, in alcoholics, in the diseases which impair its absorption from the intestine and in toxemia of pregnancy. The condition of deficiency of magnesium in the body, i.e., low serum magnesium level is called hypomagnesemia.

Excess — The condition of high serum magnesium level is called hypermagnesemia which may occur due to intake of magnesium in excess or inability of the kidneys to excrete magnesium in renal insufficiency. Hypermagnesemia rarely occurs due to excessive use of magnesium by parenteral injection in eclampsia of pregnancy.

(B) Minor Minerals or Trace Elements

1. Iron (Fe)

Fe is the chemical symbol of Iron. Iron is of great importance in human nutrition. It constitutes about 0.004% of body weight, i.e., 3 to 5 gms. Iron store in adult male is about 50 mg/kg. body weight and that in the adult female is 32 to 42 mg/kg. body weight. In the newborn iron store is 80 mg./kg. body weight. 60-70% of iron is present in the hemoglobin molecule of the red blood cells (Hb iron) which is known as circulating iron. The hemoglobin in the red blood cells is formed in the bone marrow, which gives red color to the blood. Hemoglobin consists of an iron-containing portion heme and a portion of simple protein globulin. It carries oxygen from the lungs to the tissues. The average Hb level is 14-18 gm./100 ml. of blood in men and 12-16 gm./100 ml of blood in women. Each gram of hemoglobin contains about 3.34 mg. of iron. About 10% of iron is found in the myoglobin (the oxygen-carrying and storage, protein present in the muscular tissues, resembling blood hemoglobin in function) of muscles and the rest of the iron is stored in the liver, spleen and bone marrow.

Also, iron is an important constituent of intracellular enzymes like cytochrome oxidase. The hemoglobin of the circulating blood transports oxygen from the lungs to the individual cells of the body. The iron-containing intracellular enzyme cytochrome oxidase helps in cellular utilization of oxygen.

Sources — There are two forms of iron—hem iron (portion of iron which is contained in the hemoglobin) and non-hem iron (portion of iron which is not present in the hemoglobin). Hem-iron is better absorbed than non-hem iron. Foods rich in hem-iron are animal foods as egg-yolk, fish, poultry, meat and liver etc. Sources of non-hem iron are vegetable foods, e.g., cereals, green leafy vegetables as spinach, legumes, oilseeds, nuts, dried fruits and fruits like apple etc. The bioavailability of non-hem iron is poor. Animal foods are the important sources of readily available iron (hem-iron) and they also promote the absorption of non-hem iron of the vegetable origin taken at the same time. Average normal mixed diet is supposed to contain 10 to 15 mgs. of iron. Iron is also derived from cooking in iron utensils.

Functions of Iron

Iron is essential for the following functions in the body

(1) Iron is necessary for the formation of hemoglobin in the red blood cells.

(2) It is essential for the development and function of the brain.

(3) It is necessary for muscular activity.

(4) It regulates the body temperature.

(5) It is essential for binding oxygen to the hemoglobin of the red blood cells. Oxygen combining with hemoglobin spreads throughout the body.

(6) It helps in antibody production and detoxification of drugs in the liver.

(7) It catalyzes the conversion of beta-carotene, the precursor of vitamin A, to vitamin A.

Most Important Salts of Iron Used in Medicine

1. Ferric chloride ($FeCl_3$) — It is used in tincture form as an astringent.

2. Ferric sulfate — It is an astringent and is used topically to stop the bleeding.

3. Ferrous fumerate ($C_4H_2FeO_4$) — It is a hematinic used in the treatment of anemias.

4. Ferrous gluconate ($C_{12}H_{22}FeO_{14}$) — It is an iron preparation occurring as a yellowish powder or granules. It is used as a hematinic.

5. Ferrous sulfate ($FeSo_4$) — It occurs as a pale, bluish-green crystals and is taken orally as a hematinic in the treatment of anemias.

6. Ferrous citrate — It is a hematinic.

7. Ferrous lactate — It is a hematinic.

Daily requirement — Generally the iron requirements are greater when there are expansions of the tissues and red blood cell mass, as during childhood, adolescence, pregnancy and lactation. About 10% of the iron is excreted form the body and about 20% loss of iron occurs in women who menstruates and an equal amount of iron is absorbed from the intestine, taken with food. The pregnant woman, despite of saving the menstrual loss, has more demand for iron in comparison to the non-pregnant woman, due to the needs of the growing fetus in the uterus, iron content in the placenta as well as the expansion of the maternal tissues including the red cell mass. During lactation, the requirement of iron is increased due to the iron lost in the milk, though there is saving of menstrual blood. So her basal requirement for iron is that of the non-pregnant adult woman.

***Table 21.* Daily requirement of iron**

Group	Particulars	Body weight (Kg)	Iron mg./day
Man	Sedentary work		
	Moderate work	60	28
	Heavy work		
Woman	Sedentary work		
	Moderate work	50	30
	Heavy work		
	Pregnant woman	50	38
	Lactating woman	50	30
Children	1 – 3 years	12.2	12
	4 – 6 years	19.0	18
	7 – 9 years	26.9	26
Boys	10 – 12 years	35.4	34
Girls	10 – 12 years	31.5	19
Boys	13 – 15 years	47.8	41
Girls	13 – 15 years	46.7	28
Boys	16 – 18 years	57.1	50
Girls	16 – 18 years	49.9	30

Iron losses — Iron is lost through 1. Hemorrhage—whenever blood is lost, iron is lost, the cause of which may be physiological, e.g., menstruation and childbirth or pathological as it may occur during pregnancy, ancylostomiasis (hookworm disease), hematemesis (vomiting of blood), melena, bacillary dysentery, piles and peptic ulcer etc. 2 basal losses—such as excretion of iron through the urine, sweat, bile and desquamated surface cells. Iron is also lost by the use of intrauterine devices in the family planning. Total daily loss of iron is about 1 mg., during menstruation in woman 1 mg. of iron is lost more, i.e., the iron loss in about 2 mgs.

Iron deficiency — In deficiency of iron, iron deficiency anemia or hypochromic microcytic anemia develops (size of the red blood cells is less than the normal size with less than the normal amount of hemoglobin inside the red blood cells). It is usually caused by malnutrition.

— Iron deficiency affects the immune system, it diminishes the number of T cells and the production of antibodies.

— Resistance to infection is reduced.

— Work performance is diminished.

— Morbidity and mortality rates are increased.

Causes of Iron Deficiency

(1) Menstrual loss of blood, especially if it is excessive.

(2) Dietary deficiency of iron, e.g., low protein and iron intake.

(3) Poor absorption of dietary iron due to defect in the intestinal mucosa, e.g., malabsorption syndrome. It also occurs due to presence of excess of phytates, phosphates, oxalates and medicinal antacids (which are used in hyperacidity or hyperchlorhydria)

(4) Increased requirements of iron, e.g., in pregnancy, childhood and adolescence.

(5) Intestinal worm infestation.

(6) Withdrawal of iron by the fetus in the uterus, for its immediate and future needs.

(7) Loss of blood during third stage of labor.

Excess of iron — In excessive consumption of iron, the extra iron as a waste product is excreted in the stool which becomes black. It may result in loss of appetite, constipation or even diarrhea. Excessive iron may be deposited in the liver and spleen causing their enlargement. This condition is known as hemochromatosis.

Utilization of iron — Most of the iron absorbed by the intestine is needed by the bone marrow to make hemoglobin and red blood cells. The life of a red blood cell is 120 days. It is then destroyed, the hemoglobin is liberated and stored in the reticuloendothelial system and then the iron is broken down into the bilirubin and iron compounds, the ferritin and hemosiderin. The bilirubin is carried to the liver and excreted into the bile while the iron compounds are stored in the liver and spleen for future use. Thus about 1/20th of the total hemoglobin is replaced daily in the bone marrow. This is known as conservation of iron in the body.

Storage — Iron combines with a protein to form a complex compound knows as ferritin which is chiefly stored in the liver, spleen and bone marrow. An excess of iron which can not be stored as ferritin, is stored in the liver in the form of hemosiderin. Iron stored in this form cannot be utilized by the body.

2. *Iodine (I)*

Chemical symbol of iodine is I. Iodine is an essential mineral belonging to the group of trace elements (micronutrient). A normal adult human body contains about 50 mgs. of iodine, of which 10 to 15 mgs. are found in the thyroid gland, weighing about 25 gms, in the form of thyroglobulin. Blood level of iodine is 8-12 micrograms per 100 mls. of blood.

Sources — The richest sources of iodine are sea foods, e.g., sea fishes, sea salt, vegetables growing near the sea or sea shores. Smaller amounts of iodine is found in other foods, e.g., vegetables, especially onion which is a good source of iodine, cereals, iodized salt, milk, egg-yolk, fish liver oils, meat etc. The areas nearer to the foot hills, e.g., Himalayan regions are poor sources of iodine. Water contains traces of iodine, only 1 to 50 micrograms per litre of water. About 90% of iodine comes from foods eaten, the remainder from drinking water. The iodine content of the soil determines its presence in both water and locally grown foods.

Functions of Iodine

(1) Iodine is essential for the normal growth, physical and mental development of all the humans.

(2) Iodine prevents the formation of goiter by enabling the thyroid gland to function normally.

(3) Iodine is essential for the proper function of the thyroid gland and the formation of its hormones — Thyroxine (T_4) and Tri-iodothyronine (T_3) containing 4 and 3 atoms of iodine respectively, which are required for body's metabolic functions, and also help in maintaining the body temperature. According to the body's requirement thyroid hormones are released in the peripheral blood circulation — primarily as thyroxine (T_4) and partly as tri-iodothyonine (T_3).

Goitrogens — These are chemical substances leading to the development of goiter. They interfere with iodine utilization by the thyroid gland. They may occur in food and water. Vegetables like cabbage, cauliflower, and radish etc., may contain goitrogens. Most important dietary goitrogens are cyanoglycosides and the thiocyanates.

Preparations of Iodine Used in Medicine

1. Iodized salt — It is the common salt fortified with iodine by adding potassium iodide to it in very minute quantity, which is available in the market. In India iodized common salt is used to prevent the development of goiter.

2. Lugol's iodine solution — It is a strong iodine solution used in iodine therapy, consisting of iodine 5 gms., potassium iodide 10 gms. and water to make 100 mls.

3. Radioactive iodine — Its symbol is 131I. It is an isotope of iodine with an atomic weight of 131, used in the diagnosis of thyroid diseases and in the treatment of toxic goiter and carcinoma of the thyroid gland.

4. Tincture of iodine — It is a solution of 2% iodine and 2.4% sodium iodide diluted in 50% ethyl alcohol. It is used as a disinfectant for the skin and as a germicide. It may be used to make the contaminated water safe for drinking by adding only three drops of it to a litre of water.

5. Iodoform — It is a yellow crystalline substance with a disagreeable odor, produced by the action of iodine on acetone in the presence of an alkali. It is used topically, it has mild antibacterial action.

Daily requirement — Daily requirement of iodine for adults is 150 to 200 micrograms or .15 to 0.2 mg. Infants and younger children require .05 to .1 mg. or 50-100 micrograms of iodine per day. Growing (older) children, adolescents, pregnant and lactating women, and those under emotional strain require more iodine daily.

Table 22. **Recommended daily dietary intake of iodine.**

Stages	Iodine in micrograms
Infants and children	
0 – 1 year	40 – 50
1 – 3 years	70
4 – 6 years	90
7 – 9 years	120
Adolescents	
10 – 18 years	140
Adults	
Men	150
Women	150
Pregnant women	175
Lactating women	175

Deficiency of iodine — Deficiency of iodine is more prevalent in females than in males and is more frequent during adolescence and pregnancy. It causes hypothyroidism or myxedema, formation of goiter, cretinism in children, retardation of physical development and impairment of mental function, increment of spontaneous abortion, miscarriage, intra-uterine death, stillbirth or the delivery of a deformed child.

Excess of Iodine — Intake of iodine in excess causes hyperthyroidism or thyrotoxicosis or exophthalmic goiter or Graves' disease.

3. Copper (Cu)

Symbol of copper is Cu. The total body content of copper of an adult is 100 to 150 mg. Normal serum copper level is 16 mcg./100 ml. of blood serum. Normal daily diet contains about 2 mg. of copper. Copper is an essential component of several metabolic enzymes, including those for hemoglobin synthesis and cell respiration. Copper is a constituent of the elastic connective tissue protein elastin. It is widely distributed in nature. Even poor diets provide enough copper for human needs. So deficiency or excess of this mineral is very rare. Copper is stored in the liver and excess of it is excreted in the bile or it is excreted by the kidneys.

Sources — Rich sources of copper are vegetables (roots and tubers), green leafy vegetables, legumes, fruits, pulses, nuts, and meat etc. Traces of copper are found in the liver, brain, heart and kidneys. In the fetus and newborn child, the copper content in these organs is several times higher and then decreases during the 1st year of life.

Daily requirement — Daily requirement of copper for an adult is about 2.2 mg.

Functions of copper — Copper has some role in the synthesis of hemoglobin, connective tissue formation and bone development.

Important Salts of Copper Used in Medicine

1. Cupric acetate — A stimulating local caustic to ulcers.

2. Cupric chloride — It has been used as an antiseptic in the treatment of water suppies and ponds etc.

3. Cupric citrate— Copper citrate. It is used as an astringent and antiseptic.

4. Cupric sulfate — Copper sulphate. It is used as an irritant, astringent and fungicide.

Deficiency of copper— Decreased serum copper level is known as hypocupremia. It occurs in patients with nephrosis, wilson's disease, protein-energy malnutrition and in infants fed exclusively on cow's milk for a long period.

Excess — Increased serum copper level is known as hypercupremia. It usually occurs due to excessive intake of copper which may result from eating food prepared in utensils of copper, or it may be associated with several acute and chronic infections, severe anemia, hyperthyroidism, myocardial infarction, leukemia and Hodgkin's disease. Acute poisoning occurs due to ingestion of metallic copper which is manifested by nausea, vomiting, hematemesis and melena.

4. Fluorine (F)

Chemical symbol of fluorine is F. Fluorine is an essential gaseous trace element required in very small quantity, but being so reactive, it is never found in gaseous form, it is found only in combined form. It is found in the form of fluoride. About 96% of fluoride in the body is found in bones and teeth. It is found in drinking water which is about 0.5 mg. per litre of water. When there is deficiency of fluorine in the drinking water, Government authorities add fluoride in the drinking water. In our country the quantity of fluoride in the drinking water must be .5 to .8 mg. per litre of water. It is found in the soil in combination with calcium.

Sources — *(a) Drinking water*— The main source of fluorine is drinking water. In most parts of India, the fluoride content of drinking water is about 0.5 mg. per litre of water, but in fluorosis affected areas, it may be as high as 3 to 12 mgs. per litre of water.

(b) Foods — Fluorides occur in traces in many foods of plant and animal origin, as vegetables, cheese and sea fish etc.

(c) Tea.

(d) Soil.

The average adult man ingest about 1 mg. of fluoride daily from drinking water. In addition to this, the daily diet provides 0.25 to 0.35 mg. of fluorine.

Functions of Fluorine

(1) Fluorine is essential for the normal mineralization of bones.

(2) It is essential for the formation of tooth enamel.

(3) It prevents the decay of the teeth.

Daily requirement — Recommended daily intake of fluoride in drinking water in this country is 0.5 to 0.8 mg. per litre. In the temperate countries where the water intake is low, the optimum level of fluoride in drinking water is accepted as 1 to 2 mg per litre.

Deficiency — Inadequate intake of fluoride (less than .5 mg per litre of water) through drinking water causes dental caries or tooth decay, for the prevention of which fluoride tooth paste should be applied. Deficiency of fluorine lessens the formation of enamel in the teeth.

Excess — Normally 1 part of fluoride per million (P.P.m.) i.e., 1 mg. of fluoride is added to one litre of drinking water by the authorities. By the addition of fluoride in excess to the drinking water (more than 5 P.P.m.) and intake of fluoride through drinking water for a long time causes dental and skeletal fluorosis in which there is mottling with brown color, of the teeth and sclerosis (hardness) and tenderness of the bones. The bones most often affected are those of the vertebral column, pelvis and limbs and result in apparent deformity, when the children are affected.

5. Manganese (Mn)

Mn is the symbol of manganese. Normal human body weighing 70 kgs. contains about 12-20 mg. of manganese. It is distributed throughout the body tissues and fluids. Liver, kidneys, pancreas, pituitary gland and bones contain more manganese than other tissues. Blood manganese level is very low, only 2 to 3 micrograms per 100 mls. of blood.

Sources — Manganese is found in cereals, pulses, bran, nuts, tea, coffee, green leafy vegetables, peas, beans and fruits as banana etc.

Function of manganese — Manganese plays an important role in metabolic functions. It is an essential trace element needed for normal bone metabolism and many enzyme reactions.

Daily requirement — Daily requirement of manganese for an adult is about 3.7 mg.

Deficiency — Deficiency of manganese in humans usually does not occur.

Excess — Toxicity of manganese usually occurs in mine workers due to inhalation of dust from manganese ores, which is characterized by blurred speech, tremors of the hands and spastic gait.

6. Zinc (Zn)

Zn is the symbol of zinc. Zinc is an essential trace mineral element which is present in all the living tissues of the body. The average adult body contains 1.4 to 2.3 gm. of zinc. It is an essential constituent of many enzymes in the body. Blood plasma level of zinc is about 96 μg per 100 mls. of blood plasma for healthy adults and 89 μg per 100 mls for healthy children. Its level in the blood plasma is found low in protein-energy malnutrition or PEM (kwashiorkor) or alcoholic cirrhosis of the liver.

Sources — Zinc is widely distributed in food-stuffs, of both animal and vegetable origin. Animal foods such as milk. dairy products, egg, fish, sea-foods and meat etc., are rich sources of zinc. Vegetable foods as rice, peas, beans, grain products as bread etc., are poor sources of zinc. The bioavailability of zinc in vegetable foods is low. The person taking exclusively vegetarian diet may suffer from zinc deficiency.

Functions of Zinc

(1) Zinc plays a role in growth, metabolism and normal functioning of the tissue cells.

(2) Zinc helps in wound healing.

(3) Zinc has some role in the synthesis of nucleic acid and protein.

(4) It plays a role in the maintenance of normal taste and patients with decreased taste acuity may improve with oral administration of zinc sulphate.

(5) It is required for the synthesis of insulin by the pancreas.

(6) It is required for the immunity function.

Most Important Salts of Zinc Used in Medicine

1. Zinc acetate — White, pearly crystals, used as an emetic, as astringent, styptic and antiseptic, chiefly in eye solutions, in a 0.1% to .5 % solution.

2. Zinc carbonate — It is a mild astringent, used topically in dusting powders.

3. Zinc chloride — It is a white granular powder used as an antiseptic.

4. Zinc gelatin — It is a combination of zinc oxide, gelatin, glycerin and purified water. This jelly is placed between the layers of gauze dressing to serve as a protective dressing and to support varicosities. It is removed by soaking in warm water.

5. Zinc oxide — A very fine, white powder of zinc which is slightly antiseptic and astringent and is used as a protecting ointment or as a dusting powder.

6. Zinc stearate — A zinc compound with variable proportions of stearic and palmitic acids, which is antiseptic and astringent and is used as an ointment or powder in the treatment of eczema, acne, abraisons, burns and scalds.

7. Zinc sulfate — It is an astringent used as a 0.25% solution for temporary relief of minor eye irritation.

8. Zinc undecylenate— It is an antifungal agent used in treating the fungal infection of feet.

Daily requirement—Daily requirement of zinc for an adult is 15 to 20 mgs., for infants 3.5 mgs., for children 10-15 mgs. and for pregnant and lactating women 20-25 mgs. Most of the normal mixed diets provide zinc in these quantities.

Deficiency — Deficiency of zinc causes retardation of growth, hypogonadism in adolescents, dwarfism, delayed wound healing, loss of taste, loss of appetite, anemia, dermatitis, alopecia (loss of hair), multiple infections, immunological abnormalities. Zinc deficiency during pregnancy may lead to developmental disorders in the child.

Excess—Excessive intake of zinc with food or water causes zinc toxicity which is manifested by nausea, vomiting, colic pain and diarrhea.

7. Cobalt (Co)

Co is the symbol of cobalt. Cobalt is found in small quantities in all the tissues, highest concentration is present in the liver and kidneys. Cobalt is an integral part of vitamin B_{12}, i.e., cyanocobalamin and the quantity required for maintaining normal health is very small.

Sources—Foods rich in vitamin B_{12} as whole meal flour, milk, liver and meat ae good sources of cobalt.

Functions of Cobalt

(1) Cobalt stimulates the production of red blood cells.

(2) It plays an important role in the metabolism of the sulphur-containing amino acid methionine.

(3) Cobalt interacts with iodine and affects its utilization.

Daily requirement—0.3 mg. for an adult.

Deficiency — Deficiency of cobalt rarely occurs as this trace element in required quantity is present in almost all the food-stuffs.

Excess—Excess of cobalt in children may cause death. In adults, it may cause anorexia, nausea, vomiting, tinnitis, deafness and hyperplasia of the thyroid gland with resultant compression of the trachea.

Cobalt toxicity — Cobalt administered in excess causes a condition known as polycythemia, i.e., increased number of red blood cells in the blood.

8. Selenium (Se)

Se is the symbol of selenium. Selenium is believed to be a part of the red blood cell enzyme 'glutathione peroxidase.' It is supposed to be an antioxidant and hence considered useful for the maintenance of health. Its importance in human nutrition is related to vitamin E. It resembles sulphur. Normal serum level of selenium is 13 μg/100 mls

Sources — Good sources of selenium are cereals, fish and meat.

Daily requirement — 0.15 mg. for an adult.

Important Salt of Selenium Used in Medicine

Selenium sulfide — A drug used in treating dandruff and tinea versicolor.

Deficiency — Deficiency of selenium usually does not occur. It occurs in protein-energy malnutrition (PEM) as in children with kwashiorkor disease. Selenium deficiency, especially when combined with vitamin E deficiency lessens the antibody production.

Toxicity — Toxicity of selenium can occur when selenium is ingested in excess, characterized by a sour breath odor, nausea, hypersalivation, vomiting, abdominal pain, restlessness and muscle spasms.

Note : For conditions caused by deficiency and excess of minerals, see chapter "Nutritional disorders".

WATER (H_2O)

Water is more important to life than food since man may live without food for several weeks, but for only a few days without water. The body's need for water is second only to that for oxygen. Water is a clear, tasteless and odorless fluid composed of two parts of hydrogen and one part of oxygen in chemical composition, hence its chemical symbol is H_2O. Water is the largest constituent of the body, about 65% of the body weight of an adult male and 55% of the adult female. 70 to 80% of the total water content of the body is found in the soft tissues while about 20 % is found in the bones. Infants and children contain more water, in old age the water content of the body decreases. Thin people contain more water than fatty people.

Sources — 1. Through drinking of water, milk, beverages and fruits and vegetables. Fruits and vegetables contain 75% of water and water-melon contains 90% of water.

2. The moisture or water present in food.

3. The water resulting from oxidation of the end products of food digestion as glucose, fatty acids and amino acids.

Body water is distributed as follows

I. Intracellular — Inside the cells of the tissues, i.e., in the protoplasm — 50%

II. Extracellular — Water outside the tissue cells — 20 %

The extracellular water is further subdivided into —

(1) Water in blood plasma — 4%

(2) Interstitial water — Water in tissue spaces as cerebrospinal fluid and aqueous humor (in the anterior chamber of the eye) etc.— 9%

(3) Water in lymph in the lymphatic vessels. —7%.

Functions of Water

(1) Water is the essential and main constituent of the protoplasm of all the living cells of the body.

(2) It is the essential constituent of all the vital fluids of the body, e.g., blood, lymph and cerebrospinal fluid etc.

(3) Water dissolves the food and aids in its digestion and absorption.

(4) Water plays a role in transporting the absorbed food from the intestine, to different parts of the body.

(5) It maintains the liquid state of the blood.

(6) It regulates the body temperature.

(7) All the chemical reactions taking place in the body are accomplished through water.

(8) Water acts as a lubricant to joints and mucous membranes preventing friction.

(9) It dissolves the waste and poisonous materials formed in the body and expels them from the body through feces, urine, respiration and perspiration.

(10) It is required for bathing and washing.

Different Types of Water

Drinking water — It is a clear, tasteless, odorless fluid.

Potable water — Water suitable for drinking as it is tasteless, odorless and free from pathogenic micro-organisms, and objectionable minerals.

Distilled water — Water that has been purified by distillation. It is used in preparing drugs etc.

Hard water — Water that contains salts of calcium or magnesium dissolved in it.

Soft water — Water that contains very little, if any, salts of calcium or magnesium dissolved in it.

Lime water — Aqueous calcium hydroxide solution.

Purified water — Distilled water.

Pyrogen free water — Water that has been rendered free of fever-producing micro-organisms.

Daily requirement — 6 to 8 glasses of water or 1.5 to 2 litres for an adult. Infants require 165 mls of fluid per kg. of body weight.

Intake of water — Water is taken through drinking water and with the food, milk, beverages, and fruits and vegetables. In addition, it is formed in the body by oxidation of the end products of food digestion as glucose, fatty acids and amino acids. Intake of water depends upon the climate and the nature of the job of the person. Additional quantities

FRUITS

Apple (Seb)

Orange (Santra)

Grapes (Angoor)

Banana (Kela)

Guava (Amrood)

FRUITS

Papaya (Papita)

Pine-apple (Anannaas)

Mango (Aam)

Pomegranate (Anar)

Pear (Nashpati)

FRUITS

Cucumber (Kheera)

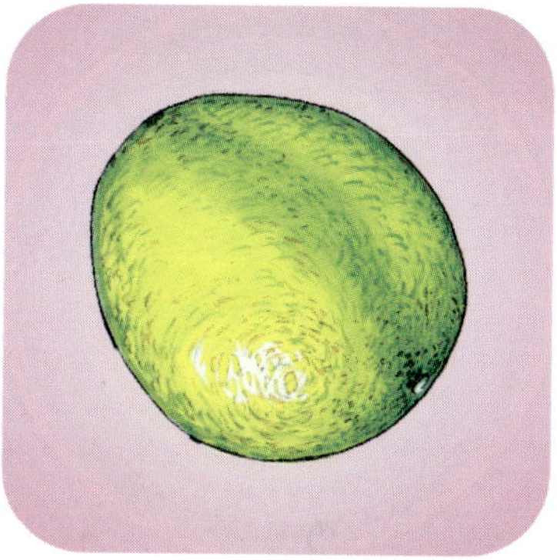
Lemon (Neemboo)

Musk-melon (Kharbooza)

Water-melon (Tarbooz)

Peach (Aaroo)

FRUITS

Sweet orange (Mausmi)

Plum (Aaloo bookhara)

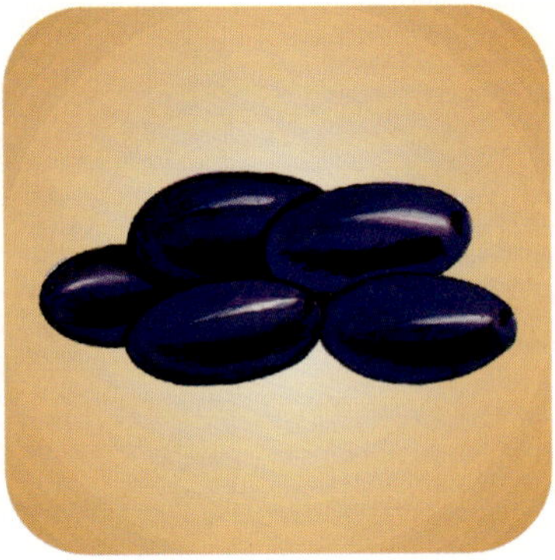

Jambul fruit (Jamun)

VEGETABLES

Cabbage (Bund Gobhi)

Radish (Mooli)

Turnip (Shuljum)

Carrot (Gajjar)

Beet-root (Chukandar)

Potato (Aaloo)

VEGETABLES

Colocasia (Arbi)

Onion (Piyaz)

Garlic (Lahsun)

Tomato (Tamator)

Cauliflower (Phool gobhi)

Brinjal (Baingun)

VEGETABLES

Bottle-gourd (Lauki)

Ribbed-gourd (Torai)

Bitter gourd (Karaila)

Round-gourd (Tinda)

Pointed-gourd (Parwal)

Pumpkin (Kashiphul)

VEGETABLES

Peas (Mutter)

Beans (Saime)

Lady's finger (Bhindi)

Jack fruit (Kathal)

of water are required in hot weather and by the persons doing hard physical labor to make up for extra loss during sweating. An excess of water results in edema, headache, hypertension, indigestion, confusion and spasms in the hands and feet.

Water loss from the body — Water is lost continuously from the body in the following ways —

— Through the kidneys in the form of urine.

— Through the skin in the form of sweats.

— Through the lungs in the expired air.

— In small quantity through the large intestine in the feces.

— In lactating women through the milk.

Vomiting, diarrhea and dysentery and cholera etc., are the pathological conditions in which an excess of water is lost resulting in dehydration. More than 10% of water loss from the body may be serious. Excessive urination as occurs in diabetes mellitus, causes an excess loss of water from the body which results in thirst.

Water intake and loss from the body per day of an adult weighing 70 Kgs.

	Temperate climate (mls)	Tropical climate (mls)
Water intake		
Drinking water	1500	2000 – 3000
In food	1000	1000 – 2000
By oxidation of glucose, fatty acids and amino acids in the tissues	300	300 – 2300
	2800	3300 – 7300
Water loss		
In urine	1500	1000 – 1500
Through skin	800	1800 – 5200
Through lungs	400	400 – 400
In feces	100	100 – 200
	2800	3300 – 7300

In a normal individual, the water intake is approximately equal to water lost from the body and the water content of the body is maintained fairly constant.

*****

CHAPTER 3

DIFFERENT TYPES OF FOOD

While planning for the balanced diet it is important to know the availability of the food-stuffs, their chemical composition, predominant function and how to combine them to increase the nutritive value of the food. Since each food-stuff has a different nutritive value, an intake of different types of food-stuffs in combination is useful to achieve a good health.

The food-stuffs are classified on the basis of their nutritive value into the following groups —

(1) Cereals

— Wheat

— Rice

— Maize

(2) Millets

— Jowar (Sorghum)

— Bajra (Pearl millet)

— Ragi

(3) Pulses (dals)

— Black gram (Urad ki dal)

— Red gram (Arhar ki dal)

— Green gram (Moong ki dal)

— Bengal gram (Chane ki dal)

— Lentils (Masoor)

— Dry peas

— Soyabean

— Lathyrus sativus (Khesari dal)

(4) Vegetables

(a) Green leafy vegetables

— Spinach (Palak)

— Bathua

— Coriander (Dhania)

— Spearmint (Podina)

— Cabbage (Band gobhi or patta gobhi)

— Fenugreek leaves (Maithee)

— Mustard (Surson)

(b) Root vegetables

— Radish (Mooli)

— Turnip (Shuljum)

— Carrot (Gajjar)

— Beet root (Chukander)

(c) Tubers

— Potato (Aaloo)

— Sweet potato (Shakarkund)

— Colocasia (Arbi)

— Onion (Piyaz)

— Garlic (Lahsun)

(d) Other vegetables

— Tomatoes (Tamator)

— Cauliflower (Phool gobhi)

— Brinjal (Baingun)

— Bottle gourd (Lauki)

— Ribbed gourd (Torai)

— Bitter gourd (Karaila)

— Round gourd (Tinda)

— Pointed gourd (Parwal)

— Pumpkin (Kashiphul)

— Peas (Mutter)

— Beans (Saime)

— Lady's finger (Bhindi)

— Jack fruit (Kathal)

(5) Nuts

— Groundnut (Peanut) or Moongphali

— Cashewnut (Kaju)

— Coconut (Narial)

— Walnut (Akhrot)

— Almond (Badam)

— Pistachio (Pista)

(6) Oil seeds

— Mustard seeds

— Sesame seeds (Til ke beej)

— Groundnuts

— Sunflower seeds

— Cotton seeds

(7) Fruits

— Apple

— Orange

— Grapes

— Banana (Kela)

— Guava (Amrood)

— Papaya (Papita)

— Pineapple

— Mango

— Pomegranate (Anar)

— Pear (Nashpati)

— Lemon

— Cucumber(Kheera)

— Musk-melon (Kharbooza)

— Water-Melon (Tarbooz)

— Peach (Aaroo)

— Sweet orange (Mausambi or mausmi)

— Plum (Aaloo bookhara)

— Jambul fruit (Jamun)

(8) Animal foods

— Milk

— Dairy products

— Eggs

— Poultry

— Fish

— Meat

(9) Fats and oils

(10) Sugar and jaggery

(11) Soup

(12) Salad

(13) Condiments and spices

(14) Miscellaneous

(a) Coffee, tea and cocoa

(b) Soft drinks —Aerated water, lemonade, pepsi cola, fruit juices etc.

(c) Alcoholic beverages — Wine, bear, whisky, and tradtional preparations. Alcoholic beverages are rich in calories.

(d) Vinegar.

(1) CEREALS

Cereals (wheat and rice) constitute the bulk of daily diet, and they are main sources of energy. They provide about 350 kcals energy per 100 gms. As cereals are consumed in large quantities, they contribute 70 to 80 % of the total energy intake. Cereals are rich in carbohydrates but poor in proteins. Their proteins are deficient in the essential amino acid lysine hence proteins in cereals are poor in nutritive value. But if the cereals (wheat or rice) are taken with pulses, as is common in the Indian diets, the proteins of cereals and pulses complement each other and provide a more balanced and *"complete"* protein intake.

Wheat

Wheat is the most important cereal and staple food in certain parts of the world. It contains 68 to 70% carbohydrates and 8 to 24% protein which is deficient in the amino acids, mainly lysine and threonine, 1 to 2% fat and 1.5 to 2% ash. The wheat grain is much less subjected to loss of essential nutrients during processing than rice. In India wheat is consumed as whole grain wheat flour or atta. White flour of wheat or maida is poor in nutrients. The whiter is the flour, the greater is the loss of vitamins and minerals. Thus whole grain wheat flour or atta is richer source of vitamins (especially vitamin B complex) and minerals than refined white flour or maida. Maida is used in making poories, biscuits, pasteries etc., but nutritionally it is inferior to atta. Maida may cause constipation.

The bran (choker) of wheat contains iron, calcium, phosphorus, potassium, magnesium, copper and zinc etc., mineral substances and cellulose. That is why bran (choker) or atta with choker is more important than wheat flour in medicine, which is usually discarded and feeded to the cattles.

Suji — It is the coarse grains derived from the outer coat of wheat. It contains high proportion of proteins, minerals and vitamin B_1 (Thiamine hydrochloride).

Rice

Rice is the staple food of majority of Indians. Rice is of the white or red color. White rice is better than red rice. White rice is of many types as Basmati and Hunsraj etc. Old rice is supposed to be better than new rice because old rice is more digestive.

Rice contains 78% carbohydrate, 8.5% protein, .6% fat, .6% fibres, 11.6% water and .7% ash. Rice proteins are richer in lysine than other cereal proteins, for this reason rice protein is considered to be of better quality. Rice is a good source of vitamin B Complex, especially thiamine. It is devoid of vitamin A, C and D. Rice is a poor source of calcium and iron.

The milling process deprives the rice grain of its valuable nutritive elements (protein, thiamine and riboflavine), so resulting white or polished rice is poor in nutritive value. Hence it is advised to take undermilled or parboiled (partially cooked) rice in place of white rice.

Washing and cooking of rice — Rice is generally washed and then cooked in excess of water. Washing in large quantities of water removes up to 60% of the water-soluble vitamins and minerals. The practice of cooking rice in large quantities of water and drawing away the excess of water at the end of cooking leads to further loss of vitamin B-complex. Thus the combined effect of washing and cooking may affect seriously the nutritive value of the rice. It is therefore best to wash in just enough water, about 2½ measures of water for 1 measure of rice.

The bulkiness of rice in the diet causes prevention of absorption of the proteins and vitamins of pulses etc., from the intestines. And it causes distention of the stomach with fermentation of its contents resulting in indigestion and bowl complaints.

Hand pounding of rice removes 25% thiamine while machine milling removes 75% of it. Hence, hand pounding is better than milling.

Maize

Maize (corn, bhutta) ranks next to wheat and rice in world consumption. It is the staple food for poor Indians and is the main source of energy for them. Maize per 100 gms. contains 66.2 gms. carbohydrate, 11.1 gms. protein, 3.6 gms fat, 1.5 gms. minerals, 0.42 mg. thiamine, 1.8 mg. niacin, 0.1mg. riboflavine and provides 342 Kcals energy. The proteins of maize are deficient in the essential amino acid tryptophan (the precursor of niacin) which is converted into niacin or nicotinic acid so on constant use of maize niacin or nicotinic acid is poorly derived from the diet which may result in pellagra. Maize is deficient in gluten so it does not form a smooth bread easily. But difficulty may be overcome by mixing it with the milk or wheat flour.

Maize flour is used in making the breads. Maize is also used in the manufacture of breakfast foods such as corn flakes. Maize flour or corn flour is widely used in the preparation of custards and table desserts. Maize is usually eaten as the grains from bhutta.

(2) MILLETS

Millets are the smaller grains which are ground and eaten without having the outer layer removed. They are as follows —

Jowar (Sorghum)

Jowar is also known as Kaffir corn or Milo. It is a staple food for poor people in India and is grown widely next to wheat and rice. Jowar per 100 gms. contains 72 gms. of carbohydrate, 9 to 14 gms. of proteins which are lacking in lysine and threonine, 2 gms. of fat, 1.6 gms. of minerals, especially calcium and iron and in minute quantities vitamins, especially factors of vitamin B complex and 2 gms. fibres , 2 gms. ash and 13 gms. moisture. Jowar provides energy 349 Kcals per 100 gms. Certain varieties of jowar have a high leucine content and consumption of these varieties is associated with pellagra.

Bajra

Bajra is grown extensively in the dry and peninsular areas of India as Rajasthan, Gujrat and Maharashtra, where it forms the staple food of a large number of people. Bajra per 100 gms. contains 67.5 gms. of carbohydrate, 11.6 gms. of protein which is deficient in the essential amino acids lysine and threonine, 5 gms. of fat, 2 or 3 gms minerals, mostly calcium and iron and minute quantities of vitamin A and factors of vitamin B-complex, especially thiamine, riboflavine and niacin. 100 gms. of bajra provides 361 kcals energy.

Bajra is very hot and laxative. Usually its bread is eaten which provides a lot of energy and causes the muscular growth and fatness of the body. Semen becomes more dense by the use of bajra.

Ragi

It is the cheapest among the millets. It is a popular food item in Karnataka and Andhra Pradesh where it is consumed in large quantity.

Ragi per 100 gms. contains, 7 to 10 gms. protein,1.5 gms. fat and 72 gms. carbohydrate, 2.75 gms. minerals, especially calcium and iron and minute quantities of vitamin B complex, especially its factors thiamine, riboflavine and niacin. 100 gms of ragi provides 328 Kcals energy. Ragi is rich in carbohydrates, but the carbohydrates in ragi are slowly digested and assimilated than those of other cereals. Ragi is known due to its high content of calcium though it is rich in carbohydrate. Ragi also contains iodine to some extent. Ragi is cooked and eaten as porridge. By increasing the intake of ragi we can help in overcoming the shortage of cereals but we also lessen the deficiency of calcium in our diet.

(3) PULSES (DALS)

Pulses are also known as dals. They give variety to the diet and make the food more palatable. They are useful in the diets because they are rich in proteins. They contain 20 to 25% protein which is double to that found in wheat and triple to that found in rice. In fact, pulses contain more proteins than that of animal origin as found in eggs, fish and meat etc., but they are inferior to animal proteins in quality. Pulse proteins are rich in lysine and poor in sulphur-containing amino acid methionine and to a lesser extent cysteine but when taken along with wheat bread, it compensates for the deficiency of lysine of wheat and thus improves the quality of protein. Pulses are rich in minerals like calcium and iron, the essential amino acids and factors of vitamin B-complex such as thiamine and riboflavine.

In the dry state pulses do not contain vitamin C. Germinating pulses, however, contain higher concentration of vitamins, especially vitamin C and B-complex. Fermentation also modifies the nutritive value of pulses in that the vitamin content particularly that of thiamine, riboflavine and niacin is enhanced.

Table 23. **Nutritive value of pulses (per 100 gms.)**

	Protein gms.	Fat gms.	Carbo-hydrate gms.	Calcium mgs.	Iron mgs.	Thiamine mgs.	Ribofl-avine mgs.	Niacin mgs.	Vita-min C mgs.	Energy (Kcals)
Urad	24	1.4		154	3.8	0.42	0.20	2	0	347
Arhar	22.3	1.7	57.2	73	2.7	0.45	0.19	2.9	0	335
Moong	24.0	1.3	56.6	140	8.4					334
Chana	17.0	5.3	61.2	202	4.6	.30	0.15	2.9	3	360
Masoor	25.1	0.7	59.7	130	2.0					540
Dry peas	19.7	1.1	56.6	70	4.4					315
Soyabean	43.2	19.5	20.9	200	6.7	.73	.39	3.2	0	432

In some people pulses being rich in purine bodies, cause feeling of heaviness and so these should not be given to persons suffering from gout or rheumatism.

Anti-nutritional factors — In the raw state, pulses have some anti-nutritional factors such as phytates and tannins which adversely affect the availability of some nutrients to the body, though most of them are destroyed by heat.

Soyabean — Soyabean is the richest source of protein among the pulses. It contains about 43% of proteins. Proteins of soyabean are of high nutritive value than that of the cereals as wheat and animal proteins as that of the eggs, fish and meat etc. Soyabean can be cooked and eaten as dal or its powder can be mixed with wheat atta for making chapaties or soyabean milk or curd can be used, or it can be used in baby foods.

Dry soyabean— supplies factors of vitamin B-complex as thiamine, riboflavine and niacin. Green soyabean provides vitamin A and vitamin C also. Soyabean contains all the essential minerals as calcium, phosphorus, sodium, potassium and iron in adequate quantity. Soyabean is deficient in the amino acids methionine and cysteine, on heating soyabean, their availability is increased. Soyabean is rich in lysine so it can supplement protein of wheat flour which is deficient in lysine. Bread containing soyabean is superior to plain wheat bread as concerned with the quality of proteins. Soyabean flour because of its low starch content does not make a smooth roti as that of maize. Hence 25-50% wheat flour may be mixed into it.

Soyabean milk — It is prepared by mixing one cup of soyabean flour with a little of water to make a smooth paste and then add the rest of the 2 litres of water very slowly consuming about 5 minutes. Then add one tea-spoonful sugar or gur and ¼ tea-spoonful salt. Stir well and then filter it through a cloth .Thus about 2 litres of soyabean milk is prepared.

Khesari dal — Among the pulses khesari dal is such a dal which when used for a long period may cause lathyrism which is characterized by irreversible muscular weakness and paraplegia, so this type of dal is of no use.

(4) VEGETABLES

Vegetables are protective foods as they contain a large amount of vitamins and minerals. They also contain a large amount of water. They are poor in protein and energy content but some vegetables such as green peas and beans etc., are good sources of protein and energy. Vegetables also contain fibres in varying amounts. Vegetables are divided into four groups —

(a) Green leafy vegetables

(b) Roots

(c) Tubers

(d) Other vegetables

(a) Green leafy vegetables — They include spinach (palak), bathua, coriander (dhania), spearmint (podina), cabbage (patta gobhi), fenugreek leaves (maithee) and mustard. The darker the green leaves, the greater is the nutritive value with the exception of vitamin B_{12} which is found mostly in animal foods as milk etc. Green leaves are rich sources of carotenes (precursor of vitamin A), riboflavine and folic acid, the factors of vitamin B-Complex, and many other micronutrients.The bioavailability of calcium and iron from green leaves is low because of the presence of high amounts of oxalates. Leafy vegetables contain a large amount of water and dietary fibres. Because of the low caloric value (25 to 50 Kcals per 100 gms) and large bulk, they have an improtant role in the diets of obese people, who are required to cut down their calories intake and reduce their weight. They should take plenty of green leafy vegetables in their diets. Diabetics are also advised to take a lot of green leafy vegetables, because of being bulky, they fill the stomach without giving many calories.

Green leafy vegetables contain a large amount of fibres and form roughage in our diet, which enhances the movement of the waste products through the intestinal tract and thus removes the constipation. Persons consuming sufficient roughage do not suffer from constipation.

The recommended daily intake of green leafy vegetables is about 40 gms. for an adult.

(b) and (c) Roots and tubers — Roots and tubers are the reserve nutrients for the use of plant itself. Root vegetables include radish (mooli), turnip (shalgum), carrot (gajjar) and beet root (chukander); and tubers include potatoes (aloo), sweat potatoes (shakarkand), colocasia (arbi), onion (piyaz) and garlic (lahsun). They vary widely in composition, some are good sources of carbohydrates such as potatoes and sweet potatoes etc. In general roots and tubers are poor in protein and fat, minerals and vitamins. Carrots are exceptionally high in beta-carotene, the precursor of vit A. When there is shortage of cereals, potatoes and sweet potatoes etc., can serve as subsidiary foods for a limited period only because they are not suitable as staple foods for a long period due to their bulk and low protein content. They can only be served as staple foods for long periods when supplemented by foods richer in protein. The recommended daily intake of roots and tubers is 50-60 gms. for an adult.

Radish, turnip and carrots etc., have many green leaves at the top which are usually removed and thrown away before serving as salad or cooking the vegetable. Actually green leaves of these vegetables are more nutritious and edible. Leaves of radish and carrots can be included in the salad. Fresh and clean leaves should be used. The leaves should be bright-green colored, free from insects, bruises and insect injuries, mud spots or holes in the leaves. They should be stored in dry and cool places or in refrigerator putting them in a polythene bag.

Vegetables should be washed properly before storing or cutting. Thorough washing is required to remove mud spots, poisonous insectisides, sprays and eggs of the intestinal worms etc.

Green leaves should not be cut into very small pieces. This may cause more loss of nutrients.

Do not soak the cut leaves for a long time, by doing so water-soluble vitamins B and C will be dissolved in water and wasted.

Addition of baking powder or soda (sodium bicarbonate) to vegetables destroys the flavor and vitamin B-Complex of the vegetable.

Do not cook in the excess of water. Avoid overcooking and reheating to avoid vitamin C loss.

Boil the water and then add vegetable to it, instead of adding vegetable to cold water and then bring to boil.

Steaming of roots and tubers is better way of cooking then boiling but their skin should not be removed because by doing so, nitrogen and minerals are lost.

Addition of acidic substances as lemon juice or tamarind juice lessens the destruction of several nutrients specially vitamin C.

(d) Other vegetables — There is a wide range of "other vegetables." They include tomatoes (tamators), cauliflowers (phoolgobhi), brinjal (baingan), bottlegourd (lauki), ribbed gourd (torai), bitter gourd (karaila), round gourd (tinda), pointed gourd (parwal), pumpkin (kashiphal), peas (mutter), beans (saime), lady's finger (bhindi) and jack fruit (kathal) etc.

They provide the variety to the diet and many of them contain a large amount of minerals, vitamins and fibres. Their daily recommended intake is 60 to 70 gms.

(5) NUTS

Nuts include groundnut or peanut (moongphali), cashewnut (kaju), coconut (narial), walnut (akhrot), almond (badam) and pistachio (pista). Nuts contain a large amount of fat and good quality of protein in small quantity. Regarding the fat content, walnut contains 64.5%, almond 58.7%, cashewnut 46.9% and groundnut 40%.

Regarding the protein content, groundnut is the richest source which contains 25-30% protein. Groundnut is known as the poor man's dry fruit as it is a concentrated source of calories like almonds and cashewnut.

Sometimes when groundnuts are stored in humid dark place, a type of fungus (Aspergillus flavus) develops which is harmful to human body. So groundnuts for human consumption should be thoroughly dried and properly stored to avoid the growth of the fungus. Groundnut does not contain vitamin C.

Nuts are good sources of vitamin B-complex. They contain minerals such as calcium, phosphorus and iron in significant amount. Almonds, cashewnuts and pistachio are good sources of iron of which pistachio is the richest source containing 14 mgs. of iron per 100 gms. Due partly to their high fat content and partly to their high cellulose content, nuts are not easily digestible but when they are eaten in a mixed diet, they become an extremely valuable source of protein and are easily digested. Combination of 3/4 groundnut proteins and 1/4 milk proteins become equivalent to class one protein.

(6) OIL-SEEDS

Oil-seeds include mustard seeds, sesame seeds, groundnuts, sunflower seeds and cotton seeds, etc., from which cooking oils are extracted. Oil seeds contain a large amount of fat and good quality of protein in small quantity. Most of the oils are rich in essential fatty acids.

(7) FRUITS

Fruits are protective foods. They are good sources of vitamins and minerals, so are very valuable in human nutrition. One special feature which distinguishes fruits from other foods is that they can be eaten raw and fresh. This makes the vitamins and minerals present in the fruit easily available. Various fruit juices are used as palatable drinks to quench the thirst, e.g., orange juice, pineapple juice and mango juice etc. Orange juice is useful for infants, invalid and sick persons. Water of green coconut (date water) is refreshing and is given usefully to the patients suffering from diarrhea. Mango is a valuable fruit of India. In the unripe stage it is used in many forms as chutney and prickles etc. It is most palatable health-promoting when ripe. Unripe fruits may irritate the intestines but as fruit ripens starch is converted into sugar which is easily absorbed from intestine.

Nutritive value of fruits (1) Vitamins — Fruits contain vitamins in large quantity. Most fruits contain significant amount of vitamin C or ascorbic acid. The orange, guava and amla are particularly rich in ascorbic acid. One medium sized orange can provide enough juice to meet the daily requirement of ascorbic acid of an adult. Several fruits contain good amounts of carotene (the precursor of vitamin A). The papaya and mango are richest sources of carotene.

(2) Minerals — Fruits are good sources of minerals, especially of sodium, potassium, iron and magnesium. Potassium carbonate (potash) combined with vegetable acids helps in maintaining the alkaline reserve of the body. Some fruits like sitaphal (custard apple) are rich in calcium. Dried fruits like dates and raisins are good sources of calcium and iron. Banana contains magnesium in large quantity, so it is useful in cardiac weakness and may be used in epilepsy.

(3) Carbohydrate — Fruits in general have a low energy value but some fruits like banana and mango contain carbohydrate in large quantity and so act as good sources of energy. When banana is in the green state, i.e., when it is unripe, most of the carbohydrates are in the form of starch which are converted into sugar during the ripening process. Pectin, a kind of carbohydrate, present in the fruits like mango or pineapple is helpful in the preparation of fruit jellies. Fruits contain carbohydrates as sugar fructose (fruit sugar) or levulose which is easily digested and completely absorbed from the intestine. The more ripe is a fruit, the higher is its sugar content.

(4) Cellulose — Cellulose is the fibrous form of carbohydrate (polysachharide). Fruits contain cellulose in large amounts. Cellulose assists in normal bowl movements and causes evacuation. So by the use of fruits containing cellulose, constipation does not occur.

Bananas supply fibres and pectin (a kind of carbohydrate) which help in normal functioning of the intestine. Banana flour is used as nutritious food for invalids. It consists of 4% protein, 0.5% fat, 80% carbohydrate, 2.5% minerals and 3% water. Papaya is used as green (unripe) as well as ripe fruit. The green papaya helps in digestion of proteins.

Daily requirement of fruits — Daily intake of fresh fruits recommended by nutrition experts is 85 grams for an adult for maintenance of good health. If green leafy vegetables are included in the daily diet, the need for fruits as an essential item in the diet is much reduced. The nutritive values of some fruits are given in the following table.

***Table 24.* Nutritive value of some common fruits (per 100 grams of edible portion)**

Name (Fresh fruits)	Calcium (mg.)	Iron (mg.)	Carotene (mg.)	Vitamin C (mg.)	Calories (energy)
Orange	26	0.32	2240	68	48
Grapes	20	1.5	0	1	71

Banana	10	0.5	124	7	104
Mango	14	1.3	2210	16	74
Guava	10	0.27	0	212	51
Papaya	17	0.5	2740	57	32
Sitaphal	17	4.31	0	37	104
Amla	50	1.2	9	600	58
Dry fruits					
Dates	120	7.3	44	3	317
Raisins	87	7.7	2.4	1	308

(8) ANIMAL FOODS

Foods of animal origin include milk, dairy products, eggs, poultry, fish and meat. They provide high quality protein (containing all the essential amino acids) and good amount of fats, besides some vitamins and minerals. Vitamin B_{12} is found only in animal foods, mostly in the milk. Among animal foods, cow's milk and hen's egg are two most perfect foods.

Milk

Milk is the best and most complete of all foods. It contains all the nutrients necessary for growth and development of the young ones. Thus milk is a good source of proteins, fats, carbohydrates (sugars), vitamins and minerals.

1. Proteins — Animal milks contain nearly three times as much protein as human milk. Milk proteins contain all the essential amino acids. The chief protein of milk is casein which occurs in combination with calcium as calcium caseinogenate. The other proteins are lactalbumin and lactoglobulin. Casein and lactoglobulin are the most common proteins in cow's milk. Lactalbumin is found in high concentration in human milk. Milk contains 3.5% protein of total weight of milk, consisting of 3% calcium caseinogenate, 0.4%

lactalbumin and 0.1% lactoglobulin. Human milk proteins contain greater amounts of tryptophan and sulphur-containing amino acids (especially cysteine) than the animal proteins.

2. Fats — Human milk contains 3.4%, cow's milk 4.4% and buffalo's milk contains double the fat content of cow's milk, i.e., 8.8%. When milk is allowed to stand for sometime, fat rises to the surface as cream.

3. Carbohydrates (Sugar) — Milk contains carbohydrate in the form of lactose or milk sugar. It is less sweeter than cane sugar and readily fermented by Lactobacillus acidophilus. Human milk contains more sugar than animal milks.

4. Vitamins — Milk is a good source of all the vitamins except vitamin C and E.

5. Minerals — Milk contains almost all the known minerals required by the human body such as calcium, phosphorus, sodium, potassium, magnesium, iodine, copper etc. Milk is particularly rich in calcium, but it is poor in iron.

Human and animal milks are compared in the following table.

***Table 25.* Nutritive value of milks compared (value per 100 grams)**

	Buffalo	Cow	Goat	Human
Fats (g.)	6.5	4.1	4.5	3.4
Protein (g.)	4.3	3.2	3.3	1.1
Sugar (lactose) (g.)	5.1	4.4	4.6	7.4
Calcium (mg.)	210	120	170	28
Iron (mg.)	0.2	0.2	0.3	—
Vitamin C (mg.)	1	2	1	3
Minerals (g.)	0.8	0.8	0.8	0.1
Water (g.)	81.0	87	86.8	88
Energy (Kcals)	117	67	72	65

Milk Products

Milk is consumed in a variety of forms, as whole milk, dried milk, condensed milk, skimmed milk (milk from which fat has been removed is known as skimmed milk), cheese, khoa, ice-cream, butter and ghee etc.

Toned Milk

Toned milk is a blend of natural milk and "made-up" milk. It contains 1 part of water, 1 part of natural milk and 1/8 part of skimmed milk powder. The mixture is stirred, pasteurised and supplied in bottles. Toned milk has a composition nearly equivalent to cow's milk. It is cheaper and yet a health-promoting product.

Vegetable Milk

Milk prepared from certain vegetable foods, as groundnut and soyabean etc., is termed as "Vegetable milk". It may be used as a substitute for animal milk. The Central Food Technological Research Institute Mysore has perfected techniques for the preparation of vegetable milk.

Egg

Hen's egg weighs 55 to 60 grams which contains all the nutrients except carbohydrate and Vitamin C. About 12% of the egg is made up of its outer layer, i.e., the shell which consists of calcium carbonate, 58% of egg white which is made up wholly of protein known as egg albumin and 30% of egg-yolk which contains mainly fat. Egg contains 6 grams of protein, 6 grams of fat, 30 mg. of calcium and 1.5 mg. of iron and supplies about 70 Kcals of energy. Egg proteins are best in quality and are taken as standard for comparing the quality of other food proteins. Egg proteins are better digested, absorbed and utilized by the body than proteins of milk or meat. Egg proteins have all the nine essential amino acids needed by the body in right proportion. Except vitamin C egg contains all the water-soluble and fat-soluble vitamins in appreciable amounts. Important minerals such as calcium, phosphorus and iron, zinc and other trace elements are present in the egg.

Raw egg white is not assimilated by the intestinal mucosa, therefore it must be cooked before consumption. Boiling of egg destroys 'avidin' a substance which prevents the body from obtaining biotin, one of the factors of Vitamin B complex. Biotin is present in the egg which is necessary for healthy and smooth skin. Boiled egg is therefore nutritionally superior to raw egg.

Cholesterol content of egg which is about 250 mgs. per egg, may cause fear of the risk of coronary heart disease, so reduction in intake of eggs is advised for those who are at the risk of coronary heart disease. Other people may eat eggs.

Fish

Fish is nutritious food rich in proteins (15 to 25%) which are easily digested and fishes are with a good biological value. Fishes contain amino acids in balance. The fat of fish is rich in unsaturated fatty acids and vitamin A and D. Fish liver oil is the richest source of vitamin A and D. Fish bones are an excellent source of calcium, phosphorus and fluorides. Fishes are a poor source of iron (0.7 to 3mgs. per 100 gms) than meat. Fishes of fresh water do not contain iodine, but sea fishes contain iodine. There is no carbohydrate in the fish.

Meat

The term "meat" is applied to the flesh of cattle, sheep and goats. It consists of muscle fibres held together by connective tissue. The proteins of meat are myosin, muscle albumin and myoglobin. Meats contain 15 to 20% of proteins which are less than that found in pulses but are a good source of essential amino acids. Meat proteins are class I proteins which are easily digested.

Clotting of protein myosin causes rigor mortis which makes the meat tough. But acids developing soon soften the myosin and make the meat tender and give it a better flavour. Hence meat should be eaten after rigor mortis has passed away.

It is better to eat the meat of younger animals because connective tissue in the older animals is in abundance which becomes tough and takes more time for cooking. Meat contains fat, and the energy provided by meat depends upon its fat content. Meat contains fair amount of vitamin B-complex and small amounts of vitamin 'A' and 'C'. Meat contains minerals as iron (2 to 4 mgs. per 100 gms) which is more easily absorbed than the iron present in vegetable foods, zinc etc. It is poor in calcium but rich in phosphorus. Liver is extremely rich in many nutrients.

Table 26. **Nutritive value of egg, fish and meat (gm/100 gms)**

	Protein	Fat	Minerals
Hen's egg	13.3	13.3	1.0
Fish	19.5	2.4	1.5
Meat goat	21.4	3.6	1.1
Liver goat	20.0	3.0	1.3

Qualities of good meat are —

- Meat should be of red color
- It should be firm and elastic to touch.
- It should have a little or no odor.
- It should not be shrunk or be wasted much on cooking.
- It should not become wet on standing for a day or two.

(9) FATS AND OILS

Fats which are liquid at room temperature are called oils. Fats and oils are used in cooking foods. They are good sources of energy, one gram of fat provides 9 Kcalories energy. Animal fats are good sources of fat-soluble vitamins and are poor sources of essential fatty acids. Pure ghee or ghee of animal origin contains saturated fatty acids which raise the serum cholesterol level and subsequently causes the heart diseases. Cow's ghee contains carotene hence it is slightly of yellow color.

Vegetable fats are rich in poly-unsaturated fatty acids except coconut and palm oils. The vegetable oils contain no fat-soluble vitamins A and D, except red palm oil which is extremely rich in carotene. Vanaspati ghee (hydrogenated fat) under various trade names as Dalda, Rath etc., made from vegetable oils do not contain fat-soluble vitamins A and D and so they are fortified with vitamin A and D. Pure ghee or ghee of animal origin contains saturated fatty acids which raise the serum cholesterol level and subsequently causes heart diseases. All fats and oils are alike in caloric content.

(10) SUGAR AND JAGGERY

Sugar and jaggery are the carbohydrate foods. Sugar is produced from sugar-cane in India. It belongs to the monosaccharide or disachharide group of carbohydrate. Refined sugar is pure sucrose and contains no other nutrients. Jaggery is prepared from sugar-cane in India and is consumed in place of sugar. It contains useful amounts of carotene , and iron derived from cooking pans.

Sugars may be of the following types —

(1) Sucrose — It is disachharide obtained from sugar-cane. In the intestine, it is hydrolyzed to glucose and fructose by the enzyme sucrase present in the intestinal juice. It contains vitamin B and C and is especially rich in the organic salts of calcium, iron and manganese.

(2) Fructose — Fruit-sugar. It is the fruit sugar derived from fruits. It is a monosaccharide and is metabolized to provide a source of energy or may be stored in the body after being converted to glycogen.

(3) Lactose — Milk-sugar. It is a disachharide that on hydrolysis yields glucose and galactose. It is obtained from evaporation of cow's milk. It is less sweeter than cane-sugar, while giving the same amount of calories. It is readily assimilable by the infant and has a laxative effect. It is used in manufacturing tablets and as a diluent.

(4) Saccharine — A sweet, white, powdered, synthetic product derived from coal tar, 300 to 500 times sweeter than sugar, used as artificial sweetner by the persons suffering from diabetes mellitus, as blood sugar level does not rise by its use, instead of cane-sugar. While cane-sugar stimulates the activity of the heart, saccharine depresses it. Use of saccharine now-a-days is restricted because it is proved to be a carcinogenic which may cause cancer.

(5) Honey — It is a sweet, thick liquid substance produced by honey bees from the nectar of flowers and stored by them for food in honey comb. Honey consists of about 75% sugars, mostly fructose and glucose and the remainder is mostly water.

(11) SOUP

Soup is a liquid prepared from vegetables or meat which is usually served at the beginning of all formed dinners and other occasions also. Soup stimulates the appetite and provides nourishment. They have no protein and caloric value, but they contribute sodium chloride, potassium and small amounts of other minerals.

(12) SALAD

Salad is a mixture of some raw vegetables which is taken with the food. Common vegetables used for salad are onions, ginger, tomatoes, radish, carrots, cucumber, corriander, green chillies and lemon etc. All the vegetables should be thoroughly washed before cutting.

All these vegetables contain Vitamin C and minerals. On cooking, these nutrients are being lost, hence they should be used in raw form. Most of these contain cellulose which is not being digested but does not allow constipation to develop. Salad does not contain calorific value.

(13) CONDIMENTS AND SPICES

Condiments are formed by mixing the spices as common salt, asafoetida (heeng), chillies (dry red mirch), caraway (jeera), turmeric (haldi), tamarind (imli), omum (ajwain), cardamom (chhoti elaichi), pepper (kali mirch) etc., with coriander (dhania), spearmint (pudina), onion (piyaz), garlic (lehsun) and ginger etc. Condiments are actually not the foods but are known as food adjuncts. Condiments give flavor to the food and stimulate the flow of digestive juices and relieve flatulent-distention occurring from the fermentation in the intestine. Excessive use of candiments causes inflammation of the mucous membrane of the stomach, and peptic ulcer.

Spices are also used in food preparation to enhance the palatability of foods and to give color, flavor and taste to the food and to stimulate the appetite. The essential oils present in the spices are carminative and may aid digestion.

Vinegar is a well known antiseptic and preservative. It is used for pickling vegetables, fruits and fishes etc. It also softens the hard muscle fibres of meat and cellulose of green vegetables. It is largely used in salad or for preserving small onions.

Medicinal Values of Some Spices

Common salt (sodium chloride) — It is used to add flavor and taste to the food. It acts as an emetic also.

Chillies (dry red mirch) — On taking chillies with the food or the presence of chillies in powdered form in the food add taste to the food and stimulate the appetite.

Asafoetida (heeng) — It is used for expelling the wind and to reduce the distension of the abdomen. It relieves toothache and earache. It is useful in the treatment of dysmenorrhea (painful menstruation) and leucorrhea.

Caraway (jeera) — It relieves flatulence and acts as anthelmintic, especially acts against hookworms. It is also useful in foul breath.

Turmeric (haldi) — Turmeric acts as hemostatic, i.e., it serves to stop the bleeding. In case of bleeding from the body, by filling the wound made by cut with the powdered turmeric, along with taking a teaspoonful powdered turmeric mixing with the milk, bleeding is stopped.It relieves pain and swelling on local application over the concealed injury and taking it with the milk. It expels the worms from intestine. It is useful in the treatment of polyuria, spermatorrhea and leucorrhea. It is very effective in chronic cough and asthma.

Tamarind (imli) — Pulp of tamarind relieves vomiting, flatulence and indigestion. It stimulates the appetite. It prevents scurvy. Its clear soup relieves cold. Tamarind juice is given in fever and dysentery.

Omum (ajwain) — It relieves indigestion, flatulence and pain in abdomen. Ajwain water has a carminative effect, Ajwain seeds with common salt and clove relieves coryza and cough. It expels the worms from the intestine. It relieves toothache.

Cardamom (chhoti elaichi) — It relieves indigestion, flatulence, pain in abdomen and stimulates appetite. It is generally used in nausea and vomiting. It removes foul smell from the mouth. It relieves hiccups.

Fenugreek (methi seeds) — Methi seeds improve the function of salivary glands. They improve sense of taste and smell. They relieve indigestion, flatulence, pain in abdomen and stimulate the appetite. Methi removes excessive mucus from the respiratory tract and hence relieves sinusitis and bronchitis. It removes foul breath and body's foul smell. It decreases the blood sugar level in diabetes mellitus. Methi is useful in dysuria.

Pepper (kali mirch) — It is useful in the treatment of fever caused by exposure to cold, especially malarial fever. It removes cardiac weakness. It relieves neuritis. It is useful in the treatment of dysuria and amenorrhea. It relieves toothache. It relieves itching, eczema and scabies.

(14) MISCELLANEOUS

Diets also includes beverages (liquid substances used for drink) and water which is essential for life (described earlier). Baverages include drinks which are appreciated for their flavor or their stimulating properties. They are classified as follows —

(a) Coffee, tea and cocoa

Coffee — Coffee is made from the seeds of coffee beans. It contains caffeine 0.6 to 2%, volatile oil and small amount of tannic acid. Caffeine is the stimulant of the nervous system and it lessens the feeling of hunger. Coffee gives feeling of comfort and increases the physical and mental vigour. Stimulation is not followed by depression.

When coffee is taken in large quantity, very hot and strong (with little milk) coffee may cause gastric irritation, dyspepsia, constipation, insomnia, heart palpitation and nervousness. Similar are the effects of tea.

Tea — Tea contains caffeine 2 to 6%, tannic acid 6 to 12%, essential volatile oils 5% and theophylline in traces. Tea is prepared by adding leaves to boiling water. When milk is added the casein of milk combines with tanin and forms a harmless complex. Due to presence of an alkaloid caffeine, tea has a stimulating effect and due to tannic acid in large quantity, tea is an astringent. Volatile oils in the tea give it a peculiar flavour. Tea is exhilerating when taken in moderate quantity, but when it is taken in large quantity, very hot or with very little milk, it may also cause gastric irritation, dyspepsia, constipation, insomnia and nervousness like coffee.

Coffee and tea both have no calorific or nutritive value, it is due to only sugar or milk which is added to them. These have high purine content, hence these should not be used in gout.

Cocoa — Cocoa is obtained from the seeds of the plant Theobroma cocoa. Fat content of seeds is removed and dried which contain theobromine that is nutritive as well as stimulating. Cocoa has a palatable taste. Chocolate is prepared from it.

***Table 27.* Chemical composition of coffee, tea and cocoa**

	Coffee	Tea	Cocoa
Protein (gms.)	1.8	0.9	7.2
Fat (gm.)	2.2	1.1	8.8
Carbohydrate (gms)	17.8	16.4	26.2
Calcium (gm.)	0.680	0.034	0.27
Phosphorus (gm.)	0.050	0.025	0.20
Vitamin A (mg.)	102	51	408
Kcals	98	79	213

(b) Soft drinks — Aerated water, lemonade, pepsicola, fruit juices, squashes and cordials etc. are soft drinks. Aerated water has a sharp pleasant taste. Some of the soft drinks are carbonated, i.e., charged with carbon dioxide under pressure, e.g., soda water incorporating carbon dioxide under high pressure, and others are non-carbonated, i.e., not charged with carbon dioxide. The principal ingredients of soft drinks are carbon dioxide, sugars, acids such as citric acid or tartaric acid, coloring and flavoring agents, Fruit beverages include fruit juices, squashes and cordials. Fruit juices are non-carbonated drinks. Orange juice contains vitamin C, mango is a good source of vitamin A. and mango juice is nutritionally very rich due to addition of milk. Fruit squashes and cordials are diluted with water before consumption.

(c) Alcoholic beverages — Alcoholic beverages include wine, beer, whisky, brandy, rum and gin.

1. Wine — Wine is derived from fermented grape juice. Grape sugar is converted into alcohol and carbon dioxide. Wine contains 10-20% alcohol.

2. Beer — It is derived from germinated barley. Starch of barley is changed into sugar which is fermented into alcohol. It contains 5 to 6% alcohol. Beer is most commonly used.

3. Whisky — It is a distilled alcoholic liquor prepared from cereal grains such as barley, maize and wheat etc. It contains 47 to 53% alcohol.

4. Brandy — An alcoholic liquid obtained by the distillation of the fermented juice of ripe grapes which usually contains 48 to 54% ethyl alcohol.

5. Rum — A spirit distilled from the fermented juice of the sugar-cane or an alcoholic beverage prepared from fermented sugar of cane juice.

6. Gin — It is distilled from a fermented mash of malt or raw grain.

Alcohol supplies about 7 Kcals per gram.

Alcohol is quickly absorbed from the gastrointestinal tract and requires no digestive process and is utilized rapidly. 25% of alcohol is rapidly absorbed from the stomach, especially if it is empty. The rest of alcohol is absorbed within 2 to 6 hours from the intestine. Within five minutes of oral administration it appears in the blood and attains highest concentration within half to one hour. Slow drinking does not lead to high blood concentration, while rapid drinking leads to high blood concentration of alcohol. Alcoholic drinks taken empty stomach is absorbed rapidly. Taking food with drinks delays absorption and blood level remains lower by 30 to 50%. Meat preparations markedly lower the rate of alcohol absorption.

About 90 to 98% alcohol is completely absorbed and reaches all the cells of the body through the blood capillaries, only 2 to 10% is excreted through urine, in the breath, sweats, milk and tears etc.

Alcoholic mothers give birth to the children with congenital abnormalities, premature or dead infants. The children remain mentally backward to a varying degree even under best environmental conditions.

Alcoholic women get their menopause earlier.

Caution — Wood alcohol or methyl alcohol should never be used as alcoholic drink because it is extremely toxic and may cause death. In those who survive, blindness may occur.

(d) Vinegar — Natural vinegar is made from fermentation of fruits, malt and molasses. It contains a minimum of 4% acetic acid. Synthetic vinegar should not be harmful if it is free from lead, copper, arsenic or mineral acids.

Synthetic vinegar should be distinctly labelled "Synthetic" according to prevention of food Adulteration Act rules.

* * * * *

CHAPTER 4

METABOLISM

Metabolism is the sum of all the physical and chemical processes occurring continuously within the body. It includes the following two processes —

Anabolism — It is a building process or the process of synthesis in which protoplasm is formed by the food ingested and the cells, tissues and organs are formed and developed and their damages are repaired by the protoplasm and the body is grown up. Anabolism is constructive metabolism and it is also known as assimilation. In anabolism muscles are built and developed and there is gain in weight. For the normal function of the body energy is obtained, and heat is produced to maintain the optimum temp. (36.8°C or 94.4°F) of the body by the chemical processes occurring in the body. Extra heat is eliminated from the body through the skin and the excretory organs of the body.

Catabolism — It is the process of metabolism opposite to the anabolism. It includes all those processes by which complex substances are decomposed into simple substances which are usually eliminated from the body through excretory organs. There is no building of the body in this process of metabolism. It is the destructive metabolism. It causes wasting of the muscle tissues and loss of fat depots of the body with the consequent loss of weight and debility or general weakness.

In an adult person provided with adequate nutrition, the processes of anabolism and catabolism are mutually balanced and the general health and body weight remain steady and satisfactory.

Metabolism of Food Involves the following processes

(1) Digestion — It is the process by which the solid foods in the gastrointestinal tract are mechanically and chemically converted into liquids, i.e., into absorbable forms.

(2) Absorption — After digestion of food its absorption into the blood takes place through villi (very small finger like projections) present in the mucous membrane of the small intestine. After the food reaches the large intestine, no digestive process occurs in the large intestine, only the water of the undigested food is absorbed in the large intestine and the food is converted into solid feces which reaches the rectum whence it is eliminated from the body voluntarily through the anus. Almost 4 litres of water is absorbed in the large intestine per day leaving only 130-150 gms. of feces.

(3) Assimilation — Digested food after absorption mixes with the blood and is carried to the cells of the different parts of the body where its oxidation occurs which results in the production of energy and the new protoplasm is formed. This is only the protoplasm which causes the growth of the body and repair of the damaged tissues. The process of formation of protoplasm from the food is known as assimilation.

Basal metabolism — The sum of total metabolic processes occurring in the condition of complete physical and mental rest. i.e., in the condition of deep sleep which is not disturbed at all and at least 12 hours after taking food (during this period even no water or fluid is taken), i.e., till then the food would have been absorbed also. In this condition, only the vital processes of the body such as respiration, heart-palpitation, circulation, kidney function, peristaltic movements of the gastrointestinal tract, maintenance of muscle tone and body temperature etc., require minimum 1500-1800 calories energy daily for a person of the normal body in the state of absolute rest. Basal metabolism may also be defined as the amount of energy required for the maintenance of life when the person is at complete bed rest. It depends on the person's sex, weight, height and age.

BMR — Basal metabolic rate. The metabolic rate which is measured by calorimeter under the basal conditions as 12 hours after eating and restful sleep with no exercise before the test, elimination of emotional excitement and in a suitable temp. It is usually 40 calories per square meter of the body surface per hour.

The following factors affect the metabolic rate——

- **Sex** — Metabolic rate is increased 6 to 10% in men in comparison to women due to sex hormone.
- **Age** — Metabolic rate goes on decreasing as the age increases. BMR is considerably higher in infants, growing children and adolescence.
- **Size of the body** — It is comparatively higher in the persons of the body of small size.
- **Weight** — It is comparatively higher in the persons of low weight or lean and thin persons.
- **Physical labor** — Metabolic rate is higher in the persons doing physical labor in comparison to those who perform mental works while sitting on the chair or lead a sedentary life.

- **Mental tension** — In mental tension respiratory rate and heart rates are increased and so metabolic rate is also increased.
- **Temperature of the atmosphere** — Metabolic rate is increased when temperature of the atmosphere is increased.
- **Temperature of the body** — Metabolic rate is increased 13% for each degree of centigrade and 7% for each degree Fahrenheit when the body's temperature is increased or fever occurs.
- **Sleep** — During the sleep hours BMR is lowered about 10% than in waking state.
- **Ingestion of food** — BMR is increased at the time of ingestion.
- **State of nutrition** — In severe undernutrition BMR is low.
- **Fast** — Metabolic rate is decreased in fast.
- Metabolic rate is increased during menstrual period, pregnancy (15 to 25% increase during the last trimester) and lactation period.
- **Exophthalmic goitre** — Metabolic rate is increased in exophthalmic goitre, as much as 75 to 100%.
- Metabolic rate is decreased in cretinism and myxedema resulting from hypothyroidism, may be 30 to 40%.

In a growing child or in the adolescent (due to growth hormones) the anabolic process is upper most in the body. But in the aged person and debilitating diseases, the catabolism is significant.

Measurement of BMR — BMR can be measured with the help of special equipment by determining the heat (in terms of Kcal) given out by the person under study in a comfortable condition at the standard normal room temperature of 37°C, 12 to 18 hrs. after a light evening meal. The result is expressed in terms of Kcal per square meter of the body surface per hr. (Kcl/sqm/hr.)

With the BMR taken as unit one, for the sedentary activity men and women require 1.6 units, for the modern physical activity their requirement is 1.9 units and for the hard physical activity requirement is 2.5 units for 24 hrs.

The currently valid ICMR recommendations regarding the daily KCal requirement of men and women respectively are as follows —

Sedentary activity 2424 Kcals and 1872 Kcals. Moderate activity 2882 Kcals and 2223 Kcals. Heavy physical activity 3788 Kcals and 2925 Kcals.

METABOLISM OF CARBOHYDRATE

When the food is ingested, its complex carbohydrates or saccharides are acted upon by the enzymes present in the saliva, pancreatic juice and intestinal juice and polysachharides are converted into monosaccharides, as glucose, fructose and galactose, mainly into glucose. Glucose is absorbed by the villi present in the walls of the small intestine and passes into the blood capillaries, mixes up with their blood. A part of glucose remains in the blood circulation which is necessary to provide energy for body activities and it maintains the blood sugar to normal, i.e., fasting blood sugar remains 80-110 mg.% and post-prandial blood sugar 110-170 mg.%. The remaining glucose is carried by the portal vein to the liver, where excess of sugar is converted into glycogen. A part of this glucose is utilized in the metabolic processes occurring in the liver. The remaining part is converted into glycogen which is stored in the liver and muscles by insulin hormone secreted by the β cells of the islets of Langerhans of pancreas, which causes the blood sugar (glucose) level to be maintained normal. In deficiency of insulin as occurs in diabetes mellitus glucose is not converted into glycogen adequately, which increases the quantity of sugar in the blood above normal, i.e., blood sugar is increased. This condition is known as hyperglycemia. On the other hand excess of insulin decreases the blood sugar level. This condition is known as hypoglycemia.

On occurrence of hypoglycemia glycogen of the liver is again converted into glucose by the hormone adrenaline, thyroxine and glucagon, which is released from the liver into the blood and increases the blood sugar level to normal. An increase in the body activity causes the glucose in the blood released from the liver to be carried to all the cells of the body to provide energy.

Some glucose from the liver reaches the muscles through circulation and deposited there in the form of glycogen which is utilized in the muscular work during physical labor being converted into glucose.

Excess of carbohydrate taken with the food is converted into fat which is deposited in fat depots which increase the body weight. A normal adult requires about 400 carbohydrate daily.

Oxidation of glucose present in the cells yields energy and heat and carbon dioxide and water are formed. Energy is utilized in physical works, heat maintains the body temp. at normal level, carbon dioxide is a harmful gas which is eliminated from the body through the lungs along with the breath, water mixes up with the water present in the body which is ultimately expelled from the body in the form of urine through the kidneys, in the form of sweats through the skin and in the form of water-vapour through the lungs.

In the deficiency of insulin the blood sugar level rises too high and neither liver nor muscles can store glucose to the normal extent. This occurs in diabetes mellitus, a condition in which the pancreas is diseased and fails to produce the normal quantity of insulin, so that the blood contains excess of sugar, and sugar is excreted through the kidneys into the urine.

Too much insulin in the blood causes insufficient sugar in the blood, i.e., hypoglycemia. This is a very serious condition which may cause convulsions, coma and death. It is chiefly seen in giving an overdose of insulin.

METABOLISM OF PROTEIN

The protein ingested with foods contains about 24 types of amino acids of which about 9 types are essential amino acids, because they are not formed in the body, these are required to be taken only with the food. The remaining amino acids are called non-essential amino acids because they are formed by many tissues in the body. The ingested protein is acted upon by the enzymes of gastric, pancreatic and intestinal juices and converted into amino acids which are absorbed by the villi of the small intestine and mix up with the blood present in the blood capillaries found inside the villi and are carried first to the liver by the portal vein and then to the general blood circulation from the liver so that they may be available for the tissue cells for their utilization. Different types of cells of the body select particular amino acids from these obtained amino acids for the growth and repair of their specific tissue and for secretions as antibodies, enzymes and hormones, which are utilized. At the same time due to occurrence of damage in the body tissues, their protein, i.e., the endogenous protein is also decomposed into amino acids. Amino acids resulting from decomposition of the protein of the tissue cells in the body are called endogenous amino acids while the amino acids resulting from the digestion of the protein taken with food are called exogenous amino acids. A normal adult requires about 100 grams of protein daily. Protein is not deposited in the body. An amino acids pool is formed in the body by both the types, the endogenous and exogenous amino acids. The body cells obtain amino acids according to their needs from the amino acid pool. When the cells do not require amino acids for the growth or repair of the tissues or the food contains a large amount of protein, the extra amino acids are decomposed in the nitrogenous and non-nitrogenous substances by deamination in the liver. Ammonia is the main of the nitrogenous substances which is converted into urea. Urea is excreted in the urine, about 30 grams a day along with traces of uric acid and creatinine. Non-nitrogenous part includes carbon, hydrogen and oxygen which are utilized in the production of energy and heat for the body. Some protein is excreted with the feces in which shedded cells from the lining of the gastrointestinal tract are found. When there is deficiency of protein in the diet or in the fasting stage not only the carbohydrate and fat stores are emptied but deficiency of protein also occurs in the body, which causes the wasting of the muscles of the body and the body becomes thin as occurs in Kwashiorkor disease of the children. Exogenous and endogenous amino acids are mixed up in the amino acid pool and the body is supposed to be in nitrogen balance at the time when the speed of expulsion of nitrogen from the pool is equal to its mixing with the pool. The quantity of excreted nitrogen is equal to the quantity of ingested nitrogen, in a normal healthy adult because nitrogen (protein) is not deposited in the body like carbohydrates and fats. In serious diseases and fasting stage, there is no remaining nitrogen in the body, i.e., the excreted nitrogen is more than the ingested nitrogen. In children nitrogen is found in their bodies, i.e., in them the ingested nitrogen is more than the excreted nitrogen. It occurs in the children due to growth of different types of the tissues.

METABOLISM OF FATS

Fatty acids and glycerol resulting from digestion of fats are absorbed through the villi present in the walls of the small intestine and enter the lacteals, i.e., lymph vessels present inside the villi and mix up with their lymph. The fatty acids and glycerol mixing with the lymph are carried to the cisterna chyli, the origin of thoracic duct, by many lymph vessels or lacteals whence these are ultimately carried to the blood stream by thoracic duct, and some of them reach the liver by portal vein, where some changes occur in them, they are desaturated in the liver by oxidation. The remaining fatty acids and glycerol circulating in the blood reach every cell of the body and utilized in providing energy to the organs, and glands and in the formation of some of their secretions.

Fat is used to serve as fuel for the production of energy and heat in the tissues. It is burnt with sufficient sugar. It is completely burnt and converted into carbon dioxide and water. Energy is utilized in the performance of physical works. Heat maintains the body temperature, carbon dioxide is expelled out of the body through the lungs during respiration and the water is excreted as urine by the kidneys and as sweats by the skin. If there is little or no sugar to burn with it, combustion is incomplete and ketone bodies (acetone and acetoacetic acid) are formed which in small quantity produce a sense of fatigue, and in large quantity by reducing the alkalinity of blood, causes acidosis which results in drowsiness, coma and finally death, if the condition is not corrected by providing the tissues with glucose. This condition usually occurs in starvation and diabetes mellitus.

Fat is also required for the building of various tissues, e.g., nerve tissue, fatty tissue and marrow.

Fat not required for immediate use as fuel, can be stored as adipose tissue in the subcutaneous layer, greater omentum, mesentery, and the muscles etc., which causes an increase in body weight.

The metabolism of carbohydrate, fat and protein is closely linked up, and the taking of food of any kind in excess of the needs of the tissues will lead to an increase in body weight.

A normal adult requires 40-60 grams fat daily.

METABOLISM OF VITAMINS

Vitamins are described in Chapter 2.

METABOLISM OF MINERAL SALTS

Total amount of mineral salts in the human body is about 4.5% of the body weight. These are taken with the foods and these are expelled from the body through urine, sweats and feces. For their metabolism see Chapter 2.

Water is the largest constituent of the body, about 70% of the total body weight of a normal adult consists of water and a normal adult requires to drink 2 to 2.5 litres of water each day. This need is increased in hot weather and hot places or on working close to the furnace etc. The water drunk or coming with the food is absorbed into the blood in the small and large intestine. From the blood it is carried to the tissues along with the nutrients and mineral salts. Water is eliminated from the body in the form of urine from the kidneys, as sweats from the skin, water vapour through the lungs, and with the fecs.

The state of dehydration occurs due to loss of water from the body resulting from vomiting and diarrhea.

Edema occurs, especially on the legs on taking excess of sodium chloride, i.e., common salt which causes increasement of the volume of the water in the blood and tissue fluid.

Medical Importance of the Study of Metabolism

Basal metabolic rate (BMR) is examined to detect the condition of hyperthyroidism or hypothyroidism, BMR is increased in hyperthyroidism which results in the development of Exophthalmic goitre. BMR is decreased in hypothyroidism which results in the development of the diseases cretinism and myxedema.

* * * * *

CHAPTER 5

ENERGY REQUIREMENTS

Energy is the capacity for doing work, which is the primary requirement for body functions and growth. For all the daily activities some amount of energy is required. The type of energy needed for various activities varies from the type of work being done. In the body also various voluntary and involuntary activities are taking place which need energy. In order to fulfil these demands we consume food.

The total energy requirement of an individual is made up of two main components (a) Basal or resting state (when the body is in the complete bed rest) — energy requirement for vital functions such as sleeping, respiration and circulation etc. (b) The energy required for actual physical activity. It is the later component which varies depending upon age, sex and occupation and climatic conditions of the surroundings. The energy required for both the components is obtained from food. Proteins supply 10-12%, carbohydrates about 60% and fats about 30% energy. The quantitative food requirements are usually estimated in terms of energy, i.e., calories. Therefore the unit of energy is Calorie, which is the amount of heat necessary to raise the temp. of one kilogram of water by 1°C from 14.5°C to 15.5°C. This is 1000 times the physical calorie unit which is the amount of heat required to raise the temp. of one gram of water by one degree. Whenever calorie as a unit is mentioned, it is the physiologic calorie written with a capital "C", or kilocalorie (kcal). Now-a-days a new unit of energy is being used which is termed as joule. A joule (J) is defined as the energy required to move 1 kg. mass to 1 meter by applying 1 Newton force.

The relationship between joule and calorie

1 calorie = 4.184 joule (physical unit)

1 kilo-calorie = 4.184 kilo joule [kj] (physiological unit)

1000 kilo-calories = 4.184 Mega joules [MJ] (MJ means million joules)

1 kJ = 0.239 kcal

1000 kJ = 239 kcal

1 MJ = 239 kcal

The energy value of foods has long been expressed in terms of the kilo-calorie (kcal), which is generally expressed as "Calorie" written with a capital "C".

The dietary sources of energy are — Proteins, fats and carbohydrates. They supply energy at the following rates —

Protein — 4 kcal/gm. (or 17 kJ)

Fat — 9 kcal/gm. (or 37 kJ)

Carbohydrate — 4 kcal/gm. (or 17 kJ)

Amount of energy is recommended by FAO committee on calorie requirements for a "reference man and a reference woman" whose profiles are described and then necessary adjustments are made for the persons who deviate from the standard reference.

Indian reference man — An Indian reference man is between 20 and 39 years of age and weighs 60 kgs. He is free from disease and physically fit for active work. On each working day he is employed for

8 hours in occupation that usually involves moderate activity. While not at work he spends 8 hours in bed, 4 to 6 hours in sitting and moving around and 2 hours is walking and in active recreation or household duties.

Indian reference woman — An Indian reference woman is between 20-39 years of age, healthy and weighs 50 kgs. She may be engaged for 8 hours in general household works or in moderately active occupational work. Apart from spending 8 hours in bed, she spends 4 to 6 hours in sitting or moving around only through light activity and 2 hours in walking or in active recreation or in household duties.

Energy requirement— The energy requirement for an individual is the amount of energy which is to be taken according to expenditure, which usually does not cause obesity or heart disease or which is most likely to prolong active life. Energy intake and expenditure of an individual should be balanced because any surplus energy consumption will be stored as fat and a continuous excess intake will lead to obesity

Energy required for basal metabolism that is about 1 kcal/hour for every kg. of body weight for an adult.

Energy is required for daily activities such as walking, sitting, standing, dressing, climbing stairs etc.

Energy is required for occupational work. This is further classified as light work (an office work), moderate work and heavy (manual physical labor) work.

The person lying on the bed requires 1200 kcals, at the time of rest 1800 kcals are required, person working while sitting requires 2500 kcals and the person doing hard physical work as a laborer requires 3500 kcals per day. Infants and developing children require more calories per kg. of body weight in comparison to the adults.

Factors affecting the energy requirement

Energy requirement vary from one person to another depending upon the following factors—Age, sex, body composition (height and weight), working condition, physical activity, physiological state and climate etc. All these factors lead to difference in food intake.

In India energy requirements are those which are recommended by Indian council of medical research (ICMR) which are given in the following table. These standards are revised from time to time in the light of new knowledge.

***Table 28.* Recommended daily intake of energy**

Group	Body weight	Energy allowance per day	
	kg.	kcals	MJ
Infants			
0-6 months	—	118 kcal/kg./day	
7-12 months	—	108 kcal/kg./day	
Children			
1-3 years	12.03	1240	5.1
4-6 years	18.87	1690	7.0
7-9 years	26.37	1950	8.1
Adolescents			
10-12 years (males)	35.4	2190	9.1
10-12 years (females)	31.5	1970	8.2
13-15 years (males)	47.8	2450	10.2
13-15 years (females)	46.7	2060	8.6
16-18 years (males)	57.1	2640	11.0
16-18 years (females)	49.9	2060	8.6
Adults			
Reference males (light work)	60	2425	10.1
Reference males (moderate work)		2875	12.0
Reference males (heavy work)		3800	15.8
Reference females (light work)	50	1875	7.8

Reference females (moderate work)	2225	9.3
Reference females (heavy work)	2925	12.2
Pregnant women	+ 300	+ 1.25
Lactating women		
(first 6 months)	+ 550	+ 2.30
(6-12 months)	+ 400	+ 1.68

Vulnerable Groups

(a) Pregnant and lactating women — The energy requirements of women are increased during pregnancy (+ 300 kcals daily throughout pregnancy) and lactation period (+550 kcals daily during the first 6 months and +400 kcals daily during the next 6 months) above their normal requirements. It is to provide the extra energy required for the formation of new tissues during pregnancy and for the secretion of milk during lactation period.

(b) Children — Because of the rapid growth of the younger children, they require proportionately more energy for each kilogram of body weight than adults. When a child's food intake is below normal, her growth slows, and if it persists, adult stature will be reduced.

A problem arises in recommending the intake of energy in communities where a large number of children are underweight because of malnutrition. Intake of energy should be based on the age rather than weight in these communities for catch-up growth during childhood. The ICMR standards are based on age, and not on body weight (except during the first year of life).

Children above the age of 13 years require as much energy as adults because they show a great deal of physical activity, almost equal to hard work done by adults. This is also the age when puberty sets in and there is a spurt in growth and increase in metabolic rate.

(c) Adults — The energy requirements decrease with the age because of a fall in BMR and a decrease in physical activity in most persons. In general there is a 2% decline of BMR for each decade for adults. FAO/WHO committee suggested that after the age of 40 years, requirements should be reduced by 5% per decade until the age of 60, and by 10% for each decade thereafter.

In normal individuals at all ages and of both sexes, there is a large variation in energy intake but the reasons for this wide range of energy requirements are not known.

Table 29. **Values of energy expenditure**

Activity	Calories *(per minute)*	Calories *(per hr.)*
Sleeping	1	60
Sitting	1.5	90
Eating and drinking	1.5	90
Watching Television	1.5	90
Washing and dressing	2.5	150
Cleaning and dusting	3.5	210
Gardening	5	300
Standing	2.5	150
Walking slowly	3.5	210
Walking briskly	6	360
Slow cycling	5	300
Fast cycling	11	660
Dancing	12	720
Skipping	8	480
Slow swimming	5	300
Fast swimming	9.5	570
Slow running/jogging	8	480
Ball-room dancing	7	420

Energy-value of commonly used food items (in raw condition) quoted from the "Dietary Guidelines for Indians" published by the National Institute of Nutrition, Hyderabad, 1998.

Table 30. Energy-value of commonly used food items

Food item	Energy value
Cereals (Wheat flour/Rice)	100 kcal per 30 gms.
Pulses (Dal)	100 kcal per 30 gms. (protein 6 gms)
Milk (Toned)	70 kcal per 100 gms. (protein 3 gms)
Egg	85 Kcal per 50 gms. (protein 7 gms.)
Fish/Chicken/Mutton (in terms of fleshy part)	100 kcal per 50 gms. (protein 9 gms.)
Vegetables (leafy)	45 Kcal per 100 gms.
Vegetables (Roots and tubers)	80 kcal per 100 gms.
Fruits in general	40 kcal per 100 gms.
Sugar/Jaggery	20 kcal per 5 gms.
Fat/oil	45 kcal per 5 gms.

Table 31. Energy-value of commonly used cooked or prepared food items

Food item	Quantity	Energy
Rice	(1 Cup)	170 Kcals.
Chapati	(2 Nos.)	160 Kcals.
Bread	(2 Slices)	170 Kcals.
Idli	(2 Nos.)	150 Kcals.
Dosa	(1 No.)	125 Kcals.
Cornflakes + milk	(1Cup)	220 Kcals.
Vegetable (dry preparation)	(1 Cup)	150 Kcals.
Egg (boiled)	1	90 Kcals.
Egg (omelette)	1	160 Kcals.
Fish (fried)	(1 large size)	110 Kcals.
Chicken curry	(3/4 Cup)	240 Kcals.

Mutton curry	(3/4 Cup)	260 Kcals.
Cream crackers	(2 Nos.)	70 Kcals.
Toast (with butter 2 tsp.)	(2 Nos.)	200 Kcals.
Samosa	(1 No.)	200 Kcals.
Pakora	(2 Nos.)	70 Kcals.
Vada	(2 Nos.)	140 Kcals.
Dahi vada	(2 Nos.)	180 Kcals.
Pea-Kachori	(1 No.)	190 Kcals.
Pizza (Prepared with cheese and tomato)	1 Slice	200 kcals.
Halwa	1/2 Cup	320 Kcals.
Sandesh	(2 Nos.)	140 Kcals.
Milk chocolate	(25 gm.)	140 Kcals.
Ice-cream	(1/2 Cup)	200 Kcals.
Fruit squash	1 glass (200 ml.)	75 Kcals.
Cold drinks	1 glass (200 ml.)	150 Kcals.
Cow's milk (with sugar 2 tsp.)	1 Cup	180 Kcals.
Buffalo's milk (with sugar 2 tsp.)	1 Cup	320 Kcals.
Lassi (with sugar 2 tsp.)	1 glass (200 ml.)	110 Kcals.
Tea (prepared with 50 ml. toned milk and sugar 2 tsp.)	1 Cup	78 Kcals.
Coffee (prepared with 100 ml. toned milk and sugar 2 tsp.)	1 Cup	110 Kcals.

Fruits

Banana (one medium size)	90 Kcals.
Apple (one medium size)	65 Kcals.
Guava (one medium size)	50 Kcals.
Mango (one medium size)	180 Kcals.
Papaya ripe (one piece)	80 Kcals.
Pineapple (one piece)	50 Kcals.

Melon (one slice)	15 Kcals.
Cucumber (one medium size)	15 Kcals.
Tomato ripe (one medium size)	10 Kcals.

1 teaspoonful	—	5 mls.
1 tablespoonful	—	15 mls.
1 cup	—	150 mls.
1 glass	—	200 mls.

* * * * *

CHAPTER 6

BALANCED DIET

Balanced diet is a diet which contains different types of food in such quantities and proportion that the requirements for proteins, fats, carbohydrates, vitamins and minerals and other nutrients are in proper quantity for maintaining the health, vitality and general well being. A balanced diet is a safeguard of the population from nutritional deficiencies. The quantities of foods required vary with the age, sex, climatic conditions and physical activity. The energy-producing macronutrients (proteins, fats and carbohydrates) are to be supplied in the diet in the following proportions suggested by National Institute of Nutrition, India — carbohydrates should provide 60 to 70 % of the total energy (Calories), proteins 15 to 20% and fats or oils 20 to 25% .

According to the recommendation of ICMR the reference man of India should have a body weight of 60 kgs. and the reference woman of India should have a body weight of 50 kgs. The recommended calories for such a man are 2425 Kcals (sedentary work), 2875 Kcals (moderate physical activity) and 3800 Kcals (heavy physical activity). The recommended calories for such a woman are 1875 Kcals (sedentary work), 2275 Kcals (moderate physical activity) and 2925 Kcals (heavy physical activity). On an average the daily requirement of calories for a healthy adult (male and female) of sedentary and moderate activity is 40 Kcals. per kg. of the ideal body weight according to the age and sex.

Classification of the Activities Based on Occupation

Men doing sedentary work.

Executives, teachers, landlords, priest, retired personnel, tailor, peon etc.

Women doing sedentary work.

Executives, teachers, tailor, housewife, nurse etc.

Men with the jobs of moderate physical activity.

Driver, weavers, basket maker, shoe maker, fishermen, porter, fitter, carpenters etc.

Women with the jobs of moderate physical activity.

Maid servant, porter, basket maker, beedi makers etc.

Men with the jobs of heavy physical activity.

Stone cutter, black smith, mine worker, wood cutter, labourer and cooly etc.

Women with the jobs of heavy physical activity.

Stone cutter etc.

Some Requirements for Maintaining Health

- There should be balanced diet.
- Diet should contain proteins, fats and carbohydrates in proper proportion to provide energy.
- Use mixed diet of cereals and pulses.
- Select fresh vegetables and fruits.
- Eat raw vegetables in the form of salad.
- Avoid dried food.

- For non-vegetarians pulses should be deducted by 50% (20-30 gms.) and one egg or 30 gms. fish or meat should be given. If there are no pulses in the diet, 2 eggs or 50 gms. fish or meat should be given.
- One should drink 6-8 glasses (1200-1600 mls.) of water every day.
- During pregnancy there will be more demands of protein, calcium, iron, folic acid, vitamin D and other vitamins.
- There will be more demand for nutrients during lactation.
- Diet should be convenient in preparation.
- Diet should be appetising and tasty.
- It should not be costly.
- It should be easily available.
- Exercise is required to maintain good health. Suitable exercise should be undertaken daily by every body, especially adults leading sedentary life and elderly people. Walking, swimming, running and cycling etc. can be undertaken daily for at least 30 to 45 minutes.

Chart showing daily requirements of proteins, fats, carbohydrates, vitamins and minerals for an adult of average body weight.

Proteins — One gram per kg. of body weight or 65 gms.

Fats/oils — 20 grams per day.

Carbohydrates — 400 grams per day or 60% of the total caloric requirement per day.

Fibres — 10-12 grams per day.

Vitamins

Vitamin A — 600 mcgs. retinol or 2400 mcgs. β-carotene

Vitamin D — 100 IU or 2.5 mcgs.

Vitamin E — .8 mg. per gram of essential fatty acids or 10 mg./day.

Vitamin K — 2 to 3 mgs. or 0.03 mg. per kg. of body weight.

Vitamin B_1 (Thiamine hydrochloride) — 1.5 mg./day

Vitamin B_2 Riboflavine — 1.6 mg. per day

Vitamin B_6 (Pyridoxine hydrochloride) — 2 mgs. per day

Niacin or Nicotinic acid — 18 mgs./day

Vitamin B_{12} or cyanocobalamin — 1 mcg. per day

Folic acid — 100 mcgs./day

Pantothenic acid — 10 mgs. per day

Choline — 10 mgs./day

Inositol — 10 mgs./day

Biotin — 50-60 mcgs./day

Vitamin C — 50 mgs./ day

Minerals

Calcium — 400 mgs./day

Potassium — 2-5 gms./day

Magnesium — 200-300 mgs./day

Iron — 28 mgs./day for men and 30 mgs./day for women.

Iodine — 150 to 200 mcgs./day or 0.15 to 0.2 mg./day

Copper — 2.2 mgs./day

Fluorine — 0.5 mg. to 0.8 mg. per litre of drinking water.

Manganese — 3.7 mgs./day

Zinc — 15 to 20 mgs./day

Cobalt — 0.3 mg./day for an a adult.

***Table* 32. ICMR recommended diet for adult Indian men (60 kg.)**

Food Groups	Sedentary work (2425 Kcals)	Moderate physical activity (2875 Kcals)	Heavyphysical activity (3800 Kcals)
• Cereals	460 gms.	520 gms.	700 gms.
• Pulses	60 gms.	90 gms.	90 gms.

• Milk	150 mls.	200 mls.	300 mls.
• Fat/oil	20 gms.	35 gms.	55 gms.
• Green leafy vegetables	100 gms.	100 gms.	100 gms.
• Roots and tubers	50 gms.	60 gms.	80 gms.
• Other vegetables	60 gms.	70 gms.	80 gms.
• Fruits	60 gms.	60 gms.	60 gms.
• Sugar and Jaggery	30 gms.	35 gms.	55 gms.

For non-vegetarians substitution of 30 gms. of pulses by one egg, or 30 gms. of fish or meat is required.

Table 33. ICMR recommended diet for adult Indian women (50 kg.)

Food Groups	Sedentary work (1875 Kcals)	Moderate physical activity (2225 Kcals)	Heavy physical activity (2900 Kcals)
• Cereals	410 gms.	440 gms.	480 gms.
Pulses	60 gms.	75 gms.	90 gms.
• Milk	100 gms.	150 gms.	200 gms.
Fat/oil	20 gms.	25 gms.	35 gms.
• Green leafy vegetables	100 gms.	100 gms.	100 gms.
• Roots and tubers	50 gms.	50 gms.	60 gms.
• Other vegetables	40 gms.	40 gms.	40 gms
• Fruits	60 gms.	60 gms.	60 gms.
• Sugar and Jaggery	20 gms.	25 gms.	45 gms.

During pregnancy on an average an additional 300 Kcals energy is to be provided every day in the second and third trimesters. Micronutrients like iron, folic acid, calcium, vitamin D, vitamin B_6, vitamin B_{12} and magnesium are to be supplemented. Protein intake should also be increased to ensure at least 1.5 gm. per kg. of body weight.

Requirements During Pregnancy

Protein — 1.5 gm.per Kg. of body weight

Fat/oil — Additional 10 gms.

Green leafy vegetables — Additional 50 gms.

Fruits — Additional 100 gms.

Micronutrients

Iron — 38 mgs./day

Folic acid — 400 mcgs./day

Calcium — 1 to 1.5 gm./ day

Vitamin D — 400 IU or 10 mcgs.

Vitamin B_6 — 2.5 mgs./day

Vitamin B_{12} — 1.5 mcgs./day

Magnesium — 500-750 mgs./day

A lactating woman during the first 6 months after delivery of the child requires 550 Kcals. energy per day over the pre-pregnant state.

Additional Requirements per day

Cereals — 100 gms.

Pulses — 30 gms.

Green leafy vegetables — 50 gms.

Fat/oil — 10 gms.

Fruit — 100 gms.

Micronutrients

Iron — 38 mgs./day

Folic acid — 150 mcgs./day

Calcium — 1 to 1.5 gm./ day

Vitamin D — 400 IU or 10 mcgs.

Vitamin B_6 — 2.5 mgs./day

Vitamin B_{12} — 1.5 mcgs./day

Magnesium — 500-750 mgs./day

Note: Extra supplementation of vitamin A is required during lactation.

Iodine — In areas where there is endemic goitre, iodised salt should be used by all.

Infants — An infant requires 120 Kcals. per kg. of body weight in the first 3 months, 110 Kcals per kg. of body weight during the period between three and six months and 100 Kcals per kg. of body weight between 6 months and 12 months. The protein requirement is between 2 and 2.5 gm. per kg. of body weight. Weaning should be started with gradual introduction of semi-solid foods, pulses, orange juice, ripe banana after 6 months of age because milk alone is not sufficient to provide all the necessary nutrients from that time onwards.

Water intake — An adult should drink about 2 litres i.e., 5 glasses of water per day.

Infants during the first 6 months of life do not require additional water because milk provides both food and water adequately during this period of life.

* * * * *

CHAPTER 7

NUTRITIONAL DISORDERS

Proper nutrition should ensure satisfactory growth and development in infants and growing children and there should be no deficiency sign of any nutrient (macronutrient or micronutrient) in the body. In the adults, both physical and mental health should be maintained at the optimum level without any deficiency sign of any nutrient, along with a sense of well being. Deficiency and excess of any nutrient causes some conditions in the body.

MACRONUTRIENTS

Proteins

Deficiency — Deficiency of protein, i.e., serum albumin level below 3.5 gm./100 mls. is called hypoproteinemia which causes the following conditions :

- Loss of weight
- Reduction in subcutaneous fat

- General debility.
- Frequent loose motions
- Susceptibility to infection
- Delay in healing wound
- Edema on legs, arms and face
- Ascites
- Anemia
- Cirrhosis of the lever

In Pregnancy Hypoproteinemia Causes

- Premature birth
- Stillbirth
- Low birth weight babies, i.e., birth weight is less than 2500 grams.

Protein-Energy Malnutrition (PEM)

Protein deficiency in children causes protein-energy malnutrition (PEM) which is most commonly found in India among the children of six months to three years of age. It occurs in poor children who do not take enough food or take food deficient in protein or both the conditions may exist. PEM causes the following diseases in children.

1. Marasmus — It is characterised by wasting of the subcutaneous fat and muscles with retardation of growth and loss of weight. The eyes are sunken. Old man facies (monkey facies) develops. The skin is dry and there are loose folds of the skin, especially on the -buttocks and thighs. Abdomen is distended (pot belly) due to wasting, hypotonia of the muscles and gaseous distention. Mental retardation occurs.

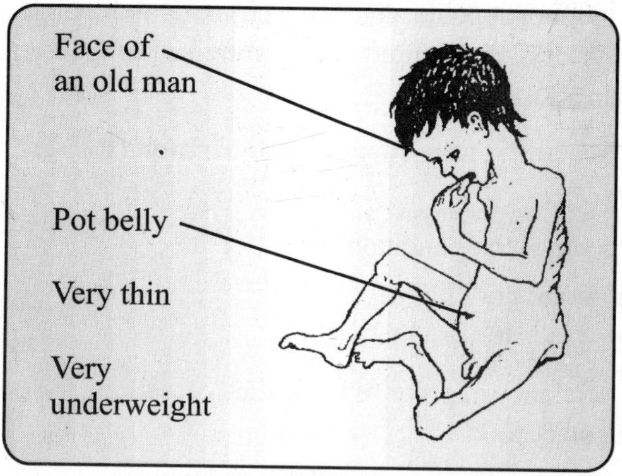

Fig. 1
The child suffering from marasmus

2. Kwashiorkor — It is characterised by the symptoms of lethargy, retarted growth, lack of proper development of the muscles, absence of muscle tone, presence of edema on the legs, arms and face (moon face), enlargement of the liver, mental deficiency, increased susceptibility

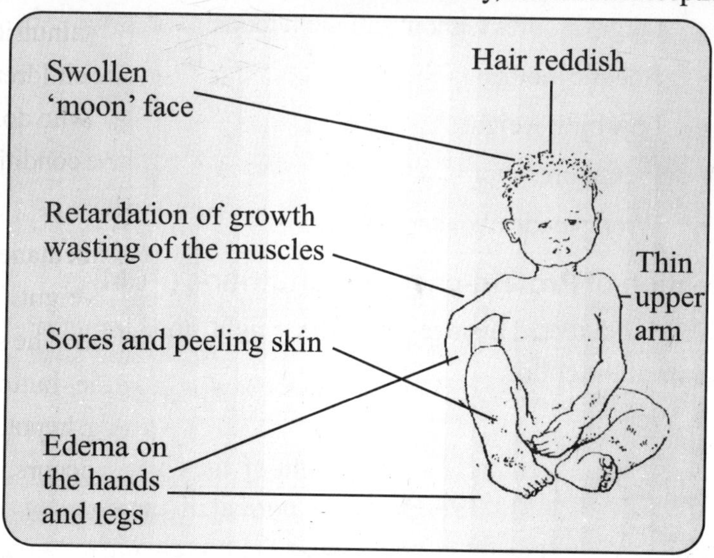

Fig. 2 The child suffering from Kwashiorkor

to infections, poor appetite, diarrhea, dermatitis and changes in the skin (the skin is dry, pigmented and flabby.) Hair become reddish. Hemoglobin is low.

Main causes of Protein-energy Malnutrition (PEM)

- Poverty
- Poor hygienic condition
- Ignorance or illiteracy
- Poor environmental sanitation
- Deficiency of proteins in the diet, cereals are the only supplementary food.
- Insufficient intake of food due to poverty
- Repeated infections such as diarrhea and respiratory infections, and intestinal worms which increase the requirements for calories, protein and other nutrients while decreasing their absorption and utilization.
- Infections present in the mother.
- Large families without sufficient foods.
- Anemic mother
- Low birth weight
- Premature labor
- Wrong medical/dietary advice.

Detection of Protein-energy Malnutrition (PEM)

PEM is detected by measuring the weight, and circumference of the arms of the child.

1. Weight —

$$\text{Weight for age (\%)} = \frac{\text{Weight of the child}}{\text{Weight of the normal of the same age}} \times 100$$

i.e., percentage of weight of the affected child is equal to her weight divided by weight of a normal child of the same age, multiplied by 100.

Percentage of weight between 90 and 110% — normal nutritional status

Percentage of weight between 75 and 89% — 1st degree, mild malnutrition

Percentage of weight between 60 and 74% — 3rd degree, severe malnutrition.

2. Measurement of the circumference of the arm — Circumference of the arm is measured after the age of one year.

An arm circumference greater than 13.5 cm.— a sign of satisfactory nutritional status.

An arm circumference between 12.5 and 13.5 cm — Indication of mild-moderate malnutrition.

Circumference of an arm below 12.5 cm — severe malnutrition.

If PEM is not checked, the child will probably develop marasmus or Kwashiorkor which are more serious conditions.

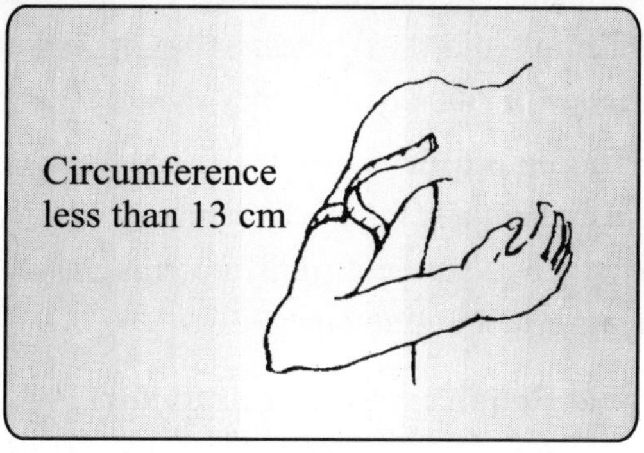

Fig. 3

Measurement of the circumference of the arm of the child after the age of one year for checking malnutrition. Circumference less than 13 cm. showing moderate malnutrition.

Prevention of protein-energy malnutrition (PEM) — PEM may be prevented in the following ways —

— Economic development to get rid of poverty.

— Family planning and spacing of births.

— Environmental sanitation should be improved.

— Measures to improve family diet.

— Promotion of breast feeding.

— Child's diet must contain protein and energy rich foods. Milk, fresh fruits and egg should be given to the child.

— Child should be made to eat more food at frequent intervals.

— Nutrition and health education.

— Immunization.

— Food fortification.

— Distribution of supplements or tonics etc., to the pregnant and lactating women.

Treatment of Protein-energy Malnutrition (PEM)

- Early diagnosis and treatment of the concomitant infection in the intestine (diarrhea), chest and skin, and of the intestinal worms and of vitamin deficiency should be undertaken.
- **Nutritional requirements** — The diet should be digestible (liquid diet initially for a week) and should contain proteins of high nutritive value, e.g., milk proteins and all other essential nutrients in required amounts.

The Nutritional Requirements are as follows : —

Calories — Intake of calories should be about 1½ times the normal requirement, i.e., 100 Kcals per kg. of body weight.

Proteins — The protein intake should be about twice or thrice the normal protein requirements, i.e., 3 to 5 gm. per kg. of body weight in the form of milk protein, usually skimmed milk powder (reconstituted) is considered the best or soya milk powder can be substituted when there is intolerance to lactose of the milk. As a general rule, in the first week only reconstituted skimmed milk powder or soya milk powder is to be fed. At the end of first week, in addition to the milk feed, mashed ripe banana, cooked mashed rice with milk and sugar are to be provided as principal meals twice a day. From the middle or end of the third week an appropriate balanced diet containing the normal dietary items should be provided gradually. Addition of pulses, leafy and non-leafy vegetables has to be made ensuring the intake of 100 Kcal. per kg. of body weight per day and 2 gms. of ideal protein per kg. of body weight per day.

Vitamins and minerals—Right from the beginning of the treatment proper supplementation of vitamins and minerals through pediatric preparations containing vitamin A, vitamin B-complex, vitamin C, iron, magnesium and zinc etc., is to be instituted. If vitamin A deficiency is present which is manifested by night blindness and xerophthalmia etc., a single dose of 50,000 IU of vitamin A should be given orally immediately followed by 5000 IU daily, or an injection of 5000 IU of vitamin A is given intramuscularly once a week for 4 to 6 weeks, on an average. Potassium and magnesium can be supplied by feeding 'Electral'. World Health Organisation (WHO) recommended Oral Rehydration Solution (ORS), a mixture of glucose and electrolytes which should be given in diarrhea for rehydration.

Anemia—For the treatment of anemia Ferrous ammonium citrate (0.8gm.) should he given daily in the form of syrup in 3 divided doses for a period of one month. Folic acid 1 mg. should be given daily for a week followed by 100 mcg. daily afterwards.

Diet—For a child suffering from protein-energy malnutrition and weighing 12 kgs., the daily intake of energy should be about 12 x 100 = 1200 Kcals. and protein intake 12 x 4 (or 5) = 48 to 60 gms.

Excess of protein—Excess of protein in the blood, i.e., serum albumin level far above 3.5 gm/100 mls. is called hyperproteinemia. Amino acids are the end products of protein digestion. When there is excess of protein in the diet, more amino acids are formed at the end of protein digestion. The extra amino acids which are not required by the body cells for the growth or repair of the tissues, are decomposed into nitrogenous and non-nitrogenous substances by deamination in the liver. Ammonia is the main of the nitrogenous substances which is converted into urea. Urea is excreted in the urine. Excess of urea (normal value 15 to 38.5 mgs/100 mls. blood serum) is retained in the blood. This condition is known as uremia which is characterised by nausea, vomiting, headache, dizziness, dimness of vision, coma or convulsions and urinous odor of breath and perspiration, dry skin, hard rapid pulse, high blood pressure and scanty urine containing casts and albumin.

Fats

Deficiency of fats — Deficiency of fats in the diet causes the following conditions.—

- **Leanness** — The body becomes lean or thin.
- Increased appetite and food intake.
- **Phrenoderma** — Deficiency of essential fatty acids in the diet causes a skin disease known as phrenoderma (toad skin) which is characterized by rough and dry skin with horny papular eruption on the posterior and lateral aspects of the thighs and on the backs and buttocks. It can be cured by giving sunflower oil which is rich in essential fatty acids, along with vitamin B complex.

Excess of fats — Excess of fats in the diet causes the following conditions :

- **Obesity** — Excessive intake of fat in the diet causes obesity. Excess of fat is deposited in the adipose tissues which constitute between 10 to 15 % of the body weight of a normal human being. In obese persons, due to deposition of fats, adipose tissues may increase upto 30 % of the body weight. One kilogram of adipose tissue corresponds 7700 Kcals. of energy.
- **Hypercholesterolemia** — Normal blood cholesterol level varies from 150 to 240 mg.% Excess of fat in the diet may in-

crease blood cholesterol level and thus may develop hypercholesteremia or hypercholesterolemia.

- **Atherosclerosis** — When large amounts of animal fats are consumed, their cholesterol may accumulate in the blood and may get deposited on the walls of the blood vessels causing atherosclerosis.
- **Coronary heart disease** — Excessive intake of fat in the diet which represents 40% or more of the energy supply and containing a high proportion of saturated fats is the major risk factor developing coronary heart disease.
- **Cancer** — Diets rich in fats increase the risk of the cancer of the colon and breast.

  Note — The World Health Organization (WHO) expert committee on the prevention of coronary heart disease has recommended only 20 to 30% of total dietary energy to be provided by fats.
- **Ketosis** — The accumulation of ketone bodies, i.e., acetone, beta-hydroxybutyric acid and acetoacetic acid in the body.

Carbohydrates

Deficiency — Deficiency of carbohydrates in the diet causes the following conditions—

- Weakness
- The body becomes thin
- Hypoglycemia — Blood glucose level (fasting) is found below 70 mg./100mls. of blood which is generally found in prolonged starvation, uncontrolled vomiting state and more commonly as a result of administration of excessive dose of insulin or other anti-diabetic drugs in a patient of diabetes mellitus. Very rarely, tumor of the β-cells of the islets of Langerhans (e.g., insulinoma) may be found to be the cause of hypoglycemia.

- Protein-energy Malnutrition (PEM)

Excess — Excess of carbohydrate causes the following conditions—

- Excessive fermentation and gas production in the intestines.
- Obesity due to conversion of carbohydrate into fat which is deposited in the fat depots and the body weight is increased.
- Hyperglycemia — Sugar (glucose) in the blood is increased which rises above 120 mg. per 100 mls. of blood (fasting sugar).
- Glycosuria — Appearance of sugar in the urine.
- Diabetes mellitus — Excess of glucose (sugar) in the blood (hyperglycemia), and appearance of glucose in the urine (glycosuria) or it is characterised by hyperglycemia (sugar in the blood above normal), glycosuria (presence of sugar in the urine), polyuria (excessive urination), polyphagia (excessive hunger), polydipsia (excessive thirst) and weakness.
- Dental caries — Intake of sweets, especially at night before going to bed may cause dental caries.

MICRONUTRIENTS

Vitamins

Vitamin A (Growth promoting factor or anti-infective vitamin) :

Deficiency — Deficiency of vitamin A causes the following conditions :—

Ocular manifestations —

- **Night blindness** — Lack of vitamin A causes night blindness or inability to see in dim light, especially when a person enter in a dark room after coming from a bright place. This condition may get worse, especially when the patient suffers from diarrhea and other infections. It is usually associated with malnutrition, especially protein-energy malnutrition (PEM)

- **Conjunctival xerosis —** The conjunctiva becomes dry and appears muddy and wrinkled, instead of looking smooth and shiny.
- **Bitot's spots —** These are triangular shiny gray, foamy spots seen on the bulbar conjunctiva on either side of the cornea which are usually bilateral.

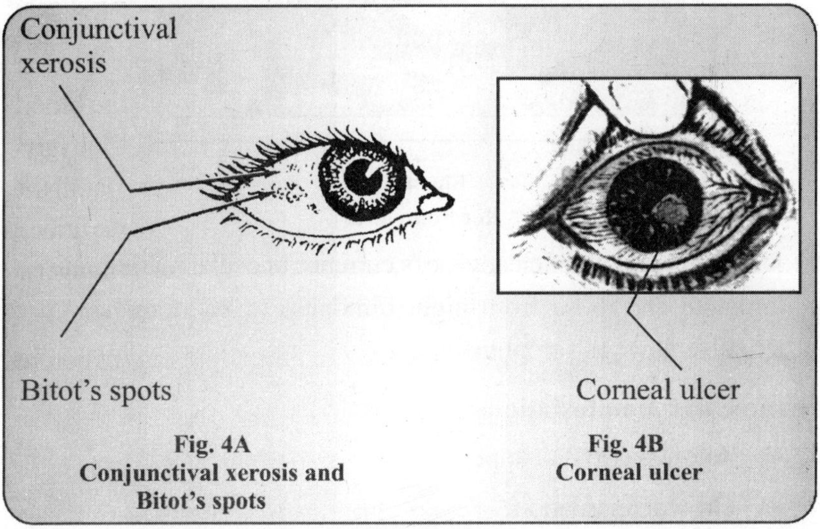

Fig. 4A
Conjunctival xerosis and Bitot's spots

Fig. 4B
Corneal ulcer

- **Corneal xerosis —** The cornea becomes dull and dry, not having a moist appearance and eventually becomes opaque. It is a serious condition. In more severe deficiency there may be corneal ulceration. The ulcer may heal leaving a corneal scar which can affect vision.
- **Keratomalacia —** Liquefaction of the cornea. A part or whole of the cornea may become soft and may burst open, then if the eye collapses, vision is lost. Keratomalacia is the commonest cause of blindness in the world, especially in India due to widespread malnutrition and under-nutrition. If keratomalacia is not

treated, it may lead to necrosis, ulceration and destruction of the eyeball.

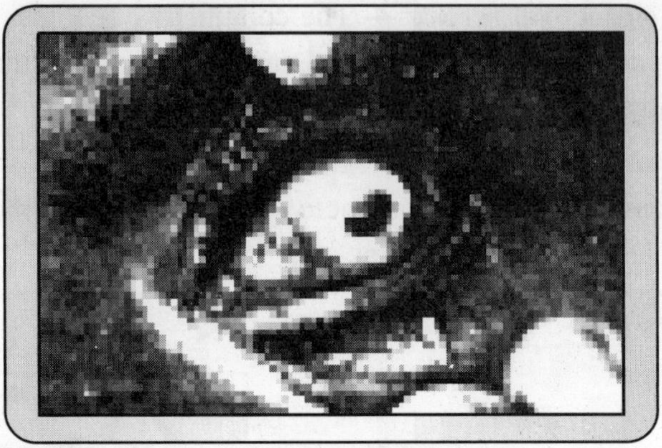

Fig. 4 C
Keratomalacia

Due to vitamin A deficiency the occurrence of ocular manifestations predominate and these from night blindness to keratomalacia are collectively known as xerophthalmia.

Extra-ocular manifestations

- Anorexia (loss of appetite)
- Growth retardation
- The skin becomes thick, dry and teared, lusterless, looking as that of the toad skin due to hyperkeratosis (excessive keratinisation of the skin).
- Changes in the epithelial tissues occur throughout the body.
- Resistance against infection is lowered due to vitamin A deficiency which may cause catarrh, cough, purulent otitis media, infection of the respiratory, intestinal and urinary tract.
- Vitamin A recently being linked to child mortality.

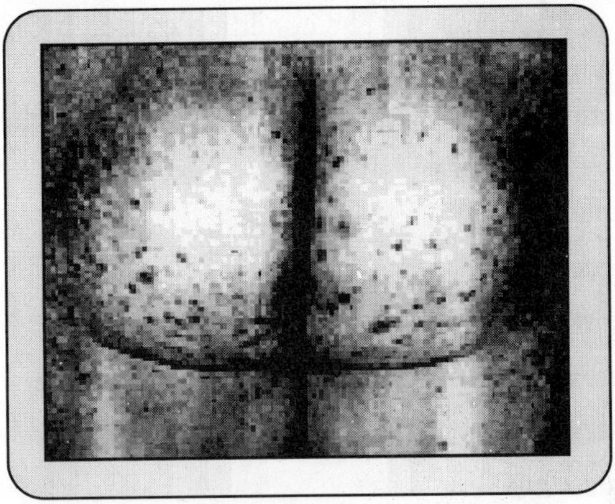

Fig. 5 Toad skin (Phrynoderma) Buttocks

Diagnostic tests : 1.Failure of dark adaptation is suggestive of vitamin A deficiency.

2. Estimation of vitamin A serum level which should not be less than 30 mg. per100 mls.

Prevention or control of vitamin A deficiency — (a) Intake of adequate foods rich in vitamin A regularly. (b) Lessening the frequency and intensity of the contributory factors, e.g., protein-energy malnutrition, respiratory tract infections, diarrhea and measles.

Since vitamin A can be stored in the body for 6 to 9 months and liberated slowly, administer a single dose of 200,000 IU of Vitamin A in oil (retinol palmitate) orally every 6 months to preschool children (1 year to 6 years), and half of that dose (100,000 IU) to children between 6 months and one year of age. Xerophthalmia and blindness can be prevented in this way.

Treatment— In night blindness and mild cases of conjunctival or skin changes, a capsule of vitamin A containing 30,000 IU should be given orally daily for a week. If there is corneal damage, 20,000 IU vitamin A should be administered by intramuscular injection daily for a week and it can be followed up by oral administration.

Excess of vitamin A — The condition caused by an excessive intake of vitamin A in the diet is called hypervitaminosis A. Excessive intake of vitamin A is toxic to both the children and adults. Common symptoms of toxicity are as follows —

- — Headache
- — Fatigue
- — Disturbances in sleep
- — Anorexia (loss of appetite)
- — Nausea
- — Vomiting
- — Hyperirritability
- — Drying and itching of the skin followed by its desquamation.
- — Loss of hair
- — Enlargement of the liver and spleen
- — Abnormal bony swellings (exostoses) over the long bones of the limbs.

Vitamin D or Antirachitic Vtamin

- **Deficiency of vitamin D** — Deficiency of vitamin D causes the following conditions —
- **Rickets** — It occurs due to diminished calcification and development of the bones and usually found in growing children with the age of 6 months to 2 years who are not exposed to sunlight and who do not drink milk. That is why vitamin D is also called antirachitic vitamin. Rickets is characterized by growth failure, general weakness; delay in walking, speaking, dentition and closure of the fontanelles; bending and distortion of the bones, craniotabes (small round soft areas of the skull due to lack of ossification), bossing of the frontal (front part of the skull), and partietal (latral parts of the skull) regions of the

skull. 'Rickety rosary' or beading of the ribs at the junctional site of cartilage, pigeon chest (chest deformity with a prominence of the sternum or breast-bone); Harrison's sulcus (a prominent depression of the chest extending laterally from the

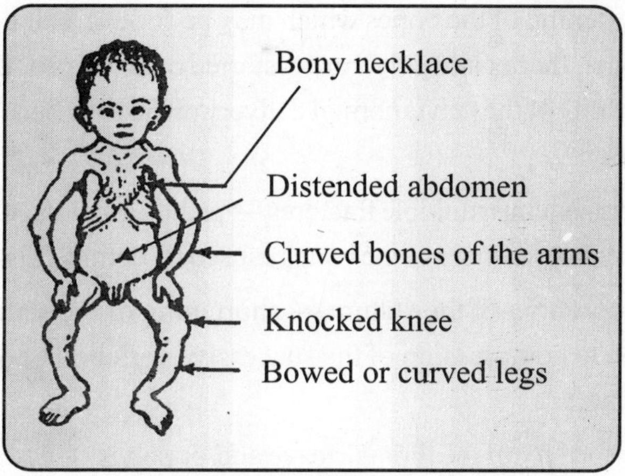

Fig. 6 Rickets

xiphoid process of the sternum), widening of the ends of the long bones as of the wrist, deformity of the pelvic bones, bowing of legs or curved legs and knock knees (due to weight-bearing on the unmineralised leg bones), muscular pain, sweating on the head at night, pot belly or distended abdomen caused by the weakness and hypotonia of the abdominal muscles, nervousness and restlessness.

- **Osteomalacia (the adult form of rickets)** — It occurs mainly in women, especially during pregnancy and lactation when requirements for vitamin D are increased. It may occur when there is interference with fat absorption, and hence absorption of vitamin D is also impaired. It is also seen in women who observe purdha system and do not expose themselves to natural light. It is characterized by — General weakness with difficulty in walking, especially difficulty in climbing the stairs or getting out of a chair.

— Pain of rheumatic type in the bones of the legs and the lower part of the back.

— Softening of the bones which may be so severe that bones of spine, thorax and pelvis are distorted or deformed. Due to deformity of the pelvis normal delivery of the baby becomes difficult.

— Spontaneous multiple fractures — pathological fractures occur due to brittleness of the bones caused by demineralisation.

— Shortening of the stature — shortening of the stature occur due to compression of the successive vertebral bodies of the spine.

— Deformity of the thoracic cage and/or pelvis.

Diagnosis : Rickets — The haziness of the outline of the wrist joints and broadening of the epiphyseal ends of the long bones will be found on x-ray examination. In blood test calcium and phosphorus levels will be found low but the level of alkaline phosphatase is increased.

Differential diagnosis of osteomalacia with osteoporosis : Calcium and phosphorus levels are low but alkaline phosphatase level elevated in osteomalacia, which are not found in osteoporosis.

Treatment of Rickets and Osteomalacia — Rickets and osteomalacia can be treated with 1000 to 5000 IU or 25 to 125 mg. of vitamin D orally daily for a month. It may be followed by 800 IU for 6 months. Depending upon the improvement, the dosage can be gradually decreased. These diseases can be prevented by supplementing the diet with 400 IU of vitamin D.

Tetany — It is caused by deficiency of vitamin D causing deficient absorption of calcium and characterized by intermittent numbness and tingling of the limbs, hyperflexion of the wrist and ankle joints (carpopedal spasm), muscular twitching, cramps and convulsions due to hypocalcemia.

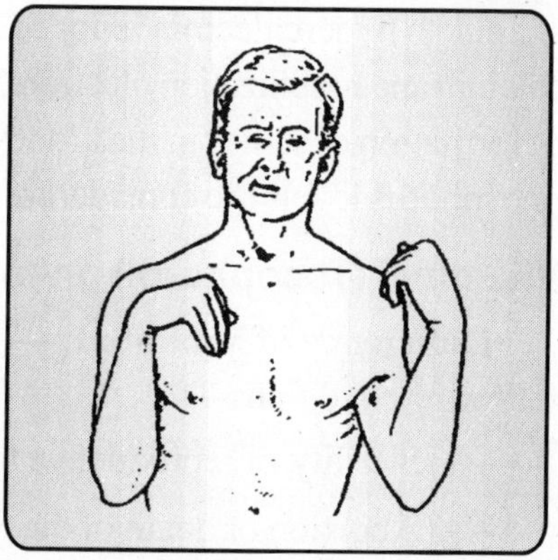

Fig. 7 Tetany

Prevention — Preventive measures include —

(a) To educate the parents to expose their children regularly to sunlight.

(b) Prophylactic dose of Vitamin D should be given to the young children periodically. Prophylactic dose is 400 IU (10 mg.) or less daily depending upon the amount of exposure in the sunlight. Along with it calcium either in the form of milk or as syrup of calcium gluconate should be given. To prevent osteomalacia one or two tablets containing vitamin D and calcium should be given from the beginning of the 4th month of pregnancy upto the middle of eighth month of pregnancy.

(c) Food, especially the dried milk for the infant feeding is to be fortified with Vitamin D.

Excess of vitamin D — The condition caused by an excessive intake of vitamin D in the diet or prolonged administration of excessive dose of vitamin D (100,000 IU daily) is called hypervitaminosis D (toxicity of vitamin D) which causes hypercalcemia.

The symptoms of toxicity of vitamin D are headache, anorexia (loss of appetite), nausea, vomiting, diarrhea, polyuria, thirst, itching, weight loss, drowsiness and weakness, etc. As the toxicity of Vitamin D increases, renal damage and calcification of the soft tissues occur which are due to hypercalcemia induced by increased intestinal absorption of calcium and mobilization of it from the bones. There is also the possibility of formation of stones in the kidney and urinary tract as the calcium and phosphorus levels are considerably raised in both blood and urine.

Vitamin E (Tocopherol) or Antisterility Vitamin

Deficiency of Vitamin E — Deficiency of Vitamin E causes the following conditions —

— Sterility, or reproductive failure

— Abortion or death of the fetus in uterus or premature labor.

— Impotency in man

— Muscular pain, weakness of the muscles and paralysis. Muscular dystrophy may occur

— Atherosclerosis and vulnerability to heart disease.

Note : Deficiency of Vitamin E in human being is unlikely to occur as it is found in abundance in food. It generally occurs in malnutrition.

Diagnosis : Blood examination will show diminished level of Vitamin E against the normal level of 0.5 to 0.7 mg. per 100 mls.

Therapeutic dose — 100 to 400 IU of vitamin E are administered orally daily in the treatment of sterility, abortion, muscular diseases. Due to its vasodilator action it is used in angina pectoris, intermittent claudication and Raynaud's disease. 300 to 2400 IU of vitamin E are administered daily orally in coronary thrombosis and angina pectoris etc., because vitamin E decreases the body's need for oxygen, while at the same time it increases the supply of oxygen to the heart.

Vitamin E when applied externally minimises wrinkles, scar and scratch marks.

Vitamin E when applied on severe burn it helps in early healing.

Hot flushes, depression and sweating of menopause have been diminished with an increased intake of vitamin E.

Tablets of vitamin E (Evion) 100, 200 and 400 mg. are available.

Excess of vitamin E — There is usually no side effect of excess of vitamin E but nausea, flatulence and diarrhea may occasionally occur after administration of large doses of vitamin E in clinical practice.

Vitamin K or Anti-hemorrhagic factor

Deficiency of vitamin K — Deficiency of vitamin K causes the following conditions —

Melena neonatorum or hemorrhagic disease of the new-born. It occurs in premature infants in the first week of life when the normal bacterial flora of the intestine is yet to grow. It is characterized by the passage of the black tarry stool due to presence of sufficient amount of altered blood. Deficiency of vitamin K prolongs blood-clotting time and causes hemorrhage.

Deficiency of vitamin K in adults may occur as a secondary manifestation of anticoagulant therapy, prolonged antibiotic therapy which causes the destruction of the normal flora of the intestine, obstruction of the bile duct due to stone formation with subsequent lack of bile and bile salts in the intestine and which interferes with the absorption of fat-soluble vitamins, and in malabsorption syndromes. This causes melena or hemorrhage from the body. There is a tendency to bleed from the skin and nose (epistaxis) due to vitamin K deficiency.

Diagnosis : Diagnosis of vitamin K deficiency can be made by laboratory test for "prothrombin time" which is found to be prolonged in vitamin K deficiency.

Prevention : During childbirth the mother is usually given an intramuscular injection of 1 mg. of vitamin K because there is always a risk of hemorrhage in cases of prematurity, complicated labor or mother receiving anti-coagulant therapy and moreover the normal bacterial flora of the intestine of permature infant has not been formed as yet. In premature infants, as a prophylactic dose of a single intramuscular injection of 0.5 mg. of vitamin K or 0.1 mg, menadione sodium bisulphite may be given to the child.

Treatment — In case of hemorrhage an intramuscular injection of vitamin K_1 1 mg. is to be given and repeated about 8 hrly for 24 hrs. In adults, in case of hemorrhage, a single intramuscular injection of 15 mg. of vitamin K is usually given, followed by one tablet of vitamin K (Kapilin) twice or thrice daily for a few days.

Excess of vitamin K — No toxic effects of vitamin K due to its excessive intake or its over dose in the treatment have been reported.

Vitamin B Complex

It includes the following vitamins (factors) which are inter-related.

Vitamin B_1 (Thiamine hydrochloride)

Deficiency of vitamin B_1— Deficiency of vitamin B_1 causes the following conditions—

(1) Beri-beri — A disease marked by peripheral neuralgic, cerebral (of central nervous system) and cardiovascular abnormalities caused by vitamin B_1 deficiency. It is of the following three types.

1. Dry beri-beri — In dry beriberi the main symptoms are related to the nervous system. It generally occurs in maize eaters in the eastern region of India. It is characterized by peripheral neuritis (inflammation of the peripheral nerves), tenderness in the calf muscles, pain, paresthesia (abnormal sensations in the affected limbs), numbness or tingling in the legs, irritability and muscular cramps, in serious cases central nervous system is affected causing Wernick's encephalopathy which usually occurs in chronic alcoholism, gastric carcinoma or hyperemesis gravidarum and characterized by bilateral, symmetrical, nystagmus and ophthalmoplegia, polyneuritis, ataxia, confusion and mental deterioration.

2. Wet beri-beri — In this type of beriberi heart is involved, so it is also called cardiac beriberi which is characterized by biventricular congestive heart failure with the enlargement of the heart and pulmonary congestion with edema, and edema on the dependent parts (legs etc.), which is the most notable feature and is due to sodium and water retention in the body, anasarca and dyspnea. Tachycardia or palpitation which is prominent and is due to myocardial weakness. Neck veins are engorged.

3. Infantile beri-beri — It is seen in infants of the age of 2 to 4 months. The affected baby is usually breast-fed by the mother with vitamin B_1 deficiency who commonly shows the signs of the peripheral neuropathy. The child becomes restless, often cries, does not sleep and there is loss of appetite. She passes urine in small quantity and shows signs of puffiness. The infant may suddenly become cyanosed with breathlessness and palpitation due to enlargement of the heart and dies within 24 to 48 hours. Other serious signs occurring are convulsions and coma.

Manifestations of minor degrees of vitamin B_1 deficiency are

(2) Loss of appetite

(3) Absence of ankle and knee jerks.

Prevention — To educate the people to eat well balanced, mixed diets containing thiamine-rich foods (e.g., parboiled and undermilled rice) and to stop alcohol absolutely. Maize should be avoided in the diet.

Treatment — In vitamin B_1 deficiency an intramuscular injection of vitamin B_1 50 to 100 mg. is given daily for a few days and then on alternate days for the next few days. Subsequently it can be given orally in a dose of 50 to 100 mg. per day for about a month. In infantile beriberi, the infant must be given 20 mg. vitamin B_1 intramuscularly and the mother should receive 10 mg.of vitamin B_1 twice daily.

Toxic effect — Sometimes anaphylactic reaction may occur with parenteral injection of Vitamin B_1

Vitamin B_2 or Riboflavine

Deficiency — Deficiency of Vitamin B_2 (Ariboflavinosis) causes the following conditions —

— Impairment of growth

— Cheilosis or angular stomatitis (fissures developing at the corners of the mouth with redness of the lips)
— Glossitis with geographic tongue — Inflammation of the tongue with numerous denuded patches on its dorsal surface resembling geographic areas on a map.
— Fissuring of the skin as of the scrotum.
— Nasolabial seborrhea.
— Photophobia — sensitivity to bright sunlight.
— Redness and burning sensation in the eyes.
— Seborrheic dermatitis.

Deficiency of vitamin B_2 generally occurs in malnutrition, alcoholism or as a adverse side effect of certain psychotrophic drugs.

Diagnosis :

Urinary riboflavine excretion is found to be less than 50 mg. per day.

Treatment

Riboflavine 5 mg. can be given two or three times a day for a long period.

Excess of vitamin B_2

Usually no sign of Nutritional Disorders is seen due to excessive intake of vitamin B_2

Vitamin B_6 or Pyridoxine Hydrochloride

Deficiency

Balanced diets usually contain pyridoxine in proper amounts, therefore deficiency of Vitamin B_6 or pyridoxine is very rare. Riboflavine deficiency impairs the optimal utilization of pyridoxine. Its deficiency usually occurs as secondary to certain medicines as Isoniazid or Isonicotinic acid hydrazide (INH) is one which is commonly used as antitubercular drug. Deficiency of vitamin B_6 causes the following conditions—

- Peripheral neuritis
- Morning sickness, i.e., vomiting during first 3 months of pregnancy in the morning.
- Irritability
- Tremors in the hands and legs.
- Epileptic convulsions may occur in severe vitamin B_6 deficiency, especially in infants.
- Mental depression
- Glossitis
- Cheilosis
- Seborrheic dermatitis
- Hypochromic anemia.

Treatment

Usually 20 to 40 mg. of Vitamin B_6 (pyridoxine hydrochloride) is given daily orally.

Excess of vitamin B_6

There is usually no sign of excess of vitamin B_6

Niacin or Nicotinic Acid

Deficiency

Deficiency of niacin occurs in malnourished people, subsisting mainly on maize diets. It is a deficiency of maize eating population. Deficiency of niacin causes the following conditions—

Pellagra

Deficiency of niacin causes pellagra, that is why niacin is called pellagra-preventing factor and pellagra is characterized by three D's—1. Diarrhea 2. Dermatitis and 3. Dementia. Niacin is used in the treatment of pellagra.

Glossitis

Red, swollen and painful tongue.

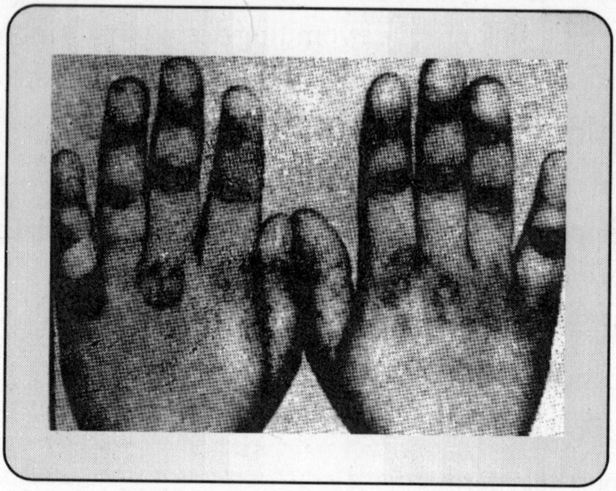

Fig. 8 Pellagra

Stomatitis – Mouth becomes sore and often shows angular stomatitis.

Dermatitis

It is bilaterally symmetrical and is found only on those surfaces of the body, exposed to sunlight, such as back of the hands, lower legs, face and neck and the lesion resembles severe sunburn. Affected areas are demarcated from the normal skin, which are red, slightly swollen and may cause itching and burning sensation. The skin becomes dry, thick and rough.

Diarrhea

Motions are usually watery and sometimes blood and mucus are seen in the stool.

— Weakness

— Loss of weight

— Loss of appetite

— Depression

— Irritability

— In severe cases delirium may occur

— Apathy

— Confusion

— Loss of memory

Treatment — Niacin or nicotinic acid 200 mg. may be given daily in divided doses when there exists some deficiency disease.

Excess — Excessive intake of niacin usually does not cause any condition.

Vitamin B_{12} or Cyanocobalamin

Deficiency — Deficiency of Vitamin B_{12} occurs in those who strictly eat food of vegetable origin and do not take animal foods, as milk etc. It is more likely to occur in strict vegetarians, who do not even drink milk. Deficiency of vitamin B_{12} causes the following conditions—

1. Pernicious anemia — A form of anemia occurring in a person, usually after 50 years of age, due to absence of Castle's intrinsic factor from the gastric juice, which causes absorption of cyanocobalamin (vitamin B_{12}) or due to deficiency of vitamin B_{12} in the diet, characterized by lemon-yellow color of the skin, soreness and inflammation of the tongue, numbness or tingling in the legs and hands, progressive weakness, loss of weight, dyspnea on exertion and palpitation. Megaloblastosis occurs due to vitamin B_{12} deficiency i.e., red blood cells become larger in size but greatly decreased in number. Average diameter of R.B.C. is greater than 7-8 μm (normal) and R.B.C. count is 1.5 to 2.5 millions per cubic millimeter of blood while normally it is 4.5 to 5.5 millions per cu. mm. of blood. Hemoglobin percentage is low, it is 7 to 9%

2. Subacute combined degeneration of the spinal cord — Degeneration of the posterior and lateral columns of the spinal cord, characterized by paresthesia (An abnormal sensation as numbness, tingling, prickling, burning or insect creeping on the body, etc.), ataxia or muscular incoordination — inability to maintain the body balance and tendency to fall down while standing with the eyes closed and the feet close together and sometimes spastic paraplegia (paralysis of the lower portion of the body with increased muscular tone and tendon reflexes).

3. Hyperglycemia

4. Anorexia (loss of appetite)

Diagnosis: Diagnosis is made by estimation of serum level of vitamin B_{12} which is normally 200 to 960 µg. per 100 mls. Finding of less than 80 µg. per 100 mls. provides a definite diagnosis.

Treatment : Ordinarily for megaloblastic anemia vitamin B_{12} is administered orally along with folic acid in an average dose of 50 to 100 µg. per day. For the neurological disorders, as in pernicious anemia 1000 µg. of hydroxocobalamin (vitamin B_{12}) is administered by intramuscular injection twice a week in the first week and then once a week for two weeks. Later on, a single injection of 1000 µg. may be given once a month which should be continued throughout life with periodic check-up of blood. Hydroxocobalamin is therapeutically more effective than cobalamin.

Excess — No clinical signs have been observed due to excessive intake of vitamin B_{12}

Folic Acid

Deficiency — Deficiency of folic acid occurs as a result of overcooking of the food which destroys folic acid, it may occur in alcoholism and it generally occurs in pregnancy. Deficiency of folic acid causes the following conditions —

- Folic acid deficiency is quite common in pregnancy. It occurs with iron deficiency anemia and causes nutritional anemia. In early pregnancy folic acid deficiency may cause abortions.

- Irritability
- Forgetfullness
- Mental sluggishness
- Megaloblastic or macrocytic anemia usually in pregnancy and to a lesser extent in pre-school children.
- Glossitis
- Cheilosis

Gastrointestinal disturbances

- Diarrhea
- Distension of the abdomen
- Flatulence
- Severe folic acid deficiency may cause infertility or even sterility.
- Congenital defects as cleft lip and cleft palate may occur in the child.

Diagnosis : Estimation of serum level of folic acid which is normally 6 to 20 ng. (ng = nanogram) per 100 mls. will surely establish the diagnosis when the level is less than 3 ng. per 100 mls. When folic acid is found just below 6 ng. per 100 mls., deficiency is most likely. RBC count is 2-3 millions per cu. mm. of blood and Hb is 6-9%

Treatment — Generally, a dose of 5 mgs. of folic acid with iron once or even two to three times a day orally should be given throughout pregnancy and continued for six weeks after delivery.

A blood transfusion will be necessary if anemia is severe or in untreated cases if delivery is imminent.

Excess of folic acid — Excess of folic acid usually does not cause any condition.

Pantothenic Acid

Deficiency : Deficiency of pantothenic acid usually does not occur as it is found in all common food-stuffs. However, its deficiency may cause the following conditions—

- Burning feet syndrome
- Tremors of the stretched hands
- Irritability
- Premature greying of hair
- Brittleness of the hair
- Alopecia
- Insomnia
- Increased flatus
- Post operative distension of the abdomen
- Paralytic ileus.
- Sterility may occur

Treatment — In mild cases pantothenic acid is given in the form of calcium pantothenate tablet 50 mg. or 100 mg, twice daily for a few days. In burning feet syndrome or paralytic ileus, it is generally given by intramuscular injection as calcium pantothenate 10 mg. daily for a few days

Choline

Deficiency — Deficiency of choline causes enlargement of the liver due to fatty degeneration which is known as fatty liver.

Treatment — Choline is given in the treatment of fatty liver and alcoholic cirrhosis of the liver.

Inositol

Deficiency— Deficiency of inositol in man is rare. However, its deficiency causes : —

— Stunted growth

— Alopecia or loss of hair or falling of hair.

Treatment — Inositol is available as one of the ingredients of multivitamin preparations. It is used for the treatment of alopecia, generally with vitamin E.

Biotin

Deficiency — Deficiency of biotin in man is rare. However, its deficiency causes the following conditions —

— Atrophy of the tongue papillae, and pale appearance of the tongue

— Anemia

— Dermatitis with scales and cracks.

— Sudden infant death syndrome.

Diagnosis — Urine examination shows the excretion of biotin in low quantity. Response of the drug will also confirm the diagnosis.

Treatment — 100 μg. of biotin is given orally daily or an injection containing 150 to 300 μg. of biotin can be administered intramuscularly per day.

Para-Aminobenzoic Acid (PABA)

Deficiency — Its deficiency causes —

Premature greying of the hair

Treatment — Para-aminobenzoic acid is often used as oral tablets and liquid preparations along with other vitamin B complex vitamins.

Vitamin C or Ascorbic Acid or Anti-scorbutic Vitamin

Deficiency — Mild form of vitamin C deficiency causes

— Malaise

— Weakness

Gross deficiency of vitamin C causes —

— Scurvy, characterized by swollen and spongy gums with a tendency of bleeding, hemorrhage into the skin characterized by pin-head size petechiae, subcutaneous hemorrhage, hemorrhages from the mucous membranes, hemorrhage in the bone joints with their swelling, anemia, weakness, pain in the limbs and joints (the infant cries when her legs and arms are moved), swelling at the ends of long bones, loosening of teeth.

— Retardation of growth in infants

— Delayed wound healing

— Increased susceptibility to infection

— Convulsions may occur in infants which sometimes result in death of the infant.

Scurvy or vitamin C deficiency generally occurs when eatable foods are heated. Heating of foods destroys vitamin C. It occurs in infants of the age of 8 to 12 months who do not drink mother's milk but take heated milk powder or condenser milk.

Diagnosis — Estimation of ascorbic acid level of blood plasma. It will be less than 0.1 mg. per 100 mls.

Treatment — 300 to 1000 mgs. of vitamin C are given orally daily in divided doses.

Toxic effects of overdose of Vitamin C — Toxic effects of vitamin C are not usually seen because it is water-soluble vitamin and is easily excreted from the body. Rarely gastric irritation or flatulence may occur. Sometimes after a long period stones of calcium oxalate are formed or there may be crystalluria (presence of crystals of calcium oxalate in the urine). This is because ascorbic acid is metabolized to oxalate.

MINERALS

Major Minerals

Calcium

Deficiency of calcium — Calcium is lost in the preparation of vegetables if their thick skins are removed or dark green leaves are discarded. There may be dietary deficiency of calcium. Deficiency of calcium in the blood is called hypocalcemia.

Causes of hypocalcemia — (1) Hypoparathyroidism, (2) Gross deficiency of vitamin D, (3) Acute pancreatitis, (4) Chronic malabsorption syndrome, (5) Chronic renal failure, (6) Uncompensated increased physiological demand of pregnancy or lactation, (7) Hypomagnesemia.

Calcium deficiency causes the following conditions : —

- Rickets in children
- Osteomalacia in women, especially during pregnancy.
- Osteoporosis — It is a condition in which decalcification of the bones occurs due to calcium deficiency in the diet. It generally occurs in old men and women, mostly in women after menopause, in which bones are rarefied and occasionally a bone is fractured.
- Brittleness of the bones
- Fracture of the brittle bones after a minor injury.
- Poor development of the bones and teeth
- Dental caries
- Retardation of growth in children.
- Hyperirritability
- Tetany — It generally occurs in infants and children characterized by intermittent numbness and tingling in the limbs, carpopedal spasm, muscular twitching, facial grimacing, cramps

of the various muscles and convulsions. If it is not treated, patient may die from prolonged convulsions.

- Hypotension
- Convulsions
- Heart failure

Prevention — A balanced diet containing 1 to 1.5 gm. calcium with vitamin D 400 IU should be given. There is increased demand of calcium in pregnancy which often produces calf muscles cramps. Hence all the pregnant women should be given foods containing calcium, as milk and egg etc., and the preparation of calcium and vitamin D in the form of tablets as calcinol, ostocalcium, calcium sandoz etc. One or two tablets daily from the onset of 4th month to the middle of the eighth month of pregnancy should be given.

Treatment — Without proper treatment, the patient may die from convulsions, hypotension or heart failure. So the patient should be given calcium gluconate by intravenous injection. Subsequently with the improvement of the condition after a few intravenous injections, tablets of calcium lactate or calcium gluconate and vitamin D should be given.

Excess of calcium — An excess of calcium in the blood is called hypercalcemia

Causes of hypercalcemia — (1) Hyperparathyroidism (2) Idiopathic hypercalcemia (3) Vitamin D intoxication which may be due to administration of vitamin D in excess for a long period. (4) Subsistence of an infant exclusively on artificial food, as cow's milk which contains 3 to 4 times more calcium than in the breast milk. (5) Vitamin A intoxication (6) Milk-alkali syndrome—this condition is caused due to prolonged and excessive intake of milk and absorbable alkali for the treatment of peptic ulcer as was the practice in the past.

Excessive intake of calcium or hypercalcemia causes the following conditions —

- Hypertension

- Phosphaturia — excretion of calcium phosphate in the urine which is deposited on the earth like white lime, at the end of urination.
- Overgrowth of a bone
- Stone formation in the kidney
- Cardiac arrhythmia.

Treatment —(1) Calcitonin hormone, the antagonist of parathyroid hormone can be given which produces hypocalcemic effect.

(2) Diuretics — A diuretic may be given in the treatment of hypercalcemia.

Phosphorus

Deficiency — Deficiency of phosphorus usually does not occur in the diet as it is found in cereals, pulses, milk and animal foods as fish etc. Fishes are the richest source of phosphorus: Low serum level (2 mg./100 ml. or less) of phosphorus is called hypophosphatemia.

Causes of phosphorus deficiency or hypophosphatemia —

— Hyperparathyroidism

— Vitamin D deficiency which may be due to inadequate intake or inadequate absorption of vitamin D as in malabsorption syndrome

— Excessive phosphaturia

— Acute renal failure

Deficiency of phosphorus causes the following conditions —

- Anorexia
- Dull mindedness
- Dizziness
- Weakness of the bones and teeth
- Waddling gait or even fracture of the bones

- Improper functioning of the nerves, so there may be the complaints of sleeping of hands and feet, feeling of creeping of ants on the body, and pain as occurs on pricking with the needles.
- Increased fragility of RBC which causes hemolytic anemia.
- Respiratory muscle weakness resulting in hyperventilation (increased exchange of air between the lungs and the surrounding air).

Treatment — A mixture of sodium and potassium phosphate should be given .5 to 1 gm. daily in divided doses.

Excess of phosphorus — High serum level (above 5 mg./100 mls.) of phosphorus is called hyperphosphatemia which usually occurs in hypoparathyroidism and chronic renal failure.

Treatment — Aluminium hydroxide antacid in appropriate doses should be given orally several times a day, after meals to prevent or control hyperphosphatemia. Treatment of the underlying disease should be done. In serious cases of renal failure haemodialysis is necessary.

Sodium

Deficiency — Certain amount of sodium is lost if vegetables are boiled in water and the water is discarded. Deficiency of sodium also occurs due to its excretion by the kidneys in the urine, 3 to 5 gms. of sodium corresponding to 8 to 12 gms. sodium chloride (NaCl) or common salt is excreted per day. Some amount of sodium is lost through the skin with sweating. Excessive sweating from working hard in the hot climate or near the furnace of the factories will result in considerable loss of sodium in the form of sodium chloride, and water. Use of diuretics and hypotensive (blood pressure lowering) drugs may also cause sodium deficiency. Diabetic hyperglycemia and Addison's disease may also be the causes of sodium deficiency. Blood serum level of sodium lower than 130 mEq/L (Normal blood serum level of sodium is 135 to 145 mEq/L) is called hyponatremia.

Deficiency of sodium causes the following conditions —

- Hypotension or low blood pressure.
- Rapid pulse or tachycardia (palpitation)
- Loss of appetite
- Vomiting
- Mental apathy
- Muscular cramps (common in the calf muscles and the abdominal muscles)
- Dehydration
- Sunken eyes
- Respiratory failure
- Coma

Diagnosis : Diagnosis of hyponatremia can be made by detecting the absence of sodium chloride in the urine by silver nitrate test. Normally, in the presence of sodium chloride in the urine, addition of silver nitrate solution to the sample of urine in the test tube will result in a white precipitate on reacting with the sodium chloride.

Treatment :— Saline water, i.e., sodium chloride (common salt) dissolved in water should be given. It may be administered as normal saline (0.9% solution of sodium chloride) through intravenous route or through transfusion.

Excess of sodium — Excess of sodium in the body may be due to inappropriate compensation with relatively inadequate quantity of water, of the loss of sodium and water occurring in excessive sweating, retention of water in the body, cardiac and renal failure which reduce the sodium excretion, increased blood volume, hyperactivity of the adrenal cortex e.g., hyperaldosteronism and Cushings's syndrome, diabetes insipidus, rarely it may occur by the administration of hypertonic saline solution either inappropriately or for longer duration by intravenous route for any disease, prolonged treatment with cortisone, ACTH and sex hormone. Blood serum level of sodium higher that 145 mEq/L is called hypernatremia. It causes the following conditions —

- Hypertension or high blood pressure
- Restlessness
- Irritability
- Edema which occurs first on the feet and ankles and then on the whole body.
- Oliguria — low urinary output in extreme cases.
- Fever
- Delirium
- Coma

Diagnosis : Diagnosis of hypernatremia may be made by determining serum sodium level.

Treatment : In profuse sweating water should be given by mouth. In severe cases 5% glucose (dextrose) solution is administered intravenously slowly. In cases of hyperglycemic hypernatremia of diabetic origin 5% glucose solution with normal saline (0.9% sodium chloride solution) with the estimated amount of neutral insulin is administered.

Chlorine

Chlorine is generally present in nature with the sodium as sodium chloride salt in which form both are taken with the food or otherwise, so these two are considered together.

Deficiency of sodium chloride (common salt) — Sodium chloride is lost from the body through urine and sweats, that which is passed out in the urine is regulated by the kidneys but that which is lost by sweating is not controlled. Deficiency of sodium chloride may occur during fasting or on taking salt-free diets. Excretion of chlorides in the urine may be decreased or only a trace of sodium chloride may be found. Deficiency of sodium chloride or common salt causes the following conditions :—

- Dehydration
- Vomiting
- Hypotension or low blood pressure
- Muscular cramps (heat cramps) in the hands and legs occurring due to loss of sodium chloride caused by excessive sweating, especially in persons doing hard physical work in hot climate, e.g., in those working in mines or near the furnaces of the factories.The loss of sodium chloride may be10-20 gms. per day.
- Coma in serious condition.

Diagnosis : Absence or presence of only a trace of sodium chloride in the urine indicates sodium chloride deficiency.

Treatment : More sodium chloride (common salt) should be added to the diet. Heat cramps may be controlled by giving 10-20 gms. of sodium chloride by adding it (in 0.3 to 0.5% strength) to the drinking water. In serious cases 5% glucose (dextrose) with normal saline (0.9% sodium chloride solution) is administered by transfusion.

Excess of sodium chloride (common salt) — Excess of sodium chloride in the body may be due to excessive intake of sodium chloride. It causes the following conditions —

- Hypertension or high blood pressure
- Edema which appears first on the feet and then on the whole body.

Treatment — Salt-free or salt-restricted diet. Strictly low salt diet contains 200-300 mgs. of sodium chloride and moderately low salt diet contains 400-500 mgs. sodium chloride.

- Use of diuretics.

Potassium

Deficiency of potassium — Deficiency of potassium in the body or the lowered blood potassium level is called hypokalemia. Causes of hypokalemia are —

— Deficient intake of potassium in the diet.

— Excessive loss of potassium through gastrointestinal tract due to persistent vomiting.

— Diarrhea

— Use of diuretic drugs for a long time.

— Prolonged use of steroids in the treatment of diseases.

— Tissue damage or wasting that is likely to occur in protein-energy malnutrition (PEM) or starvation.

— Hyperaldosteronism .

— Cushing's syndrome

— Metabolic alkalosis

— Uncontrolled insulin therapy

— Prolonged and excessive dose of common anti-asthmatic drug with beta-adrenergic drugs.

Deficiency of potassium causes the following conditions —

- Fatigue
- Muscular weakness
- Cramps
- Vertigo
- Thirst
- Mental confusion
- Cardiac arrhythmias.
- In severe potassium deficiency there may be paralytic ileus (due to weakness or paralysis of the intestinal muscles).

- In severe potassium deficiency paralysis of the skeletal muscles may occur.

Diagnosis : Diagnosis can be made from the estimation of serum level of potassium which will be found lower than normal.

Treatment : Tomato juice or orange juice one to two spoonful should be given repeatedly or mixture potassium chloride may be given. In serious cases injection lactated Ringer's solution containing potassium chloride may be administered intravenously.

Excess of potassium — Excess of potassium in the blood is known as hyperkalemia. Causes of hyperkalemia are —

— Excessive intake of potassium

— Uncontrolled diuretic therapy with potassium sparing diuretic (e.g., spironolactone) therapy.

— Addison's disease

— Hypoaldosteronism

— Metabolic acidosis

— Insulin deficiency

— Renal insufficiency causing diminished urine volume

Excess of potassium causes the following conditions —

— Muscular weakness

— Even paralysis may occur

— Abdominal distension

— Diarrhea

— Cardiac arrhythmias, e.g. ventricular fibrillation or even cardiac arrest may occur.

Diagnosis :— Diagnosis can be made from the estimation of serum level of potassium which will be found higher than normal.

Treatment :— Principles of treatment are as follows —

- Elimination of potassium-rich diet.

- Stoppage of potassium sparing diuretic therapy
- Stoppage of potassium supplementation in any form
- In cases where there is hypofunction of the adrenal cortex, apropriate dose of mineralocorticoid hormones should be administered.

Magnesium

Deficiency — Usually deficiency of magnesium does not occur, as it is found in about all the food-stuffs. However, its deficiency may occur in the following conditions. Serum level of magnesium below normal is called hypomagnesemia.

— Malabsorption syndrome which impairs its absorption from the intestines.

— Chronic diarrhea

— Severe vomiting

— Alcoholism — Absorption of magnesium is being affected.

— Cirrhosis of the liver

— Vitamin D deficiency

— Hypocalcemia

— Parathyroid disorders

— Toxemia of pregnancy

— Hyperaldosteronism

Deficiency of magnesium causes the following conditions —

- Muscular weakness
- Irritability
- Anorexia
- Vomiting
- Mental depression

- Confusion
- Malaise
- Vertigo
- Cramps and tremors in the hands and legs
- Convulsions
- Cardiac arrhythmias

Treatment — Magnesium oxide 250-500 mgs. may be given orally 2-4 times a day. In serious cases, an injection of magnesium sulphate may be administered intramuscularly, especially when hypertension is an accompanying feature.

Excess of magnesium — Serum level of magnesium above normal is called hypermagnesemia. Its causes are as follows —

— Renal insufficiency in which the kidneys are unable to excrete magnesium.

— May rarely occur due to excessive use of magnesium by injections in cases of eclampsia of pregnancy.

— Excessive intake of magnesium.

Excess of magnesium causes the following conditions —

- Sedation
- Mental confusion
- Muscular weakness, especially of the respiratory system causing hypoventilation.
- Respiratory acidosis
- Paralysis
- Bradycardia (decreased pulse rate)
- Hypotension
- Cardiac arrest and ultimately death may occur.

Treatment — Furosemide (Lasix) is administered intravenously with the drip of 5% glucose in normal saline to improve the renal function. Simultaneously, calcium chloride in appropriate dose should also be introduced in the intravenous infusion. In late cases or those refractory to the above treatment, hemodialysis will be required.

Minor Minerals or Trace Elements

Iron

Deficiency — Causes of Iron deficiency have been described earlier. Iron deficiency causes the following conditions —

Iron deficiency anemia or nutritional anemia. It is the microcytic (red blood cells are less than 5 μm in diameter) and hypochromic (hemoglobin is less than 10% i.e., less than 10 gms/100 mls. of blood) anemia with the mean corpuscular hemoglobin concentration (MCHC) less than 34%. It is characterized by weakness, general fatigue, poor appetite, gastrointestinal upsets, paleness of the body, whiteness and spooning (koilonychia) of the nails, giddiness, dyspnea on exertion, palpitation and rapid pulse, in severe cases edema of the ankles.

Diagnosis : Diagnosis of iron deficiency anemia can be made by the following tests —

(i) Hemoglobin concentration estimation — Hemoglobin level below 11 gms. per 100 mls. of blood is considered as anemia. Hemoglobin level 6-8 gms/100 mls. of blood occurs in severe anemia.

(ii) Estimation of iron concentration — Normal range of iron is 0.80 to 1.80 mg./L blood serum. Values below 0.50 mg./L indicate the iron deficiency.

Treatment — Ferrous sulphate 0.2 gm tablet (providing 60 mgs. Iron) or ferrous fumerate or ferrous gluconate is administered orally 3 times a day after meals with a 5 mg. tab. of folic acid once a day for 10 days and then ferrous sulphate 0.2 gm. tablet twice a day with folic acid 2 mg. tablet once a day from 11th day to 40th day should be administered.

For infants a sweetened syrup containing 0.2 gm. ferrous ammonium citrate (providing 20 mg. iron) should be given thrice a day. When hemoglobin level is very low, iron is administered by intramuscular injection. Generally inferon injection one ampoule is given deep intramuscularly in the gluteal region (buttock). Sometimes in critical cases with significant loss of blood due to hemorrhage, fresh blood transfusion is required to compensate the deficiency of hemoglobin and the blood volume.

Side effects : Oral iron therapy—constipation, diarrhea, gastric discomfort and even colicky pain in the abdomen.

Parenteral iron therapy — Local pain, tenderness and discolouration of the skin may occur following an injection of iron. Headache, nausea, chest pain, breathlessness and even anaphylactic shock may also occur. Hence the patient should be closely observed so as to adopt appropriate measures promptly.

Iodine

Deficiency — Deficiency of Iodine causes the following conditions.

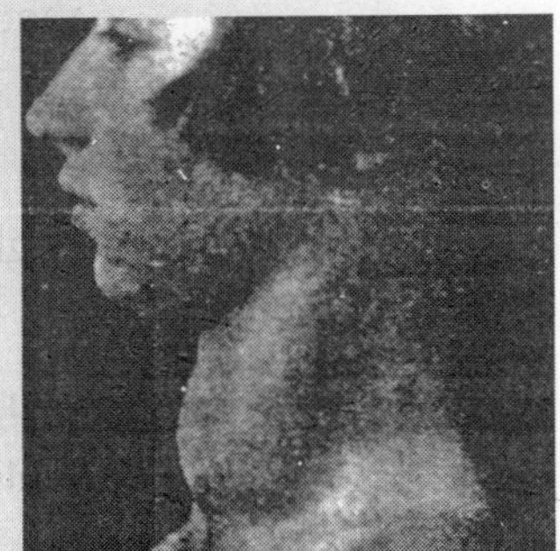

Fig. 9 A
Diffuse goitre

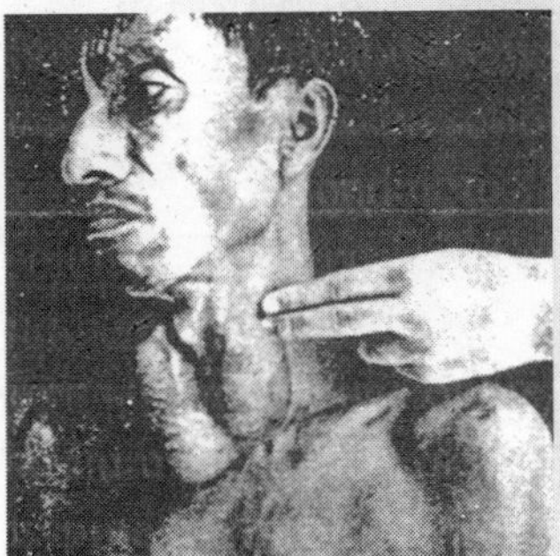

Fig. 9 B
Nodular goitre

Hypothyroidism — Hypofunction of the thyroid gland resulting in a decreased basal metabolic rate and characterized by obesity, dryness and lustrelessness of both the skin and the hair, low blood pressure, slow pulse, sluggishness of all the functions, mental deficiency with hearing and speech defects, depressed muscular activity, intolerance of cold and goitre formation.

Goitre formation — Deficiency of iodine leads to the formation of goitre. Goitre is the enlargement of the thyroid gland causing swelling in front of the neck, which may be diffused or nodular and usually occurs in the damp regions of Himalaya from Kashmir to Assam due to deficiency of Iodine in drinking water. The thyroid gland of an adult which normally weighs about 25 gms. may weigh upto 200 to 500 gms. or even more in the goitre.

Myxedema — It is a condition resulting from hypofunction of the thyroid gland which occurs in children and adults, more commonly in women. Myxedema occurring in children is called juvenile myxedema. Myxedema occurs due to iodine deficiency in the diet, surgical removal or atrophy of the thyroid gland, or secondary to hypofunction of the anterior pituitary gland, which is characterized by dry, coarse and thickened skin with loss of hair, puffiness of the hands and face, stunted growth with dwarfism with moon-face, poor memory, mental retardation, large tongue, slow speech, anemia, sensitivity to cold and drowsiness.

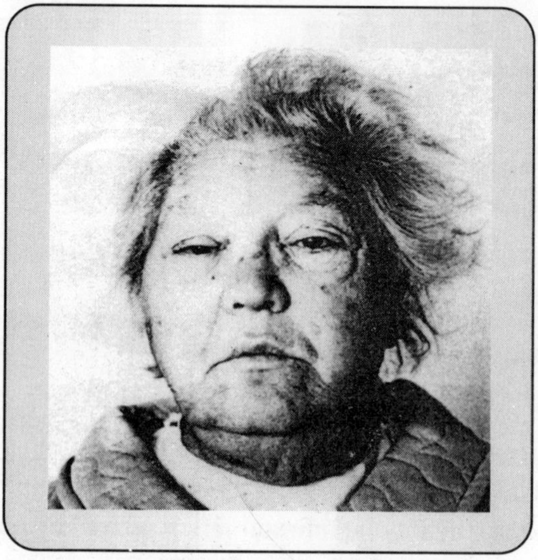

Fig. 10 Myxedema

The adult type of myxedema is more commonly found in women. There are menstrual disorders like amenorrhea, hypomenorrhea or diminished menstruation and other menstrual irregularities. There is lethargy, fatigue, constipation, obesity, sub-normal temp. of the body, susceptibility to cold, slow pulse rate and high blood cholesterol level.

Cretinism — Thyroid gland is usually found to be rudimentary since birth and so there is a lack of thyroid secretion which causes deficient function of the thyroid gland. There is failure of physical and mental development of the child. Growth of the child is retarded, hairs are thin and lustreless, there is pallor of the skin, puffiness of the face and the protrusion of the tongue.

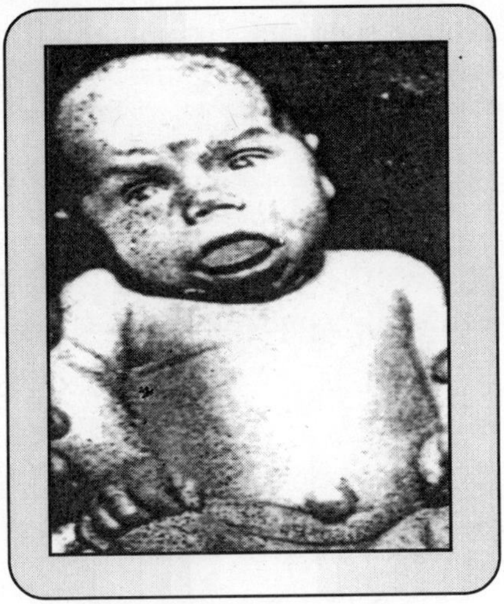

Fig. 11 Cretinism

- Retardation of physical development
- Impairment of mental function
- Increments in spontaneous abortion and stillbirth.
- Birth of the deformed child.

Prevention — To prevent the recurrence of goitre common salt is fortified with iodine, i.e., Iodized common salt is used which is available in the market. It is a salt containing 1 part of potassium iodide to 10,000 parts of sodium chloride or common salt. By adding one gram of potassium iodide to 10 kgs. of common salt provides 1 mg. of potassium iodide in 10 gms. of daily salt intake, i.e., it also provides 1 part of potassium iodide to 10,000 parts of common salt.

Treatment — In the treatment of hypothyroidism thyroxine hormone is used orally throughout life. Both types of goitres, i.e., uniformly enlarged and nodular type are treated with surgical operation.

Excess — Excessive ingestion of iodine may cause hyperactivity of the thyroid gland, the condition is known as hyperthyroidism, thyrotoxicosis, exophthalmic goitre or Graves' disease, which is characterized by enlargement of the thyroid gland, bulging of the eyes, tremors of the fingers and tachycardia (palpitation), frequent diarrhea, weight loss, irritability, restlessness, insomnia and hot sweats.

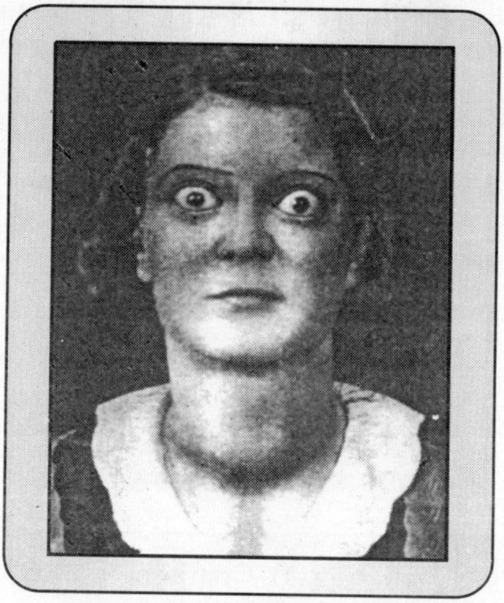

Fig. 12 Exophthalmic Goitre

Treatment — Usually anti-thyroid drugs like Thiourea derivatives are used for the control of the hyperactivity of the thyroid gland. However, major part of the thyroid gland substance is generally removed by operation (subtotal thyroidectomy).

Copper

Deficiency — Deficiency of copper causes the following conditions —

— Weakness

— Severe anemia

— Abnormalities of hair and skin pigmentation

— Impairment of respiration

— Retardation of growth

— Rupture of the great arteries due to defective elastic tissue formation in them

— Faulty development of bones

— Faulty development of nervous tissues

— Chronic diarrhea in premature infants

— Neutropenia (diminished number of neutrophil cells in the blood).

Diagnosis — Serum level of copper below 16 mcg/100 mls.(normal) is considered deficiency of copper (Hypocupremia)

Excess — Excessive ingestion of copper or acute poisoning causes the following conditions —

— Nausea

— Vomiting

— Hematemesis

— Melena

Copper sulfate poisoning — It occurs due to ingestion of excessive amount of copper sulfate. Its symptoms are as follows —

- Disagreeable coppery metallic taste
- Tightness in the throat
- Nausea
- Vomiting
- Thirst
- Abdominal pains

- Cramps
- Suppression of urine.

Diagnosis : Serum level of copper above 16 mcg./100 mls. is supposed as excess of copper (Hypercupremia).

Fluorine

Deficiency of fluorine (less than 0.5 mg. per litre of water) through drinking water causes dental caries or tooth decay, for the prevention of which fluoride tooth paste should be applied on the teeth and fluoridation (addition of fluorides to the water supply) of the community water supplies should be done. Its deficiency lessens the formation of enamel in the teeth.

Excess — Consumption of drinking water containing excess of fluorine (more than 5 PPM) causes the following conditions :

Dental fluorosis — Teeth loose their shiny appearance and chalky white patches develop on them, especially on the incisors of the upper jaw. This gives the appearance of mottled enamel. These patches later on become brown or black. Later on pitting may be seen, especially in the upper incisors due to loss of enamel. This disease usually occurs in young children.

Skeletal fluorosis — It occurs in old people which affects the bones. There is first a tingling sensation in the legs and feet which is followed by pain and stiffness of the neck, back and then of both the limbs. X-ray shows exotosis (formation of new bone) and calcification of tendons, ligaments as well as interosseous membranes.

Prevention and control of fluorosis — It is of utmost importance to prevent the development of fluorosis as there is no specific treatment. The normal content of fluoride in water should be below 1 mg./L. For this purpose defluoridation of water is done. According to Nalgonda Technique of National Environmental Engineering Research Institute, Nagpur for defluoridation of water, at first lime powder is added to water and mixed well with it at the rate of 30 mg. per litre of water. Then alum at the rate of 500 mg. per litre of water is added to the water and the water is stirred for 10 minutes. The contents are allowed to settle down for an hour. The sedimented portion of water will contain excess of fluorides.

— To provide safe (free from excess of fluorine) drinking water from another source.

— In such areas where fluorosis is prevailing, fluorine containing medicines are to be banned.

— Marketing and sales of tooth pastes fortified with fluorine (as for preventing dental caries) are to be banned in such areas.

Zinc

Deficiency — Deficiency of zinc causes the following conditions—

- Retarded growth
- Hypogonadism or degenerative changes in male and female reproductive organs.
- Loss of taste
- Hyposmia — A decrease in odor acuity.
- Loss of appetite
- Anemia
- Delay in wound healing
- Alopecia (loss of hair)
- Dermatitis
- Immunological abnormalities
- Zinc deficiency during pregnancy may lead to developmental disorders in the child.

Treatment — Food-stuffs rich in zinc should be supplemented.

Zinc toxicity — It may result from excessive ingestion of zinc in food and beverages which is mainfested by —

— Nausea

— Vomiting

— Colic pains

— Diarrhea.

Water

Deficiency — Loss of water from the body causes the following conditions —

- Thirst
- Dehydration
- An adult who has lost 5 to 10 litres of water from the body will be seriously ill and death will occur when the water loss from the body is about 15 litres.
- Hypotension or low blood pressure
- Rapid decrease in body weight
- Oliguria : Reduced urinary output, the urine is thick.
- After a few days blood circulation failure occurs due to reduced cardiac output resulting from decrease in plasma or blood volume.
- An excess of sweating in tropical region
- Stone formation in the kidney.

Treatment — One packet of powder of oral rehydration mixture is dissolved in one litre of water (ORS — Oral Rehydration Solution) and is given to the patient in divided doses within 24 hours or 5 gms. common salt with 20 gms. sugar dissolved in one litre of water may be substituted. In serious cases of dehydration 5% glucose with normal saline can be transfused intravenously from the bottle.

Excess of water — Excess of water in the body causes the following conditions —

- Indigestion
- Headache
- Hypertension — High blood pressure

- Confusion
- Spasms in the hands and feet
- Edema.

Treatment — Water intake should be restricted or should be totally abandoned.

— Antihypertensive drugs with diuretics should be used.

* * * * *

CHAPTER 8

OBESITY (OVERWEIGHT)

Obesity means excessive accumulation of fat in the adipose tissues, located especially in the waist, hips and breasts with increased body weight by 10% or more above the standard reference weight for the age, sex and height. When the eaten food provides more energy than required, the extra energy is converted into fat which is deposited in the adipose tissues in the body. Fat deposition in the adipose tissues causes obesity. On the other hand, if all the adipose tissues are used and there is continuous supply of inadequate food, the body becomes lean and thin. Obesity is most commonly found initially in the 25 to 50 years of age group and is more common in women.

Causes of Obesity

- To lead sedentary life.
- Lack of adequate physical labor.
- Genetic factors — When father or mother is obese, there are 50% chances that their child will be obese. When both father

and mother are obese, the chances of obesity of the child are increased to 80%.

Eating habits

- Overeating
- Eating faster, taking less time for chewing, thereby consuming more food.
- Irregular timings of taking food
- Taking snacks in between the meals.

Endocrine Factors

- Hypothyroidism — It is confirmed by estimation of serum T_3, T_4 and TSH
- Hypogonadism
- Cushing's syndrome — Accumulation of fat over the central part of the body manifested by moon-face, buffalo hump (around the neck and shoulders) and pendulous abdomen.
- Puberty
- Pregnancy
- Menopause

Other causes

- Excess of alcohol intake
- Taking of contraceptive pills regularly
- Mental depression in which the people are found to indulge in over eating.
- Injury to hypothalamus—Injury to the hypothalamus after a head injury may lead to obesity.

Body weight may be increased by more than 10% due to edema caused by cardiac, renal or hepatic disorders, which can be excluded by appropriate tests.

Assessment of Obesity

Assessment of obesity can be made by the following criteria—

1. Relative body weight—It is determined by the ratio of actual body weight with the desirable body weight in kilograms.

2. Skin-fold thickness—It is determined by measuring the skin-fold thickness in centimeters with the help of a skin-fold measuring calipers. The measure is taken at the sites like abdomen, pectoral region or the anterior upper portion of the chest, back, outer side of the arm and thigh. This is done to assess the subcutaneous fat in the body. The indices obtained in this way are compared with the standard values.

3. Body mass index (BMI) or Quetelet's index — It is the value obtained by dividing the actual body weight in kilograms by the height of the body in square meters. If the body mass index or BMI is 20 to 25 kg./ square meter or more, treatment is required.

4. Waist hip ratio (WHR)—It is the ratio obtained by dividing the circumference in centimeters of waist by the circumference in centimeters of the hip. High WHR (waist : hip ratio) more than 1.0 in men and 0.85 in women indicates the accumulation of fat in the abdomen and there is the high risk of cardiovascular diseases.

5. Corpulence index $= \dfrac{\text{Actual body weight}}{\text{Desirable body weight}}$

This should exceed 1.2

6. Broca's index = Height of the body in centimeters — 100 = ideal weight

For example, if a person's height is 160 cms.

His ideal weight is 160 — 100 = 60 kg.

Types of Obesity

Obesity is of the following three types—

Grade I—The persons of grade I obesity have body mass index (BMI) more than 25 (25 BMI is normal) but less than 29.9. The excess of weight or obesity does not affect the health of these persons. They generally reduce their weights themselves.

Grade II — The persons of grade II obesity have body mass index (BMI) between 30 and 39.9. Though they maintain good health, but on little exertion they are tired. They are more at risk for developing diabetes mellitus, hypertension, atherosclerosis, fatty liver, gallbladder diseases, hernias, etc.

Grade III — The persons of grade III obesity have body mass index above 40. They have very limited physical activity due to too much body weight. They are more susceptible to all the diseases of grade II.

Effects of Obesity

Obesity may cause the following conditions —

- Diabetes mellitus
- Hypertension (high blood pressure)
- Coronary heart disease as angina pectoris and coronary thrombosis or myocardial infarction.
- Congestive heart failure
- Atherosclerosis — Thickening and hardening of the arterial walls due to the formation of atheromas in their intimas resulting in narrowing of their lumen.
- Osteoarthritis of the weight-bearing joints, e.g., knees and hip joints.
- Varicose veins
- Abdominal hernia
- Formation of gall stones.
- Intertrigo — An erythematous eruption occurring on the opposite surfaces of the skin from friction or rubbing.
- Infection at the skin flexures and under the breast of the obese woman.

- Flat feet
- Obesity lowers the life expectancy
- Obstetrical risk — Fatty pregnant women are at greater obstetrical risk due to diabetes and hypertension and the delivery of the child is very difficult in obese women.
- Fertility is lowered
- Psychological disturbance — Adolescents feel inferiority complexion due to obesity.
- Prone to accidents — Obese people are more prone to accidents due to slipping and falling down.
- Death — Sudden death may occur of the persons with more than 20% overweight. Death may also occur due to renal failure.

Twenty percent or more body weight than the average body weight is called obesity. Classification of different degrees of obesity based on the body weight is given below —

Body weight excess %	Degree of obesity
20	Mild
30	Moderate
40	Severe
50	Very severe

Obesity can be controlled by reducing the body weight for which we should know the average body weights of normal adults.

Management of Obese Persons

Energy — About 20 Kcals per kg. of body weight is prescribed for a sedentary person and about 25 Kcals. per kg. of body weight for moderately active person. Food energy intake should not be greater than what is necessary for expenditure. It should always be lesser than the energy consumed.

The most common methods of reducing the obesity are as follows—

(1) Dietary control

(2) Exercise

(3) Drug therapy

(1) Dietary Control— The quantity of food which one is taking should be halved to start with. Initially it should be of 100 Kcals and it should contain a large amount of fibres. Small quantities of food should be taken frequently to control appetite, and one should eat food slowly than to gulp it down in hurry. Diet should contain 1 gm. of protein per kg. of ideal body weight. Ghee, butter, eggs, fried foods and fatty preparations, sweets, potatoes and alcohol should be avoided. Vegetable oils except coconut and palm oil may be consumed to provide the required essential fatty acids. Emphasis should be on taking lightly prepared soup-like preparations, green vegetables as spinach, bathua, cabbage, coriander, spearmint, fenugreek leaves, bottle-gourd, ridge-gourd or ribbed- gourd etc., salad and fresh fruits. Cucumber and/or tomatoes should be taken in between the principal meals to prevent hunger. Skimmed milk should be taken.

Restriction of salt intake — Salt intake should be restricted. Amount of salt present in the food naturally as its constituent is sufficient which is about 3 gms. So no extra salt should be added to the diet.

Fluids — Fluids should be taken in abundance as they give filling sensation. A glass of water consumed before a meal lessens the food intake.

Starvation — Some scientists introduced fasting for 2 to 14 days which may be repeated if necessary as a treatment of obesity. The purpose is to encourage weight loss and to produce post-starvation anorexia (loss of appetite). In about 50% patients hunger subsides mostly in 7 days.

On dieting weight of the body is lost rapidly, say ½ to 2 pounds per week for about 6 months. Initially this is due to loss of excess of water content of the body as evidenced by increased frequency of micturition and polyuria. Therefore, the weight is somewhat stationary for a few months, when one adopts oneself to new weight and then one starts to lose weight again. In this way, when the desired weight is reached, one should maintain it.

(2) Exercise — Generally obese persons lead sedentary lives. They have to lose their body weight. For this purpose a low caloric diet with moderate exercise as walking for increasing calorie expenditure (for loosening body weight calorie expenditure is to be increased) should be advised.

Brisk walking for 30 to 45 minutes with pleasure daily in the morning and evening is to be insisted. Walking at a speed of about 5 kilometers per hour will involve expenditure of 300 Kcals. in one hour. Moreover, obese persons can also take part in light outdoor games as badminton, table tennis, swimming and cycling etc., which will provide exercise, entertainment, close company and at the same time will prevent social isolation. For housewives household activities like mopping, sweeping the floor, cleaning the utensils and gardening etc., are the forms of exercise. Yogabhiyas is one of the best methods of reducing the body weight.

(3) Drug therapy — Laxative — Patient should take husk of isubghol 2-3 teaspoonful with milk at bed time, or some other laxative containing fibres in abundance should be taken.

Anti-obesity drugs—Any one of the following anti-obesity drugs may be used.

(1) Amphetamine sulfate (Benzadrine)—It is anorexic, i.e., causes loss of appetite in obese people but is not very effective as its large doses are toxic, and its prolonged use may cause drug dependence. It is available in the market in the form of tablets or capsules.

(2) Fenfluramine hydrochloride (Pondimin)—It is most widely used medicine in obesity which acts by causing loss of appetite like

amphetamine but has many side effects as dryness of the mouth, palpitation, insomnia, depression and hypertension (high blood pressure) and drug dependence. So it should not be given in case of hypertension, heart disease, epilepsy and pregnancy.

(3) Phentermine — It is also an anorexic (causing loss of appetite) used as a single capsule daily.

(4) Diethylproplon hydrochloride (Dospan) — It acts like amphetamines in the treatment of obesity.

(5) Leptin — It is a hormone affecting the hypothalamus and consequent food intake and appetite. It is administered now-a-days in the form of injection and it is the ideal drug for obesity without side effects.

(6) Orlistat — It is a drug approved by the food and drug authority of USA for the treatment of obesity by reducing fat absorption from the gastrointestinal tract.

Surgical Treatment

I. Liposuction — Excess of fat from the body is removed but it is generally associated with recurrence and a few complications.

II. Gastric plication — Some surgical staples are placed across the upper portion of the stomach due to which capacity of food Intake is reduced.

* * * * *

CHAPTER 9

UNDERWEIGHT

When the body weight is decreased by 10% or more below the standard reference weight for the age, sex and height, the body is underweight. The underweight person looks lean and thin and emaciated and is more prone to be afflicted with the infectious diseases as tuberculosis etc. There is anorexia (loss of appetite) so the main aim in the management of underweight is to improve the appetite.

Causes of Underweight

- Imbalanced diet — As inadequacy of proteins in the diet may cause low body weight (LBW)
- Underweight may be caused by wasting diseases such as tuberculosis, diabetes, cancer, malabsorption syndrome, diarrhea, dysentery and cholera etc.
- Fasting — Excessive fasting causes underweight which most commonly occurs in women.

— Starvation — There is marked emaciation, loss of hair and low blood pressure.

— Consumption of food in lesser quantity as occurs in persons who are more active and busy, nervous and tense.

— Aversion to eating

— Lack of interest in eating and food

— Alteration of taste

— Inability to ingest food

— Psychological factors — As anorexia nervosa in which the person eats very little food, which usually occurs due to certain rigid ideas (as overeating will cause obesity) occurring in the age group of 15-25 years. If untreated, it can lead to progressive starvation.

— Marasmus in children

REMEDY

Dietary considerations

The afflicted person should take high calorie, high protein, high fat and high carbohydrate food with vitamins and minerals in abundance.

Energy — Requirements of the calories depend upon the activities of the person. If there is excessive intake of high caloric foods, digestive troubles as diarrhea may occur. Therefore an increase of 50 Kcals to the normal requirement should be given.

Proteins — Intake of 1.2 to 1.5 gm. of proteins per kg. of body weight is recommended for the building of the tissues. Proteins of high biological values should be included in the diet as they can be completely utilised by the body.

Fats — Fats as ghee, butter and oils etc.,should be increased in the diet as they increase the body weight but fried foods and the foods containing excess of oil should be avoided as they may cause diarrhea or may lessen the appetite.

Carbohydrates — Carbohydrates are the main sources of energy for our body and these are the base, and form the bulk of our diet. Underweight persons should take food containing an excess of carbohydrates to increase their body weight. Carbohydrates include cereals as wheat, rice, maize, pulses, underground vegetables as potatoes, and sweet potatoes etc. Nuts as groundnuts, almonds, walnuts and cashewnuts should be supplemented. Initially the intake will be less to counter balance. Underweight persons should take food in small quantity but frequently. They should take easily digestible food.

Vitamins and minerals — In a liberal diet all the essential vitamins are generally found in adequate amounts and so usually they are not required to be supplemented.

Fluids — Underweight persons should drink water and other fluids after meals as their consumption before a meal suppresses the appetite. Enough fluids in the form of fresh fruit juices and soups should be included in order to avoid constipation. Underweight persons should have a good appetite. They should not consume such beverages as alcohol etc., which suppress the appetite.

Altered nutrition — Less than body requirement

A state in which a patient experiences an intake of nutrients insufficient for the body. This condition may be due to imbalanced diet, as a side effect of some medicines, nausea, vomiting, alteration in mode of food intake, forgetfulness of taking food regularly, radiation and chemotherapy (treatment with chemical agents) etc., causing lack of interest in eating and food. Hence the body weight is reduced due to insufficient intake of food.

Methods of improving appetite and so food intake

- Avoid the noxious environmental stimuli as unpleasant sight and foul smell etc.
- Mouth of the underweight person should be cleaned before taking food as it promotes eating.
- Cut the food items into small pieces which promotes eating. One should eat food slowly and should take adequate time in chewing, it also promotes eating.

- There should be no fluid intake during meals. Fluid intake during meals reduces food intake, so fluid intake should be after meals.
- Tasty food promotes eating, so the taste of the food should be improved.
- Encourage exercise which stimulates appetite.

* * * * *

CHAPTER 10

FOOD HYGIENE

Food is more liable to be contaminated by micro-organisms, so it is a potential source of infection at any point during its transportation from the producer to the consumer. Food hygiene implies hygiene in the production, handling, distribution an serving of all types of food. The aim of food hygiene is to prevent food poisoning and other food-borne diseases, which may be infectious or toxic and caused by the agents that enter the body through ingestion of food.

Food poisoning is caused generally by the bacteria of the genus Salmonella, Staphylococcus aureus, Clostridium botulinum and Clostridium perfringens.

Food-borne diseases are classified as follows —

A. Infections :

(1) *Bacterial diseases* —

- Acute diarrhoea

- E. coli diarrhoea
- Gastroenteritis
- Bacillary dysentery
- Cholera
- Typhoid fever
- Paratyphoid fever
- Septicemia
- Gas gangrene
- Streptococcal infection causing various diseases.

(2) *Viral diseases* —

- Viral gastroenteritis
- Viral diarrhoea
- Viral hepatitis.

(3) *Parasitic diseases* —

- Amoebic dysentery caused by the protozoon Entamoeba histolytica.
- Ascariasis caused by Ascaris lumbricoides (Round-worm).
- Enterobiasis or Oxyuriasis caused by Enterobius or Oxyuris vermicularis (Threadworm).
- Taeniasis caused by Taenia saginata or Taenia solium (Tapeworm).
- Trichuriasis caused by Trichuris trichiura (Whipworm).
- Trichinosis caused by Trichinella spiralis.
- Giardiasis caused by a protozoon Giardia lamblia.

B. Diseases caused by toxins :

- *Lathyrism* — It is caused by the toxin Beta-N-oxalyl-amino-L-alanine, naturally occurring in Kesari dal.

- *Epidemic dropsy* — It is caused by consumption of mustard oil contaminated with argemone oil.
- *Botulism* — It is caused by a toxin botulin, produced by Clostridium botulinum bacteria.
- Toxins produced by Staphylococci.
- *Aflatoxicosis* — It is caused by a toxin aflatoxin produced by the fungi Aspergillus flavus an Aspergillus parasiticus. Groundnuts, wheat, rice, maize, sorghum and tapioca etc. are contaminated with these fungi under conditions of improper storage.

Hygiene of Vegetables and Fruits

Vegetables and fruits, especially the vegetables which are eaten raw, e.g., tomatoes and radish etc., can be a source of infection. Those which are grown in sewage irrigated land, are particularly dangerous, if eaten raw and unwashed as they transmit the pathogenic bacteria as Salmonella typhi causing typhoid fever, protozoa and the eggs of the worms. Vegetables which are to be eaten raw in the form of salad should be treated in a weak solution of potassium permanganate and later washed in running water. Fruits should be thoroughly washed in tap water before consumption.

Milk Hygiene

The sources of infection or contamination of milk may be —

1. The dairy animal
2. Human handler
3. The environment, e.g., contaminate vessels, polluted water, flies and dust etc.

The important milk-borne diseases are as follows —

(1) *Directly from the dairy animal*

- Bovine tuberculosis — It is the main milk-borne disease transmitted directly from the dairy animal or cattle to the human being. The infection is transmitted through drinking the milk of the infected or the sick cattle, especially the cow's milk. Usually children suffer from tuberculosis of the abdomen (Koch's abdomen) through drinking milk of the sick cow.

- Brucellosis
- Streptococcal infection
- Staphylococcal enterotoxin poisoning
- Foot and mouth disease
- Anthrax.

(2) *Indirectly from the human handler or environment*

- Typhoid fever
- Paratyphoid fever
- Streptococcal infection
- Staphylococcal food poisoning
- Tuberculosis
- Bacillary dysentery (Shigellosis)
- Cholera
- Viral hepatitis.

Clean and safe milk

For the production of clean and safe milk the following conditions should be maintained :

— There should be a healthy and clean animal. Milk from a healthy udder contains only a few micro-organisms and these are relatively unimportant.

— The premises where the animal is being kept in the house and milked should be clean and hygienic.

— Milk vessels must be sterile and kept covered.

— Water supply should be pathogens free.

— Milk handler must be free from communicable diseases.

— Milk handlers should wash their hands and arms before milking. Where possible, milking machine should be used.

— Milk should be cooled immediately to below 10°C after it is drawn, to retard the bacterial growth.

— For the production of good quality milk, all the containers and equipments in which milk is handled, should be clean.

A hygienic and good quality milk should be white with no deposit, disagreeable smell or taste. An average specific gravity of cow's milk and buffalo's milk is 1032, which is determined by lactometer. Its reading should not be less than 1026.

Methylene blue reduction test — This test is carried out for detection of micro-organisms in the milk. It is based on the observation that bacteria growing in milk bring about a decrease in the color imparted to milk. In this test a definite quantity of methylene blue is added to some samples of milk, each of 10 mls. and the samples are held at a uniform temperature of 37°C until the blue color has disappeared in all the samples. The sample of milk which remains blue for the longest time is considered to be of the best quality as it indicates the absence or a small number of bacteria.

Milk is made sterile by the process of pasteurization. For pasteurization of milk and phosphatase test for checking the efficiency of pasteurization, see chapter "Preservation and Storage of Food".

Eggs

Although the freshly laid eggs are sterile inside, the shell may be contaminated by the fecal matter of the hen, pathogenic bacteria can penetrate the cracked shell and enter the egg causing it to be infected. Eggs become stale on prolonged storage and storage under unsatisfactory conditions. The freshness of the eggs may be tested as described in the chapter "Contamination of Food".

Meat Hygiene

The term "meat" is applied to the flesh of animal origin which consists of muscle fibres held together by connective tissue and the proteins myosin, muscle albumin and myoglobin. Clotting of protein myosin causes rigor mortis which makes the meat tough, but acids developing soon soften the myosin and makes the meat tender and give it a better flavor. Hence meat should be eaten after rigor mortis has passed away.

It is better to eat the meat of younger animals because connective tissue in the older animals is in abundance which becomes tough and takes more time for cooking.

Meat can be a source of infection if it is bad or unwholesome. Meat-borne diseases are —

(1) Taeniasis (Tapeworm infestations) — Taeniasis caused by Taenia solium and Taenia saginata, Trichinosis caused by Trichinella spiralis.

(2) Bacterial infections :

- Food poisoning
- Tuberculosis
- Anthrax
- Actinomycosis.

Inspection of meat —

Antemortem (before killing the animal) and postmortem (after killing the animal) inspection of the animal intended for slaughter should be done by a qualified veterinary doctor.

Antemortem inspection — The meat becomes unfit for human consumption in the conditions of emaciation, exhaustion, pregnancy, actinomycosis, brucellosis, fever, diarrhea and other diseases of an infectious nature and so the meat is to the rejected.

Postmortem inspection – If there is tuberculosis, parasitic and nodular infections of the liver and lungs, septicemia, an abscess in the body, cysticercus infection, liver fluke and hydatidosis etc., the meat is to be rejected.

Signs of good meat :

1. *Color* — Meat should not be pale, pink or deep purple, but of red color.
2. *Touch* — Meat should be firm and elastic to touch, it should not be greasy or shiny.
3. *Smell* — The odor of the meat should be agreeable.
4. It should not be shrunk or be wasted much on cooking.
5. It should not become wet an standing for a day or two.

Slaughter houses :

Slaughter houses are the places where animals whose meat is eaten, are killed. The hygiene of the slaughter house is very important to prevent the contamination of meat during the process of dressing. The following minimum standards for slaughter houses have been suggested under the Model Public Health Act (1955) in India.

1. *Location* — A slaughter house should be away form the residential area.
2. *Structure* — Floors, and walls upto 3 feet of a slaughter house should be impervious and easy to clean.
3. *Disposal of wastes* — Blood, carrion and garbage etc. should not be discharged into public sewers but should be collected separately.
4. *Water supply* — It should be independent, adequate and continuous.
5. *Examination of the animals* — Antemortem and postmortem examination should be arranged. Animals or meat found unfit for human consumption should be destroyed or denatured.
6. *Storage of food* — Meat should be stored in fly-proof and rat-proof rooms; for overnight storage, the temp. of the room should be maintained below 5°C.

7. *Transportation of meat* — Meat should be transported in fly-proof covered vans.
8. *Miscellaneous* — Animals other than those to be slaughtered should not be allowed to stay inside the shed.

Prevention :

1. Infected meat should be destroyed.
2. The meat should be cooked thoroughly. Uncooked or half-cooked meat should never be used.
3. Pigs and cattles should not be allowed to eat the human excreta.

Fishes

Fishes decompose quickly after death because of the autolysis and the bacteria with which they become infected. Stale fishes should be discarded. The signs of fresh fish are :

1. The fish should be in a state of stiffness or rigor mortis.
2. The gills should be bright red.
3. The eyes should be clear and prominent.

The following diseases are produced by fishes —

1. *Tapeworm infestation* — Diphyllobothrium latum is the broad and largest tapeworm living in the intestine of fish-eating humans. Its infection occurs after the man eats raw (since fish is not eaten raw, its infestation is a rare disease) or improperly cooked fish, which can be prevented by thoroughly cooking the fresh water fish or by keeping the fish frozen at –10°C (14°F) for 48 hours prior to eating.
2. *Fish poisoning* — Consumption of certain types of fish infected with bacteria or viruses may cause fish poisoning.

Inspection of tinned fish :

It is necessary to inspect the tin or cane before consuming its contents (fish, meat or any food), the following points should be noted :

I. The tin must be new and clean.
II. The tin must be without rusting.
III. There should be no holes or sealed openings in the tin.
IV. On shaking the tin, there should be no sound.
V. On opening the tin, the contents should not be blown out which indicates decomposition, on the other hand there should be a hissing noise.

Sanitation of eating places

The following minimum standards have been suggested for restaurants and eating houses in India under the Model Public Health Act (1955).

1. *Location* — An eating place should not be near any accumulation of filth or open and dirty drain, stable, dairy and other sources of contamination of food.
2. *Floors* — Floors should be higher than the adjoining land, made with impervious material and easy to keep clean.
3. *Rooms* — (a) Rooms where meals are served should not be less than 100 sq. feet which should provide accommodation for a maximum of 10 persons. (b) Walls upto 3 feet should be smooth, impervious and easily washable. (c) Lighting — There should be ample natural light and arrangement of artificial light also. (d) Ventilation — There should be good circulation of air in the rooms through ventilators.
4. *Kitchen* — (a) Floor space should not be less than 60 sq. feet. (b) Floor of the kitchen should be impervious, smooth, easy to keep clean and no slippery. (c) Window area should be 25% of the floor area. (d) Doors and windows should be fly-proof, rat-proof and of the self-closing type. (e) Ventilation area should be 2% of the floor area, in addition to smoke pipes.

5. *Storage of cooked food*— Separate room should be provided for storage of cooked food. Temperature should be controlled for long storage.
6. *Storage of the uncooked foodstuffs* — Perishable and non-perishable articles should be kept separately, in rat-proof and insect-proof space; for storage of perishable articles temperature should be controlled.
7. *Furniture* — It should be strong and easy to keep clean and dry.
8. *Disposal of refuse* — Refuse should be collected in covered, impervious container and disposed-off twice a day.
9. *Water supply*— Water supply should be independent source, adequate, continuous and safe.
10. *Cleaning of the utensils and crockery* – It should be done in hot water and then by disinfection.

Sanitation of food handlers :

The infections which are likely to be transmitted by the food handlers are diarrhea, dysentery, streptococcal and staphylococcal infections, typhoid and paratyphoid fevers, viral hepatitis, protozoal cysts, eggs of helminths (worms) etc.

At first it is essential to have complete medical examination carried out of all food handlers at the time of employement. Any person with a history of typhoid or paratyphoid fever, diarrhea, dysentery, tuberculosis or any other communicable disease should not be employed. Persons with wounds or skin infections and otitis media should not be permitted to handle food or utensils. Daily medical check-up of food handlers is important, those who are ill should be excluded from food handling. It is also important that any disease occurring in a food handler's family should at once be notified.

Education of food handlers — Food handlers should be educated in food handling, handling and cleaning the utensils and crockery and control of insects and rats. The following aspects of personal hygiene are to be considered —

1. Hands — The hands should be clean at all times. These should be scrubbed and washed immediately after visiting the toilet, and as often as necessary at other times. Finger nails should be kept trimmed and free from dirt.
2. Hair — Head coverings should be provided, especially to the women to prevent loose hair entering the food-stuffs.
3. Gown — All food handlers should wear a clean white gown.
4. Coughing and sneezing should be avoided in the neighbourhood of food.
5. Smoking on food premises should be avoided.

* * * * *

CHAPTER 11

CONTAMINATION OF FOOD

Food-stuffs may be contaminated by the bacteria, viruses, fungi or their toxins, protozoa (unicellular parasites), ova or eggs of intestinal parasites, poisons derived from plants and animals, inorganic chemical substances and adulterants etc. Ingestion of contaminated foods or the preparations of contaminated food-stuffs may cause the diseases in man as follows: —

Food-borne Diseases

Food-borne diseases are those which are toxic or infectious in nature, caused by the causative organisms entered the body through ingestion of food.

Food-borne diseases are as follows :

LATHYRISM

It is a nervous disease caused by eating Kesari dal (Lathyrus sativus pulse), due to the presence of the toxin Beta-N-Oxalyl- amino-L-alanine

(BOAA) in it which produces the toxic effects upon the nervous system. Diet containing 30% of kesari dal (Lathyrus sativus pulse) if consumed for 4 to 6 months, as more common among the poor people, will cause the disease. It is prevalent mostly among the landless agricultural laborers who consume this pulse in excess due to poverty. Males between the age of 10 and 35 years are affected more in the month of July and August. More than 50% persons suffering from this disease suddenly fall down in the field while at work. There are 5 stages of this disease.

1. Warning stage — Sudden agonizing pain occurs in the calf muscles or back of the thigh along with the spasmodic contractions of these muscles. If during this stage, the patient stops eating kesari dal, the disease does not progress.

2. First stage (Non-stick stage) — The patient walks with the short steps and jerky movements with the heels not resting on the ground. The patient can walk without the help of the sticks and may remain in this stage throughout the life. Most of the patients are found in this stage.

3. Second stage (One-stick stage) — Knees are flexed and the patient walks on toes with muscular rigidity. The patient requires one stick for supporting and maintaining balance.

4. Third stage (Two-stick stage) — The patient becomes very weak. For walking even for a short distance, the patient requires two sticks for support.

5. Crawler stage — The knees become completely bent and the patient crawls on the knees and palms.

Preventive Measures

Ban on farming of kesari dal — Farming of kesari dal should be banned.

Removal of toxins — Kesari dal is soaked in boiling water for one hour. About 90 to 95% of its toxins will be drained in the water with water-soluble vitamins.

Parboiling method — In this method, water-soluble vitamins are not lost. Kesari dal is first soaked in lukewarm water and after that steamed for 15 minutes. By this method 80 to 90% toxins are being removed.

EPIDEMIC DROPSY

It is caused mostly by the consumption of mustard oil contaminated with argemone oil and attacks many people at the same time in the same geographical area. Argemone oil is added to the mustard oil intentionally or mustard oil may be adulterated unintentionally on account of argemone growing in mustard fields, the seeds of which are similar in shape and size to that of mustard seeds and so these are mixed up easily with the mustard seeds. To produce the disease adulteration should be upto or more than 4%. The toxic factor is an alkaloid 'Sanguinarine'. The disease is characterised by loss of appetite, diarrhea followed by edema over the feet which occurs especially after walking and late in the evening, which is pitting on pressure, tender and hot. There is fever, temperature usually 102°F. Some patients develop sudden bilateral swelling on the legs, often associated with diarrhea, dyspnea, cardiac failure and death.

Test of argemone oil

Argemone oil is of orange colour with an acrid odor. Nitric acid test is done to detect argemone oil. Oil is taken in a test tube and a few drops of nitric acid is added to it. The tube is shaken and the development of a brown to orange colour indicates the presence of argemone oil.

Toxicity generally disappears if the oil is kept for some months.

AFLATOXICOSIS

This disease is caused by ingestion of groundnuts, maize and parboiled rice etc., contaminated with the fungi Aspergillus flavus and Aspergillus parasiticus, that produce a toxin aflatoxin. Aflatoxin is a potent hepatotoxic and produces cirrhosis liver in the childhood and possibly a carcinogenic too. Moisture level above 16% and temperature ranging from 11 to 37°C favour its formation.

Prevention — Avoid hot humid atmosphere for its growth for which proper storage of nuts and seeds and avoiding water soiling is required.

DIARRHEA

Frequent passage of loose or watery stools. It is generally caused by the bacteria of the genus Salmonella which are found in the contaminated food and after 12 to 24 hours (incubation period) of the ingestion of bacteria with the food diarrhea occurs which usually lasts for 2 to 3 days.

Prevention — Vegetables should be washed and food should be cooked properly before consumption. Half ripe, decayed and stale food-stuffs should never be used.

Treatment — For the control of diarrhea rehydration therapy is adopted through which the water expelled from the body in loose motions is replaced. In mild cases of diarrhea oral rehydration solution—ORS is administered orally and in serious cases fluid (glucose 5% with normal saline) is administered intravenously. One of the antibiotics as deoxycycline, tetracycline, chloramphenicol and furazolidine may be given.

CHOLERA

Cholera is an acute infectious disease caused by the infection with the coma-shaped bacterium Cholerae vibrio which is generally found in contaminated drinking water, and food. The disease is characterized by sudden occurrence of very frequent watery, white rice-water type motions, vomiting, dehydration, oliguria, muscle cramps and low blood pressure and marked weakness.

Prevention — Water should be boiled before consumption. Food should be properly cooked. Flies should be killed and their reproduction should be destroyed. Rubbish and other waste matter should be disposed of properly. All the edible and drinkable materials should be covered.

Treatment — Treatment is the same as that of diarrhea.

BACILLARY DYSENTERY

It is an acute infectious disease marked by the inflammation of the intestinal mucosa caused by the bacterium Shigella dysenteriae ingested with the contaminated edible materials and characterized by abdominal pain, tenesmus, fever and diarrhea. The stools contains blood and mucus also. In severe cases the stool looks like purulent matter.

Prevention — Same as for diarrhea and cholera.

Treatment — Oral rehydration therapy should be adopted. Antibiotic as tetracycline or ampicillin may be administered orally.

AMEBIC DYSENTERY

It is the infection of the colon caused by ingestion of the unicellular parasite Entameba histolytica with the contaminated edible and drinkable items and characterized by spasmodic pain in abdomen followed by diarrhea, the stools containing a large amount of mucus with foul smell. Sometimes a tinge of blood is seen in the stool.

Prevention — Hands should be cleaned thoroughly with soap and water after defecation and before and after taking food. Edible and drinkable materials should be protected from contamination of the feces, and from the flies. Water should be used for drinking after it has been filtered and boiled

Treatment — Metronidazole (metrogyl) 400 mg. tab. is given three times a day for 5-7 days. Metrogyl syrup 5 mls. (200 mg.) for elder children and 2.5 ml (100 mg.) for younger children is given three times a day for 5 to 7 days.

GIARDIASIS

It is the infection with the protozoan parasite Giardia lamblia which is ingested with the food or beverages. The lower part of duodenum and upper part of jejunum are inflamed. The disease is characterized by abdominal distension with gurgling sound due to formation of air in excess, and diarrhea of sudden onset producing sound with yellowish, frothy, watery stools that have very offensive smell.

Prevention and treatment — Similar to that of amebic dysentery.

FOOD POISONING

Food poisoning is an acute gastro-enteritis caused by ingestion of food or drink contaminated with either living bacteria or their toxins or inorganic chemical substances and poisons derived from plants and animals.

The bacteria causing food poisoning are generally the bacteria of the genus Salmonella, Staphylococcus aureus,Clostridium botulinum and Clostridium perfringens.

1. Bacteria of the genus salmonella — Food poisoning caused by Salmonella is an extremely common form of food poisoning. Man is infected by consumption of contaminated milk, curd, milk products, egg, egg products, sausages, meat etc. Rats are often heavily infected and contaminate food-stuffs by their urine and feces. The causative organisms, on ingestion, multiply in the intestine and give rise to acute enteritis and colitis. The onset is generally sudden with chills, fever, nausea, vomiting and profuse watery diarrhea which usually lasts 2-3 days. Mortality rate is about 1%.

2. Staphylococcus aureus — This type of bacterium produces enterotoxins which are heat stable and resist boiling of the food or drink for 30 minutes or more. It is found on the skin, nose and throat of men and animals. It produces boils and pyogenic infection of the skins. Food poisoning usually occurs when the milk or milk products consumed are of the cow suffering from mastitis. The foods involved are salads, custards, milk and milk products which are contaminated by Staphylococcus aureus.

Food poisoning results from ingestion of enterotoxins preformed in the food in which bacteria have grown. Enterotoxins, being heat-stable may remain in food after the organisms have died. Enterotoxins act directly on the intestine and central nervous system. The disease is characterized by sudden onset of vomiting, abdominal cramps and diarrhea. In severe cases blood and mucus may appear in the stools. Fever usually does not occur. Death is uncommon.

3. Clostridium botulinum — Botulism is a severe form of food poisoning but it occurs rarely. It kills two-thirds of the patients. It is caused by food containing the exotoxin of the bacterium Clostridium botulinum. The bacteria are widely distributed in the soil, dust and the intestinal tract of the animal and enter the food as spores. Foods most frequently responsible for botulism are improperly preserved foods such as home- canned vegetables, home-made cheese and similar low acid foods, and smoked or pickled fishes.

The toxin is preformed in the food under anerobic conditions. It acts mainly on the parasympathetic nervous system. Botulism differs from other forms of food poisoning in that the gastrointestinal symptoms are very slight. The prominent symptoms are dysphagia (difficulty in swallowing), diplopia (double vision), ptosis (dropping of the upper eyelid from paralysis), blurring of vision, dysarthria (difficulty in speaking), muscle weakness and even guadriplegia (paralysis of all the four limbs). Digestive symptoms such as nausea, vomiting, diarrhea and abdominal pain may or may not be present. Fever is generally absent, and the patient remains conscious. The condition is usually fatal, death occurs 4-8 days later due to respiratory or cardiac failure. Since the toxin is thermolabile, the heating of food to the tempreature of 80°C (170°F) for 30 minutes or boiling of it at 100°C (212° F) for 10 minutes before use will make it quite safe for consumption.

4. Clostridium perfringens (Welchii) — This bacterium is found in the soil, water, air and in the feces of the men and animals. The meat is prepared and cooked 24 hours or more before consumption, and allowed to cool slowly at room temperature and then heated immediately before consumption. By doing this, the spores which are being survived during cooking are carried to the large intestine where an enterotoxin is produced from them, which causes food poisoning after an incubation period of 6-24 hours after consumption of food (if the meat is not cooled enough), which is characterized by abdominal cramps, diarrhea, mild fever or the fever may be absent, nausea and vomiting is rare and the illness is usually of short duration, usually of one day or less. Recovery is rapid and usually no death occurs.

Prevention of Food Poisoning

- Floor of the kitchen and utensils and equipments should be cleaned thoroughly regularly.
- The persons engaged in handling, preparation, cooking and serving food should live with hygiene.
- The persons suffering from infected wound, boils, eczema, dermatitis, diarrhea, dysentery, throat infection or cough should be excluded from food handling.
- Food should be cooked properly, half-cooked food should never be consumed.
- Time between preparation and consumption of food should be shortest.
- Food premises should be free from dust, flies and rats.
- Food-stuffs as raw vegetables and fruits and eatable materials prepared in the house should not be left on warm places, if these are not consumed immediately, because a few germs

can multiply to million by the next morning. Foods not eaten immediately should be kept in refrigerator below the temperature. of 4°C to prevent bacterial multiplication and toxin production, "cookand eat the same day" is the golden rule.

- The food animals must be free from infections which can be confirmed by getting them examined by the veterinary doctor before and after slaughter.
- Health education — food handlers should be educated in matters of clean habits and personal hygiene such as frequent and thorough hand washing.

TYPHOID FEVER

Typhoid fever is the fever caused by the infection with the bacillus Salmonella typhi which is found in dirty water, ice, eatable matters, milk and the soil. By consumption of eatable materials, water, especially milk and milk products contaminated by the patients and carriers, by flies, by infected cloths etc., by utilizing such vegetables which are grown in sewage manure or washed with contaminated water, this disease is transmitted into the healthy person.

Usually after the incubation period of 1 to 3 weeks (the period between the entrance of the disease-producing organisms into the body and the appearance of the symptoms of the disease) typhoid fever occurs.

The disease runs the course of three weeks as follows —

First week — The patient complains of general weakness, frontal headache, aching in the limbs, loss of appetite, constipation, insomnia, and fever. The temperature gradually rises (step-ladder pattern) which drops ½ to 1 degree each morning and by the end of week may reach 102°F to 103°F. The pulse is slow in comparison to the rise of temperature and is dicrotic. It is usually 90 to 100 per minute. The tongue is coated with white fur with the edges and tip clean. Typhoid spots (rose spots) may appear about the seventh day on the trunk and abdomen, fading on pressure. Spleen becomes palpable.

Second week — The patient is more prostrated and headache is less marked. Insomnia may be troublesome and delirium may occur. The temperature remains sustained at about 101°F to 103°F. It often rises abruptly very high, 104°F to 105°F. Abdomen is distended and there is great tendency to diarrhea.

Third week — In the third week toxemia increases and the patient may pass into coma and may die but there is usually improvement toward the end of this week, and the temperature begins to fall. There is however, risk of hemorrhage and perforation of ulcers of the small intestine. The patient becomes very weak.

Prevention

- After defecation or urination and before cooking food you should wash your hands thoroughly with soap and water.
- Clean water should be used for drinking.
- The house, especially the kitchen should be maintained clean.
- Personal sanitation should be attended. One should live in hygienic conditions.
- Fresh and clean edible food-stuffs should be consumed, decayed fruits and stale food should not be consumed.

Immunization — Anti-typhoid vaccine is used for immunization against typhoid which is administered by injection subcutaneously in the arm, or orally. It is available in 5 ml. vial for injection.

Typhoral oral vaccine — It is available in the form of capsule. It is given to the children of the age above 6 years and to adults for immunization against typhoid. One capsule is given on the Ist, 3rd and 5th day one hour before lunch and dinner with cold or lukewarm water. Protection occurs for at least 3 years against typhoid fever since 2 weeks after taking the last capsule.

Treatment — An antibiotic chloramphenicol is used. One 500 mg. capsule is given 4 hourly for a week and then 6 hourly for the next 14 days.

PARATYPHOID FEVER

Paratyphoid fever is an infectious fever resembling typhoid. Its causative organism is the bacterium Salmonella paratyphi. Its incubation period is less than that of typhoid fever, so it comparatively occurs more abruptly. It is characterized by rigor followed by fever but it is less severe and of short duration than typhoid fever. Gastroenteritis with fever is the main characteristic of this disease. Vomiting and diarrhea occur due to gastroenteritis or only diarrhea occurs. It is also transmitted to the healthy person like typhoid fever, by living in contact with the patient, by carriers and by infection of the food.

Prevention and treatment — These are the same as described for typhoid fever, only Bivalent anti-typhoid vaccine is used for its prevention.

VIRAL HEPATITIS

This disease was previously called infective hepatitis. It is caused by Hepatitis A virus (HAV). It is acute hepatitis. Hepatitis A virus is transmitted to the healthy person by consumption of water, milk or food contaminated with the feces of the patient of jaundice or hepatitis. This disease is also caused by eating the vegetables as raw or half-ripe grown up in the sewage. This disease is characterized (after an incubation period of one month) by shivering with cold, fever, headache, muscular pain, general weakness followed by loss of appetite, nausea, vomiting and pain in the right upper portion of the abdomen. On examination liver is found to be enlarged and tender. Jaundice occurs, due to which the colour of the urine becomes brownish yellow and that of the stool becomes muddy.

Prevention

- The hands should be thoroughly washed before taking food and after defecation.
- Stool should be disposed of with sanitation, so that drinking water, food and milk may not be contaminated.
- There should be arrangement of killing the flies.
- For purification of water, chlorine should be added to the water supply of the public in sufficient quantity by municipality or municipal corporation.
- One should drink boiled water during epidemic days.
- An intramuscular injection of human immunoglobulin is given for producing immunization for the prevention of this disease.

ASCARIASIS

This disease is caused by the parasite Ascaris lumbricoides which is also called roundworm .Its eggs are found in the stool of the persons suffering from Ascariasis. Ascariasis occurs by ingestion of the eggs of the roundworm with infected edible or drinkable materials by man. The eggs in the small intestine passing through the liver and lungs are carried again into small intestine where they are converted into the adult form of the roundworms passing through the larva stage. The life period of an adult roundworm is one year after which it is escaped spontaneously from the intestine.

This disease is characterized by pain in the umbilical region, gas formation in the abdomen, indigestion, nausea, vomiting, diarrhea occasionally, sometimes urticaria may also be hopped, excessive hunger but the patient suffers from anemia which causes dyspnea (breathlessness) on walking a little distance and marked weakness.

Complications of Ascariasis

— Occasionally the bunch of roundworms causes intestinal obstruction.

— Especially the children suffer from malnutrition.

— Children are not developed physically and mentally.

— Eosinophilia may occur.

Prevention

- Human excreta should be discharged and disposed of with sanitation and sewage must be expelled so that the soil may not be contaminated.
- Hygienic latrines should be made in the rural areas.
- Pure water should be managed for drinking.
- Pure food should be taken and stale and decayed food should never be consumed.
- Hands should be thoroughly washed with soap and water or clay after defecation.
- Wash your children's hands thoroughly with water and then clean them with dry toil before lunch and dinner.
- The vegetables should be thoroughly washed with water before they are being utilized in the form of salad.

Treatment: — Piperazine phosphate 260 mg. tab. three times a day to the adult and piperazine citrate syrup 1 tea-spoonful three times a day to the children should be given for 2 days and a purgative is given at night before going for sleep.

OXYURIASIS OR ENTEROBIASIS

It is a disease caused by white, thread-like worm called Oxyuris vermicularis or threadworm. It generally occurs in children, in which irritation and itching occurs around the anus, especially at night and it is the main symptom of the disease.

On scratching the anus with the fingers, the eggs of the threadworms are adhered to the fingers and nails. Without cleaning thoroughly the infected fingers and nails, if eatable and drinkable materials contaminated by these fingers and nails are consumed, the eggs of threadworms are carried to the small intestine passing through the stomach, where these are converted into adult worms passing through the larval stage. Gravid female threadworm reaches the rectum passing through the cecum and colon and from there it comes out in the night and lays thousands of eggs due to which excessive itching occurs around the anus, especially at night.

Complications : Occasionally cystitis occurs, especially in young girls.

— Salpingitis may occur in women.

— Appendicitis may occur.

— Rectum may be prolapsed.

Prevention

- Cut the nails regularly. Do not allow them to grow.
- Special attention should be paid toward the personal hygiene.
- The hands should be washed thoroughly with water after defecation and before going to take food.
- Tight underwear should be worn to prevent scratching of the anus.
- All the members of the family should be treated at the same time on occurrence of the disease.

Treatment — Syrup piperazine citrate two teaspoonfuls to the adults and one teaspoonful to the children is given three times a day for 7 days. Again this course is repeated after 2 weeks.

Or only one tablet of mebendazole 100 mg. is given. One more tablet is given after two weeks. It is not given during pregnancy.

Or oxytetracycline hydrochloride (Terramycin) 250 mg. or 500 mg. one capsule is given 6 hourly for two or three days.

MILK-BORNE DISEASES

Milk is an important vehicle or medium for the transmission of disease-producing organisms, e.g., tubercle bacilli and typhoid bacilli.

The contamination of milk may arise from Three sources

1. The dairy animal, e.g., tubercle bacilli
2. The human handler, e.g., typhoid bacilli.
3. The environment, e.g., through contaminated vessels, polluted water, dust and flies.

The important milk-borne diseases are as follows —

1. Directly from the dairy animal

- Bovine tuberculosis — It is the main milk-borne disease transmitted directly from the dairy animal or cattle to the human being. The infection is transmitted through drinking the milk of the infected or the sick cattle, especially the cow's milk. Usually children suffer from tuberculosis of the abdomen (Koch's abdomen) through drinking milk of the sick cow. It can be eradicated, especially in children by supplying pure milk to them. It can be accomplished by not feeding the child with the infected cow's milk but the milk should be of the healthy cow, or it can be done by killing the pathogenic bacteria of the milk by pasteurizing the milk before feeding.
- Brucellosis
- Streptococcal infections
- Foot and mouth disease
- Anthrax

2. Indirectly from the human handler or environment

- Typhoid fever
- Paratyphoid fever
- Cholera
- Dysentery
- Viral hepatitis

FRUITS AND VEGETABLES

Fruits and vegetables, especially those which are eaten raw, e.g., tomatoes and radish can be a source of infection. Those which are grown in sewage irrigated land, are particularly dangerous, if eaten raw and unwashed. They can transmit pathogenic bacteria like the 'typhoid bacilli' and the eggs of the worms. Vegetables which are cooked and eaten are free from this danger. Vegetables which are to be eaten raw in the form of salad are best treated in a weak solution of potassium permanganate, and later washed in running water.

EGGS

Eggs become stale on prolonged storage, and storage under unsatisfactory conditions. The freshness of the eggs may be tested as follows:—

(a) Candling — When a strong light is projected, the egg must appear transparent. The eggs should be rejected if there are any spots or internal blemishes.

(b) Floating in saline water — Fresh eggs sink in 10% saline solution, stale egg will float.

FISHES

Fish decomposes quickly after death. The signs of fresh fish are as follows :

(1) It must be in a state of stiffness or rigor mortis.

(2) The gills should be bright.

(3) The eyes should be clear and prominent.

The following diseases are produced by fishes —

(a) A tapeworm disease known as 'D' latos, but since fish in not eaten raw, D latos, infestation is a rare disease.

(b) Fish poisoning

Tinned fish — many people are eating tinned fishes now-a-days.

It is necessary to inspect the tin or cane before consuming its contents. The following points should be noted when examining the tinned fish, meat or any other tinned food.

(I) The tin must be new and clean.

(II) There should be no holes or sealed openings in the tin. Such tins should be discarded.

(III) On shaking the tin there should be no sound.

(IV) On opening the tin, the contents should not be blown out, on the other hand there should be a hissing noise.

MEAT

The term "meat" includes various tissues of animal origin. It can be a source of infection if it is bad or unwholesome. The meat-borne diseases are as follows —

Taeniasis — It is the disease caused by the worms which are long and flattened like the tape and so these are called tapeworms. The worms are found sticking with the small intestine. They cause indigestion, nausea, pain in abdomen occasionally, sometimes diarrhea and the other times constipation occurs, and there is itching on the anus. Sometimes the patient looks the proglottides of the motile tapeworm in his stool, on his body and clothes. There is excessive hunger, the patient eats too much but the weakness goes on increasing and the body weight decreases continuously and anemia develops.The last gravid proglottides of the tapeworm in the intestine of the patient go on separating and coming out with the stool or the proglottides burst open even in the intestine of the patient, so their eggs come out into the intestine whence they are excreted with the stool through the anus.

There are two types of tapeworms which are similar in shape.

I. Taenia solium — Taenia solium causes taeniasis through eating of the half-cooked meat of the pig. The stool of the persons consuming half-cooked meat of the pig contains the eggs of the Taenia solium.

II. Taenia saginata — Taenia saginata causes taeniasis through eating of the half-cooked meat of the cow or buffalo. The stool of the person consuming half cooked meat of cow or buffalo contains the eggs of Taenia saginata.

Prevention

- Infected meat should be destroyed.
- The meat should be cooked thoroughly. Uncooked or half-cooked meat should never be used.
- Pigs and cattle's should not be allowed to eat the human excreta.

Treatment — The drug niclosamide is used. Its 2 tablets (1 gm.) are chewed on empty stomach in the morning at one hour interval and then ingested with a little water. After 2-3 hours magnesium sulphate is given as purgative.

Bacterial infections

— Tuberculosis

— Anthrax

— Food poisoning

Signs of good meat

1. **Color** — Meat should not be pale, pink or deep purple.
2. **Touch** — The meat should be firm and elastic to touch, it should not be greasy or slimy.
3. **Smell** — The odor should be agreeable.

Different processes of making food more nutritious

- **Sprouting** — Many cereals and pulses as Bengal gram (Chana or Chane ki dal), black gram (urad ki dal) and green gram (moong ki dal) etc. can be sprouted. For sprouting soak any of the food-stuffs in water for 24 hrs, then spread it out on a damp cloth and keep the cloth damp for one or two days until there is a half inch sprouting. It must be taken raw or slightly cooked (for a short time) in order to preserve the nutrients. Vitamin C is increased upto 10 times in sprouted food-stuffs, while vit. B complex is often doubled. Iron becomes free and therefore becomes more available to the body. Sprouting also increases the digestibility of the foods. Sprouting of fenugreek seeds (maithee) reduces its bitter taste also.

- **Fermentation** — In preparing curd from milk, its sugar called lactose or milk sugar is fermented by lactic acid bacilli and milk is converted into curd. In making idli and dosa in South India, rice mixture is to be fermented. It is being done by micro-organisms which are multiplied speedly when the conditions are in favor. In fermentation vitamin B complex (thiamine, riboflavine and nicotinic acid) is also doubled and this increases the availability of iron to the body. Fermented foods are soft and spongy.
- **Parching (Roasting)** — By this process the cereals as wheat, rice and maize are puffed or swollen, if they are heated suddenly when they are wet. The water escapes by puffing out the grain. Best example of the parched food is corn. Starch becomes more digestible after parching.
- **Cereal millet mixture** — Mixture of a millet such as bajra or jowar and a cereal adds extra nutrients to the diet.
- **Cereal pulse mixture** — If a pulse is added to the rice or chapati, the protein value of the meal is increased.
- **Milk porridge** — Instead of using milk alone, if porridge is made by mixing it with the grains of wheat, it will be more nutritious. An infant will get more proteins and calories than milk alone.
- **Powdered protein food** — It can be prepared by grinding into powder a large amount of groundnuts, grams, pulses and

beans etc. Dried fishes can also be powdered. The protein-rich powders can be kept in tins. They need to be cooked and should therefore be added to the cereal flour before cooking. This makes very nutritious meal for a child.

- **Pounded dark green leaves** — The dark green leaves may be pounded either fresh or dried. Dried leaves will be converted into a green powder which can be used to enrich the porridge. It can also be added to the dough for making roti or chapati, to enrich the family diet. It is rich in protein and iron.
- Certain fruits and vegetables change their colour when exposed to air. Hence brinjal should be cut into water and apples should be covered with sugar and lime juice.
- When milk is heated, it becomes a little brown due to reaction of sugar (lactose) with amino acids giving a pleasant flavor.
- **Preparation of salad** — Use fresh fruits, vegetables, green leaves, nuts etc., in the preparation of salads. Wash the vegetables and fruits and then cut them in water with the stainless steel knife so that vegetables and fruits are not discolored. Fruits and vegetables can be served and decorated. Sprouted grams and fresh peas can be used in salad.

* * * * *

CHAPTER 12

ADULTERATION

Adulteration of food is the mixing or substitution of an impure, weaker, cheaper or inferior, possibly toxic substance to the food-stuff which affects the quality of food. According to the Indian Prevention of Food Adulteration Act (PFA),1954 any ingredient which when present in food is injurious to health is an adulterant. The act has been amended several times, the latest amendment is of 1986 to make the act more astringent.

Although it is a central Act, its implementation is largely carried out by the local bodies and the State Governments.

Bureau of Indian Standards — The ISI mark on any article of food is a guarantee of food quality in accordance with the standards prescribed by the Bureau of Indian Standards (BIS) for that commodity.

ADULTERATION OF FOOD ADDITIVES

Food additives are of two types —

I. Intentionally added substances — These are added intentionally to the food, generally in small quantities, to improve its appearance, colour, flavour, taste, texture or storage properties (shelf life). These substances may be as follows —

- Colouring agents, e.g., turmeric, saffron etc.
- Flavouring agents, e.g., vanilla essence
- Sweeteners, e.g., saccharin
- Preservatives e.g., sodium benzoate etc.

The agents are generally considered safe for human consumption. Uncontrolled or indiscriminate use of food additive may cause health hazards. Generally the processed foods such as breads, cakes, biscuits, sweets, lozenges, toffees, jams, jellies, soft drinks, ice creams and refined oils etc., contain food additives.

II. Contaminants incidental — These are added to the food incidentally during cultivation as insecticides, process of food preparation, through packing of food or through environmental conditions.

The use of food additives is subjected to Government regulations throughout the world. In India Prevention of Food Adulteration Act governs the rules and regulations of food additives. Any food that contains food additives that are not permitted is considered to be adulterated and if the permissible limit of an additive exceeds, then also the food is considered to be adulterated.

The nature and quantity of the additives should be clearly written on the label to be affixed on the container. Whenever, any extraneous colouring matter has been added to any article of food, the words "Artificially coloured" should be written on the label.

Adulteration of Foods

Adulteration of food is done through the following ways —

- Mixing
- Substitution
- Abstraction
- Concealing the quality

- Putting up decayed foods for sale
- Wrong advertisement of a food
- Affixing of false labels on the containers
- Addition of toxicants

Food adulteration practices vary from one part of the country to another, and from time to time.

The types of adulteration commonly found in India and the tests for their detection are as follows —

Cereals such as wheat and rice—Clay, gravels, pieces of stones and marbles etc.

Test—By visual examination adulteration can be detected.

Wheat flour—Low grade flour from which maida or semolina (Rava) has been extracted. Stone powder is mixed.

Pulses — Clay, pieces of stones, gravels and kesari dal.

Test — By visual examination clay, pieces of stones and gravels can be detected.

If Kesari dal is consumed regularly for a long time, it leads to lathyrism characterized by muscular weakness and paraplegia and ultimately death may occur.

Test for Kesari dal — Add 50 mls of dilute hydrochloric acid to a small amount of dal and allow it to stand in boiling water for 15 minutes If pink colour appears in it, it indicates the presence of kesari dal.

Ghee or butter	—	(a) Dalda or Vanaspati ghee
		(b) Mashed potatoes or sweet potatoes, or some starch powders
		(c) Animal fat as pig's fat
Edible oils	—	(a) Argemone oil
		(b) Mineral oil
		(c) Castor oil
Sugar	—	Chalk powder

Test — Dissolve in a glass of water, chalk will be settled down.

Milk — (a) Addition of water to increase the bulk of the milk.

(b) Starch or maida or arrowroot after extraction of fat to make the milk thicker.

Examination of the milk

1. Milk should be white with no deposit or disagreeable smell or taste.
2. An average specific gravity of cow's milk and buffalo's milk is 1032. Lactometer is the instrument which is used to determine the specific gravity of the milk. Its reading should not be less than 1026.

Sweetmeat — Non-permitted colours.

Ice-cream— Cheap quality, non-permitted coaltar dye, cellulose, starch.

Sharbat — Cheap quality, non-permitted coaltar dye.

Khoa — Starch.

Tea — Dried used tea leaves, husk of red gram (arhar), leather and saw dust.

Test — Tea leaves are sprinkled on the wet filter paper, it would immediately release colours.

Coffee — (a) Chicory

(b) Tamarind seed powder

(c) Date seeds powder

Test — Gently sprinkle a little amount of coffee powder on the surface of water in a glass. The coffee will float over the water but chicory etc. will be settled down at the bottom.

Common salt — Chalk or powdered stone.

Test — Stir a spoonful of common salt in a glass of water. The presence of chalk will make the solution white and other impurities as powder of stone will be settled down.

Turmeric (Haldi) — Coloured saw dust.

Test — Take a tea-spoonful of turmeric powder in a test tube and add a few drops of concentrated hydrochloric acid. A violet colour will be appeared immediately which disappears on dilution with water.

Chillies powder — Brick powder.

Test — Take a tea-spoonful of chilli powder is a glass of water. The brick powder will be settled at the bottom.

Dried powder of coriander (Dhania powder) — Starch, cow-dung powder, horse dung powder.

Asafoetida (Hing) — Sand, gums, resins, grits.

Black pepper (Kali mirch) — Dried papaya seeds.

Test — Black pepper is spherical. On biting the black pepper a repulsive pungent flavour is escaped, which is the important sign of black pepper. Dried papaya seeds can be separated as they are oval and shrunken in shape.

Honey — Molasses (the end products in the manufacture of sugar or jaggery).

Test — A cotton wick dipped in pure honey when burned, it will burn with good flame, if adulterated it will produce crackling sound not allowing the honey to burn.

Saffron — Dried fibers of corn-cob.

Mustard seeds — Seeds of prickly poppy — Argemone.

Any food that is not according to the minimum standards laid down under the Prevention of Food Adulteration Act 1954, is said be adulterated.

Food fortification

According to WHO "Food fortification" is the process whereby nutrients are added to foods (in relatively small quantities) to maintain or improve the quality of the diet of a group, a community or a population.

For example

1. Foods artificially fortified with vitamin D, e.g., Milk, margarine, vanaspati and infants' food.

2. Foods fortified with vitamin A, e.g., Margarine, milk and vanaspati.

* * * * *

CHAPTER 13

FOOD ALLERGY

Allergy is a hypersensitive reaction to a substance called allergen which normally does not cause any reaction. It is due to release of histamine or histamine-like substances from the damaged tissue cells. Food allergy is an abnormal or a hypersensitive reaction of an individual to the food he eats. Food allergen may be introduced into the body by ingestion of food. Usually food allergen is protein in nature but it may be a carbohydrate, lipid or a chemical present in the food.

Food allergy may occur after ingestion of wheat, milk and milk products as cheese etc., eggs, meat, fish, chocolate, strawberries and tomatoes etc. Other food allergens (foods causing allergy) which are not so common, are oranges, spinach, cabbage, onions, nuts, spices and condiments etc.

Signs and symptoms of food allergy — Food allergy causes the following signs and symptoms—

- Skin lesions
  - — Nettle rash
  - — Urticaria
  - — Eczema
- Nausea
- Vomiting
- Diarrhea
- Colitis
- Headache
- Redness, swelling, burning and itching of the eyes.
- Allergic rhinitis or coryza
- Bronchial asthma
- Hypotension or low blood pressure
- Shock
- Fever

Diagnosis — The procedures adopted for the diagnosis of allergy are as follows —

(1) History — A complete history of the food item taken by the person prior to and after the onset of allergic reactions should be obtained. This may give some clue regarding the food item responsible for the allergy.

(2) Skin tests — Water extracts or solution in water of the suspected food is applied to the skin in the following ways —

1. Scratch test — A few scratches are made on the arm or back of the patient and a few drops of the extract or solution of food are dropped into each scratch. If the person is allergic to any of the extracts used, a wheal surrounded by a red or inflamed area will develop within a few minutes.

2. Patch test — The powder of suspected food or food extract is put on a filter paper which is placed on the skin, covered with cellophane and kept for 24 hours. If a red inflammation or wheal appears at the site of the scratch or point of contact, the food material is suspected as allergen.

3. Intradermal test — A few drops of a food extract are injected intradermally (within the skin). If a wheal appears within a few minutes at the site of injection, the food material is suspected as allergen.

(3) Leukopenic index test — Total Leukocytic Count (TLC) should be done of the fasting patient at ten minutes interval. Then a small portion of the food which is to be tested is served to the patient. Then again total leukocyte count is done at 15 minutes interval for one to one and half hours. Decline of total leukocyte occurring between 0.5 hour to 1.5 hours following intake of food indicates that the food is allergic, i.e.,causing allergy.

Treatment of food allergy

Food allergy may be treated by the following five methods —

(1) Drug therapy

(2) Synthetic diet

(3) Elimination diet

(4) Restricted diet

(5) Desensitization

(1) Drug therapy —Antiallergic drugs such as corticosteroids or antihistamines as Anthisan or Avil 50 mg.l tablets are administered. Mild cases are treated with antihistamines. The allergic reactions usually disappear after treatment. Ephedrine hydrochloride 30 mg. 2 to 3 times a day before meals may be given if there are frequent attacks of allergy. Attacks of allergy of night and morning may be prevented by taking 60 to 120 mg., i.e.,1 to 2 grains of phenobarbitone at night with an additional dose of ephedrine. In serious condition or in case of anaphylactic shock an injection of adrenaline or epinephrine may be administered. The patient may learn to inject it in a small dose to prevent the attack.

(2) Synthetic diet — Patients who are allergic to common foods show improvement when they are fed on a synthetic diet. The diet consists of amino acids, sugar, salt mixture, vitamin concentrates, emulsifying fat and water. None of the constituents of the synthetic diet causes allergy. Synthetic diet can be given through nasogastric tube in serious cases. Patients who are allergic to food show marked improvement with the synthetic diet in a few days. The patient after cure should be put on diet consisting of natural foods. Care should be taken to avoid the foods which produce allergy.

(3) Elimination diet — Rowe in the year 1944 suggested elimination diets which can be used for the treatment of allergy. The patient is first treated with anti-allergic drugs. When the allergic reactions are cured, he is put on one of the diets given in the following table, which on the basis of dietary history and skin tests do not cause allergic reaction. The diet should be consumed for 2 to 3 weeks unless severe allergic reactions occur soon after intake of the diet. It the patient does not develop any allergic reaction, then he can continue on taking the diet. Otherwise, diet ll in the table is consumed for 2 to 3 weeks. A period of 2 to 3 weeks is essential to make sure whether any of the foods included in the diet caused allergic reactions in the patient. If the patient reacts well to the second diet, he should try the remaining two diets in the table in the above manner. If the patient tolerates the foods included in all the four diets in the table, all the foods listed in the four diets can be used.

***Table 34.* Elimination diet (Rowe 1944)**

Diet I	Diet II	Diet III	Diet IV
Rice	Corn	Tapioca	Milk
Tapioca	Rye	White potato	Tapioca
Rice biscuits		Breads made of any	Cane
		combination of	sugar

Rice bread	Corn-rye muffina	soya, Lima bean and
	Rye bread	potato starch and
	Rye-Krisp	tapioca flours.
Lettuce	Beets	Tomato
	Squash	Carrot
Spinach	Asparagus	Lima beans
Carrot	Artichoke	String beans
Sweet potato		Peas
or yarn		
Lamb	Chicken	Beef
	Bacon	Bacon
Lemon	Pineapple	Lemon
Grapes	Peach	Grapes
Pears	Prunes	Peach
	Apricot	Apricot
Cane sugar	Cane or beet sugar	Cane sugar
Sesame oil	Mazola oil	Sesame oil
Olive oil	Sesame oil	Soyabean oil
Salt	Salt	Salt

(4) Restricted diet — When someone tolerates one of the elimination diets described in the above table, other food such as milk, wheat and meat should be added (one at a time) to the elimination diet. The new diet should be continued for 2-3 weeks. If the new food added to the diet does not cause any allergic reaction, it can be consumed for a longer period in order to make sure that it is well tolerated by the patient. On the other hand, if it causes allergic reaction, it should be eliminated completely from the diet. In this way, the foods which cause allergic reaction in the patient can be found out and the same should be completely eliminated from the diet.

(5) Desensitization — The object of desensitization is to develop tolerance to the food allergy in a person. For this purpose the person takes food which he tolerates well. Allergy-producing food is given to the person in very small quantities. If he tolerates the small quantities of the food, he can be given slightly larger quantities of the food. It he is continuously tolerating the food, it is given in increasing quantities gradually. In this way, tolerance to an allergic food can be developed in that person. If that person does not tolerate even minute quantities of the food, it may be difficult to develop resistance in the body to that particular food.

Hypersensitivity to a food allergen may decrease or even disappear spontaneously as the patient grows older, and therefore re-inclusion of a food item in the diet should be considered from time to time. This is particularly important in case of infants and children, where food allergies usually do not persist.

Allergy in Infants

Food allergy is observed frequently among the infants who drink cow's or buffalo's milk. Mother's breast milk does not cause allergy or causes a slight allergy. A child born in a family where her father or mother or both of them are allergic or hypersensitive to some foods, the child is likely to show allergic reaction to the same foods. Generally cow's milk is allergic to some infants witch should be replaced by fortified soyabean milk. Mother's breast milk is the best.

* * * * *

CHAPTER 14

COOKING AND ITS EFFECTS ON FOOD

Cooking food brings about desirable changes in the foods being consumed. The sources of heat provided may be by the burning of wood or charcoal, kerosine oil or gas, by electric heater, electric oven, hot plate or by a microwave cooker.

Causes of Cooking Foods

(1) Cooking improves the appearance of the foods.

(2) It develops the flavour of the foods.

(3) Cooking makes foods more appetizing and palatable.

(4) It changes the taste of food.

(5) Cooking improves the digestibility of food. It makes mastication easier. Heat causes the starch of the cells to swell leading to the burst out of the cell walls, so that digestive enzymes act easily upon the starch.

(6) It sterilizes the food by destroying the harmful micro-organisms, parasitic ova and eggs, and toxins present in the food.

(7) Cooking introduces a variety of foods, i.e., many different types of dishes can be prepared with the same ingredients.

(8) Food becomes nutritious on cooking.

Methods of Cooking

There are 9 methods of cooking foods as follows —

(1) Boiling
(2) Simmering
(3) Steaming
(4) Baking
(5) Roasting
(6) Frying
(7) Grilling
(8) Poaching
(9) Stewing

(1) Boiling

Cooking of food in water at 100°C (212°F) temperature is called boiling. Rice, pulses, roots, tubers and other vegetables are cooked in this way. Boiling in excess of water may result in loss of vitamins and minerals. Therefore boiling of food-stuffs should be done in minimum amount of water.

(2) Simmering

Cooking of food below boiling point, i.e., at about 84°C is called simmering. Meat and fishes are best cooked by simmering, because at high temperature the fibres of them are hardened.

(3) Steaming

Steaming is also a method of cooking food in which steam of water is applied to the food-stuffs. This principle is employed in pressure cookers. Because of the increased pressure of the steam, the temperature attained is higher than100°C, it becomes 121°C. Pressure cooker is better method of cooking since it saves nutrients, fuel and time.

(4) Baking

In this method food is cooked by dry heat. It is done in hot air oven. Food is enclosed by hot air, so that it gets heat from all sides. The cooking temperature may vary from 250°F to 500°F. It is a slow method of cooking.

(5) Roasting

In this type of cooking when heat reaches the food, only the surface of food-stuff is heated. Heat does not penetrate the food. The rest of the food is cooked mostly by conduction and also to some extent by convection, e.g., toasting of bread. Bread piece is smeared with a little butter and exposed directly to heat or flame or the bread piece is exposed directly to heat or flame and then it is smeared with a little butter.

(6) Frying

Cooking of food in fat or oil is called frying. Frying increases the taste but destroys the vitamins. It is of the following two types —

Shallow frying — In this type of frying fat or oil in the pan needs to be only about 1/8 inch deep. The fat should be hot and quite smooth on the surface when the food is put into it. When food becomes brown on one side, it should be turned and let it be browned on the other side. Only thin pieces of food are cooked by this method. This method of cooking is satisfactory for cakes, dosa, pre-cooked food, for preparing amlets of eggs, fish, cutlets and thin pieces of meat etc. This method prevents food from sticking to the pan.

Deep frying — In deep frying, food is completely immersed in large quantity of hot (to the boiling point) ghee or oil in the pan. At this temperature the food usually becomes hard, crisp and brown in colour. It is suitable for making puri, pakora etc. By this method a large amount of fat is absorbed by the food-stuffs, which also raises the calorific value of food.

(7) Grilling

In this method of cooking dry heat is applied directly on the food-stuffs. Cooking is quickly done under a grill, e.g., fishes and meat etc.

Food can be cooked by a combination of media e.g., Upma or Halwa involves the combination of fat and water.

(8) Poaching

Cooking is done gently in water which is hot to just below the boiling point, e.g., egg and fish etc.

(9) Stewing

Stewing is used for cooking meat. Low degree of heat (usually 200°F) is applied to the liquid being used in cooking, for a long time. The food is half covered with the liquid and as soon as it reaches the boiling point, the heat is reduced to make it simmer for a long time. For each kilogram of food approximately 7 litres of the liquid are required. For a better result, use pan with a well-fitting lid to prevent evaporation. The nutrients which escape while stewing are not lost,

Cooking media — Air, water, steam, and fat or the combination of these are used as cooking media. Baking, roasting and grilling take place in the air. Boiling and simmering take place in water. In these methods the medium transferring heat is water. Method of steaming generally takes place in pressure cookers. Frying is carried in fat or oil.

The effects of heat on the nutrients in foods :

To understand the way in which cooking affects the digestibility of food, it is necessary to know the effect of heat upon the nutrients in food. The following changes occur in the nutrients in the food by the effect of heat.

Changes in Proteins

— Destruction of micro-organisms of the food.

— Destruction of the toxic substances of food, as trypsin inhibitor present in the legumes, which affects the digestibility and availability of protein.

— Inactivation of certain enzymes present in the food.

— Proteins are coagulated on heating or cooking the food. This takes place at a temp. of about 140° F or 60°C. Above this temp. the protein of animal foods, with the exception of eggs, shrinks and becomes slightly less digestible. Vegetable proteins also coagulate on cooking, but they are usually found along with the starch which swells up in moist heat and the cellulose covering is ruptured. Cooking thus makes the vegetable soft and protein more digestible. Some loss of protein from the vegetables occurs when these are boiled in water particularly when salt is used in cooking.

Changes in Fats

Fats are not affected by heat so much as proteins and carbohydrates. Fat which is solid at room temperature melts on heating. When fat is heated further, i.e., .at high temperature it starts smoking, known as smoking point, and begins to decompose. At this point it becomes brown and thickens with a change in taste and flavour. Fat becomes rancid due to oxidation, and watery due to hydrolysis by the enzymes.

Changes in Carbohydrates

Starch of the carbohydrates is mostly affected by heat. Cellulose walls of the cells are not digested in man, which must be broken down for the cell contents to be digested. If water is used in cooking, the cellulose walls are softened, but moreover, the starch grains within the cells absorb water and swell up and eventually the cellulose walls are ruptured causing the quicker digestion of starch by the enzymes, thereby increasing the digestibility of carbohydrates. When starch is subjected to dry heat, it is broken down into dextrin which is responsible for the brown colour and slightly sweet taste of the baked foods, e.g., crust of the bread.

Changes in Vitamins

Vitamin A or carotene is not affected when food-stuffs are cooked in water. But in shallow frying or roasting there may be considerable loss of vitamin A.

Vitamin B complex of rice and dal is lost upto 50% by scrubbing and washing them repeatedly before cooking, while vitamin C is lost upto 45%.

Vitamin C is the most heat-labile (destroyed by heat) vitamin which is readily lost or destroyed in food preparation or by cooking food.

Thiamine, riboflavine and vitamin K are destroyed in the presence of an alkali, e.g., sodium bicarbonate, and may be lost by solubility in water.

Changes in Minerals

There is no loss of minerals during cooking of food but they may be lost by solubility in water if cooking water is thrown out.

The effects of cooking on different types of foods —

Cereals

Cereals consist mainly of starch with a little protein enclosed within a cell wall of cellulose. By cooking the food adequately, the cellulose walls of the cells are broken so that the digestive juices can reach the starch within the cells. Moreover, boiling of cereals causes the starch grains to swell and burst the cellulose wall.

Rice absorbs water twice of its own weight during cooking and so the weight of cooked rice is three times of its dry weight.

If much water is used in cooking cereals, the thiamine is lost from the food by solubility in water. Thiamine will also be destroyed if soda bicarbonate is added to the food during cooking.

The protein of cereals is also coagulated on cooking food and it depends upon the breaking of the cellulose walls, for digestion.

Well-cooked cereals are thus more easily digested than the cereals in the raw state.

Pulses

Pulses contain less carbohydrate but more protein than cereals but the effect of cooking is much the same. Pulses also contain some carbohydrate which is not digestible, and they also contain an anti-trypsin substance which prevents the action of trypsin enzyme. The undigested carbohydrate may be broken down by the bacteria present in the large intestine and cause flatulence. The anti-trypsin substance is destroyed by adequate boiling so that it is very important that pulses or dals should be properly cooked.

VEGETABLES

Green Leafy Vegetables

Green leafy vegetables provide a little caloric value but give most of the vitamins and minerals of a normal diet. They are usually cooked by boiling method. If much water is used in boiling, thiamine, vitamin C and some of the minerals are lost by solubility in water. Thiamine may also be destroyed if sodium bicarbonate is used in cooking. Vitamin A and carotene content are not much affected by domestic methods of cooking.

Roots and Tubers

Root vegetables do not suffer much loss of nutrients by either wet or dry methods of cooking because their skin prevents the leaking of the nutrients. Hence, these should be boiled with their skin intact and vegetables should be washed just before cutting and cutting of the vegetables should not be done long before their cooking, they should be cut just before cooking. Vegetables should be cut into big pieces and not in small pieces because vitamins are lost from their cut ends.

Tubers, e.g., potatoes contain a large amount of starch, more than other vegetables. They must be adequately cooked so that the starch grains may swell and burst the cell walls of cellulose. They should not be soaked in water for a long time, because it causes the loss of vitamins. Nutrients in tubers are retained by cooking them with their skin intact, but if they are old, a strong flavor is also retained. New potatoes should be scrapped rather than peeled off to preserve the mineral layer. Tubers should be cooked or boiled slowly as rapid boiling breaks up their skin.

Other Vegetables

Other vegetables vary in food contents, but like green leafy vegetables they also contribute vitamins and minerals to the diet. The same precautions should be taken in the preparation and cooking of food to preserve their food value.

FRUITS

Fruits consist mostly of water with a little carbohydrate as cellulose and sugar. The protein, fat and mineral content is very low. Some fruits as guava, orange, apple, ripe mango, ripe papaya, pine apple and lime or lemon etc., are good sources of vitamin C. Generally, the fruits are eaten raw, and if are eaten fresh, they will supply vitamin C to the body. Cooking makes the fruits more digestible by softening the cellulose but usually results in the loss of sugar by solubility is water. If the fruit is cooked by stewing and the juice is taken with the stew, the sugar loss is very little, but even then there will be loss of vit. C.

MILK

On cooking or boiling the milk following changes occur in the milk.

— Vitamin C is destroyed.

— Partial loss of vitamin B-complex occurs.

— Certain enzymes are destroyed.

— Micro-organisms are destroyed. Organisms of producing lactic acid are killed.

— Caseinogen (principal protein of the milk) becomes more digestible.

— Lactalbumin and lactoglobulin (proteins of the milk) are coagulated at the temp. of 160° F and 168° F respectively.

— Calcium, magnesium and phosphorus are precipited.

— After sometime a thin scum is formed on the top of the milk which consists of milk fat, lime salt, partly dried casein and coagulated lactalbumin.

EGG

On boiling egg-white and egg-yolk are coagulated. 'Avidin' a substance present in the egg is destroyed on boiling the egg, which prevents the body from obtaining biotin, one of the factors of vitamin B-complex present in the egg. Boiled egg is therefore nutritionally superior to raw egg.

FISH

There are three main kinds of fish.

1. White fish — It has white and opaque flesh when cooked, which contains protein but very little fat. It is regarded as the most easily digestible kind of fish.

2. Oily fish — It has flesh of pinkish brown color when cooked, which contains a higher proportion of fat than white fish, and as a result is easily digestible.

3. Shell fish — As crabs and prawns, etc., with flesh which is very dense and tough and difficult to digest.

MEAT

Meat is protein food of animal origin but it also contains variable amounts of fat. Cooking makes the meat softer to be chewed easily. On cooking or boiling the meat , water content of it is reduced, protein is coagulated, fibres are softened due to conversion of the connective tissue into gelatin and the fat is melted. If meat is cooked by roasting or grilling, the protein on the surface is coagulated quickly, sealing the juices inside the meat.

Some of the mineral salts may be lost in the process of boiling or stewing, but this is of little importance if the liquid is also used, as soup or gravy.

Prolonged cooking, especially by dry heat as in roasting, causes the protein to become hard and indigestible.

Changes in Colour

There are various colours of food which make the food more attractive and acceptable. The plant pigments such as chlorophyll of green leaves, carotenoid of carrots, flavonoids of white potatoes and anthocyanins of beet root, onions and red cabbage and myoglobulin of the meat, etc., are affected by heat. The soluble pigments such as anthocyanins may leach in the cooking water.

Some Suggestions on Cooking

- Keep all the ingredients ready before cooking.
- Close the lid of the container while cooking.
- While cooking green vegetables, keep the lid on to preserve green color.
- Use little amount of soda or baking powder as it irritates the intestine.
- Frying increases the taste but destroys vitamins.
- Boiling and steaming are good methods of cooking.
- Avoid use of food colours.

* * * * *

CHAPTER 15

PRESERVATION AND STORAGE OF FOOD

Food gradually undergoes deterioration or spoilage when it is manufactured, slaughtered or harvested. Some foods are spoiled readily and others take a long time to be spoiled. Due to deterioration, physiological, chemical and biological changes occur in the food, which make the food unfit for human consumption. In order to prevent deterioration, the foods should be carefully stored and preserved for future use. Any condition opposing the growth of bacteria, and causing their destruction aids in preservation of food.

Methods of food preservation are as follows —

1. Refrigeration or cold storage and freezing
2. Heating
3. Drying
4. Canning
5. Salting and pickling

6. Jams
7. Vinegar
8. Use of chemical preservatives
9. Smoking
10. Irradiation

(1) Refrigeration or cold storage and freezing :

A number of food-stuffs, e.g., fruits, vegetables, fish, meat and butter etc. are stored and preserved in the refrigerator, widely used at home and in the commercial plants. Potatoes are generally stored in cold storage in the season. Fruits and vegetables should be kept just above the freezing point, i.e., 0°C. Meat and butter are kept at much lower temperatures. Though the freezing process does not destroy the micro-organisms, it stops their growth and multiplication. It does not affect the taste and flavour of the food. Fruits, vegetables, fishes, meat and butter etc., can be preserved by this method for a long time.

(2) Heating :

Food is also preserved by heating. The liquid food is heated in containers or by other means to a temperature below the boiling point of water, usually at 60°C for a definite period, usually 30 minutes. Other method of heat treatment is dipping the food material in boiling water for two or three minutes. This process destroys the pathogenic organisms present in the food material without changing the chemical composition of the food and so the shelf-life (the period for which a food may be kept safely to eat, on a shelf) of the food is increased.

Boiling of milk—Boiling of milk is an ancient method of rendering the milk safe for human consumption. In India much of the milk is treated by boiling.

Sterilization—This is done by raising the temperature to 100°C and then maintaining it for 15 minutes in a closed vessel.

The disadvantages of boiling or sterilization of milk are as follows:-

- Boiling kills all the organisms present in the milk, including the useful bacteria Lactobacillus acidophilus producing lactic acid.

- It destroys most of the vitamin C and partially vitamin B complex.
- Boiling gives "Cooked taste" to the milk, due to burning of lactose during boiling.
- Proteins in the milk (lactalbumin and lactoglobulin) are coagulated.
- The enzymes are destroyed.
- Calcium, magnesium and phosphorus are precipited.

In short, boiling alters the taste, flavor and nutritive value of the milk considerably.

Pasteurization of Milk

Pasteurization has been defined by an expert committee of WHO (1970) as "the heating of milk to such temperatures and for such a period of time as are required to destroy any pathogens that may be present, while causing minimal changes in the composition, flavour and mutritive value".

In pasteurization of milk, pathogenic bacteria are destroyed by heating the milk at 62° C for 30 minutes, or by "flash" heating to higher temperatures for less than 1 minute. Pasteurization destroys the causative organisms of the diseases typhoid, tuberculosis, diarrhea, dysentery and cholera etc., of the milk by 97 to 99%.

Advantages of Pasteurization

1. Pasteurization destroys only the harmful pathogenic bacteria, but not the lactic acid-producing bacteria.
2. The vitamins are not destroyed by pasteurization .
3. Pasteurization is the simplest, safest and the cheapest method rendering the milk safe.

Phosphatase Test

This test is employed to find out whether the milk has been properly pasteurized or not. The test is based on the principle that the enzyme phosphatase which is present in raw milk is destroyed during pasteurization. If phosphatase enzyme is present after pasteurization, it indicates that the milk has not been properly pasteurized.

(3) Drying

Drying is also an ancient and moreover natural method of food preservation. Drying is the process by which the moisture content of the food-stuff is removed. In the absence of water in the food-stuff, micro-organisms can not grow as moisture or water in the food-stuff is important for their growth. Many fruits, vegetables, fishes and meat are preserved by drying. In drying vitamin C is destroyed, but other nutrients are preserved.

Drying of fruits may be done by exposing them in the sun. Salting removes the moisture and dries up the food-stuff. Milk and juices can be dried mechanically. Dehydration by heat is done for eggs, fishes and meat etc. Cut pieces of meat are dried by roller process or under low pressure. Loss of water from the meat inhibits putrefaction.

Drying of milk — Milk is passed over heated rollers where it is evaporated and a thin film is formed which is powdered finally. This powder is free from dangerous micro-organisms and is easily digested by infants.

Condensed milk — Milk is usually pasteurized and is gradually heated under pressure in vacuum pans, till its water is evaporated to one-fourth of the original water content.

(4) Canning

In canning, the food-stuffs are sterilized at high temperatures (275°F to 350°F) for a short time (for a few seconds only), then cooled and filled in pre-sterilized sealable tin containers in a sterile atmosphere, which are closed and sealed. Various foods such as fruits, vegetables, milk, baby foods, soups, fishes and meat are preserved by the method of canning. There is some loss of heat labile vitamins during the process of canning.

Note : One should not use rusty, foul smelling and damaged tins.

(5) Salting and pickling

Salt is a preservative. Salting does only a superficial preservation for a shorter time because it inhibits the growth of bacteria, while in pickling, i.e., the use of salt along with certain condiments and spices penetrates and kills the bacteria. Mango, vegetables, fishes and meat may be preserved by this method. Salt helps to remove the moisture of the food-stuffs.

(6) Jams

Jams are usually fruits preserved in the form of pulp. These are formed by the addition of sugar to the fruit pulp which is cooked and then chemical preservatives like sodium benzoate, potassium metabisulphate or citric acid is added. This is also an ancient method of preservation of food.

(7) Vinegar

Vinegar is also a preservative, foods were preserved in ancient time which is continuous to the present day. Vegetables like onions, pieces of radish and lemon etc. are preserved in vinegar in which suitable amount of salt is added.

(8) Use of chemical preservatives

Certain chemicals are used as preservatives which retard the growth of the micro-organisms by increasing or decreasing the pH of food. They help in retaining the quality of food for long periods. The common chemical preservatives used are sodium benzoate, sodium nitrate, potassium metabisulphate, citric acid, vinegar and ascorbic acid etc. Sodium nitrate is used in the preservation of cheese and meat. Ascorbic acid prevents the growth of mould in confectionary, wines, cheese and pickles etc. The aim of the use of chemical preservatives is to eradicate the pathogenic and spoilage bacteria during manufacture so that food remains safe for a long time.

(9) Smoking

Smoking is also a method of preservation, as meat is salted and then hung up in a big hall and exposed to smoke produced from sawdust.

All the bacteria and even spores of the meat are killed by creosote present in the smoke.

Smoking also add flavour.

(10) Irradiation

It is done by gamma rays or x-rays by which micro-organisms of the food are destroyed. Foods may be treated after packing. Wheat, potatoes and onions may be preserved by irradiation. Fruits, vegetables and fishes can be kept fresh. Perishable goods can be kept for a long time without loosing their qualities.

* * * * *

CHAPTER 16

NUTRITION EDUCATION

Nutrition education is very important for improving the health of the families in the community in the developing countries like India. Lack of awareness about the dietary requirements and nutritive value of different food-stuffs is the main cause of malnutrition occurring in school going children, pregnant women, lactating mothers and other vulnerable section of the community. So, nutrition education programme should become a part of the community. Its main aim is to improve the nutritious status of the community by the available means.

The course of nutrition education should be short, practical and it should emphasize on the current nutritional problems prevailing in the community and their prevention by the use of locally available food.

Factors to be considered in relation to Nutrition Education are —

- Culture
- Religion

- Food habits
- Food available locally
- Water supply
- Educational level of the people of the locality
- Economic status of the families
- Land available for food production
- Housing and environmental sanitation

Methods of nutrition education of the community

The various important methods of nutrition education are as follows :

- Lectures
- Demonstrations
- Film and slide shows
- Posters
- Charts
- Pamphlets, newspapers and books
- Radio and television
- Exhibition

Lectures — A lecture on nutrition should be consice, to the point, in simple language and easily understandable. It should be easily adoptable by the people attending the lecture.

Demonstrations — A demonstration should be simple and it should make use of locally available resources by which it can be easily adopted by the community.

Film and slide shows — These are very effective methods of nutrition education. They should be practical, illustrative and easily understandable.

Posters — Posters should be simple and their matter should contain a few words of very large size written in the regional language which should be clearly and easily visible from a distance too. The posters should immediately attract the attention of the viewers.

Charts — Charts should not be of many colours, they should be of a few colours. These should be attractive and should create interest in the people.

Pamphlets, newspapers and books — They contain printed matter about nutrition education which are suitable for educated persons. Their matter should be available in regional languages and should provide sufficient information.

Radio and television — Radio and television programmes involving the nutritional problems help to create awareness on a large scale.

Principles of Nutrition Education

- First observe and ask the questions to obtain the information about the culture and food habits of the people.
- Ask the questions about the availability of foods, i.e.,which food are available in that area.
- Do not expect that the people will change their food habits easily. So new ideas should be introduced gradually and only one thing is taught at a time. Your any suggestion should be acceptable by the people of that area.
- Help the people to see that good nutrition is important for them, e.g., if they want that their children should grow strong and do well in their schools, sufficient nutritious food should be given to them.
- Find out the local words for food so that there will be better communication.
- In teaching nutrition, use actual foods whenever possible, especially home-produced foods.
- Teach nutrition, also with the help of pamphlets, posters and charts etc.
- Encourage the people to ask the questions, and for discussions, to clear the doubts.

— Do not teach the people those things which are not possible for them to do, nor about the foods for which they cannot afford to purchase or cannot obtain them.

— Have a connection of your teaching on nutrition with mother and child health activities and with other health education.

— Follow up and find out whether the families are changing their food habits. Use the information in modifying your teaching.

The Means of Nutrition Education

Nutritional survey in a community can give proper information about the nutrition problem prevailing in the community which needs nutrition education, especially in the vulnerable group like infants, pre-school children, pregnant women and lactating mothers of the community. Nutritional survey gives the information of nutritional status.

The assessment of nutritional status is accomplished by carrying out the following investigations.

1. Dietary survey
2. Assessment of ecological factors
3. Study of vital statistics
4. Anthropometric examination
5. Clinical examination
6. Laboratory tests
7. Biochemical tests

1. Dietary survey — A dietary survey may be carried out by either of the following methods:–

(a) Weighing of raw foods

(b) Weighing of cooked foods

(c) Checking of stock inventory

(d) Oral questionnaire method — The following questions are asked —

— Are you vegetarian or non-vegetarian ?

— What do you eat morning, noon, afternoon, evening, night and other times ?

— What foods do you like or dislike and why ?

— How often do you consume the following foods:—

Daily, weekly, once in 15 days, monthly, yearly or rarely ?

- Cereals
- Sugar or jaggery
- Pulses
- Green leafy vegetables
- Roots and tubers
- Other vegetables
- Milk and milk products
- Eggs
- Fish
- Meat

Any modification for certain groups within the family ?

— Infants and pre-school children

— Elderly

— Pregnant women and lactating mothers

— Illness

— Foods consumed

Methods of preparation or cooking foods as —

— Chapati

— Rice

— Vegetables

— Dals

— Fish

— Meat

Do you have :

Garden

Cattles

The data collected using any of the above methods are analysed for —

- Mean intake of food in terms of cereals, pulses, vegetables, fruits, milk, egg, fish and meat etc.
- Mean intake of calories, proteins, fats, carbohydrates, vitamins and minerals.

2. Assessment of ecological factors — In nutritional survey it is necessary to collect the ecological factors of the given community in order to make the assessment complete. The ecological factors related to malnutrition are as follows —

(a) Cultural influence — Food habits, feeding of infants and pre-school children, feeding of the pregnant women and lactating mothers, cooking practices, religious beliefs, customs and traditions affecting the dietary patterns, and prohibitions.

(b) Socio-economic factors — Family size, occupation, income, education, housing and prices of food.

(c) Food production — Customs related to the methods of cultivation, food storage and distribution.

(d) Conditioning influences — Bacterial, viral, fungal, and parasitic infections as amebiasis and ascariasis etc.

(e) Health and education services — The number of hospitals and health centres, distribution of health presonnels, preventive (as immunization) and curative measures, number of primary schools, middle schools, high schools and inter colleges or degree colleges.

It is necessary to detect the etiological factors which may co-exist with other factors responsible for malnutrition in a community, before the measures are taken for the prevention and control of malnutrition.

3. Study of vital statistics — Study of the morbidity (sick or diseased state) and mortality (number of deaths). Data of morbidity and mortality from a community in a particular area are collected and they are analysed. Morbidity data are more important which can be obtained from the hospitals and community health centres etc., which would enlighten the problems related to protein-energy malnutrition (marasmus, kwashiorkor), anemia due to iron or vitamin B complex deficiency, xerosis, night blindness and keratomalacia due to vitamin A deficiency, endemic goitre due to iodine deficiency in drinking water and parasitic infection etc. For mortality data information should be obtained about antenatal and neonatal deaths, deaths of the infants and of the children of 1 to 4 years of age.

4. Anthropometric examination — Anthropometric measurements such as height and weight of the body, circumference of the head, chest and arm, and skin fold thickness are the indicators of the nutritional status. Anthropometric measurements recorded from time to time show the patterns of growth and development. Height is an indicator of growth in infants, children and adolescents and height below normal for age indicates malnutrition. Weight for height is an index of current nutritional status. Circumference of the head, chest and arm below normal in children indicates protein-energy malnutrition. It is also an indicator of body fat. Skin fold thickness measured with skin calipers over the subscapular area is an early indication of malnutrition.

5. Clinical examination — Clinical examination plays a vital role in nutritional surveys. Its main aim is to assess the level of the people in a particular area in relation to the food they consume. The people of a particular area can be examined clinically as follows —

- General appearance — Normal built/thin/obese/sickly or weak/ gait normal or abnormal.

- Hair — Alopecia (loss of hair)/normal/white, greyish reddish/ depigmented/dry/Lustureless/thin and sparse/ brittle.
- Face — Normal/diffused/puffy/mask like/depigmented/ lethargic with open mouth/sunken cheeks with sallow skin/moon face/ nasolabial dyssebacea.
- Eyes — Normal/blinking/sunken/bulging.

  Conjunctiva — Normal/pale/white/brown pigmentation/Bitot' s spot/dry and wrinkled/angular conjunctivitis.

  Cornea — Normal/dry/hazy/opaque.
- Lips — Normal/dry/scaly/fissured/inflammation/cheilosis.
- Tongue — Normal/dry/coated with white patches/pale/fissured geographical/inflamed/protruded.
- Teeth — Normal/dental caries/mottled enamel/attrition.
- Gums — Normal/spongy/bleeding
- Glands :

Thyroid gland — Normal/enlarged, diffused or nodular.
Parotid glands — Normal/enlarged

- Skin — Normal/inflamed/pigmented/depigmented/thick/thin/dry, rough and fissured/scaly/loose folds, flabby.
- Nails — Normal/whiteness/Koilonychia or spooning of the nails.

  Edema — In the dependent parts or on the ankle, edema on the face, arms and legs due to protein deficiency.
- Abdomen — Normal/distention/ascites/enlargement of the liver/enlargement of the spleen/ wasting of the subcutaneous fat and muscles.

Examination for rickets in children — Fontanelles are not closed, presence of craniotabes, bossing of the frontal and parietal region of the skull, pigeon chest, Harison's sulcus, rickety rosary or beading of the ribs at the junctional site of cartilage, bowing of the legs or curved legs, bending and distortion of the bones, general weakness, growth failure, delay in walking, speaking and dentition, and distended abdomen.

6. Laboratory tests

- **Hemoglobin** — Hemoglobin percentage in the blood is determined for the confirmation of anemia.
- **Stool** — Stool is examined for ova of intestinal parasites.
- **Urine** — Urine is examined for sugar and albumin.

7. **Biochemical tests** — Biochemical tests are time consuming and very expensive, hence they are not performed on large scale. However, following biochemical tests are usually performed.

- Serum protein — Albumin and globulin
- Vitamins — A,C,D, thiamine, riboflavine and niacin
- Minerals — Iron, iodine.

National Programmes in Nutrition

The government of India has started several programmes in nutrition on a national scale to control/prevent major nutritional problems. These programmes may be classified as follows —

1. **Programmes to improve the nutritional status**

   (a) Applied nutrition programme

   (b) Supplementary feeding programmes

   (c) Mid-day meal programme for school children.

2. **Programmes to overcome specific deficiency diseases**

   (a) Naitional goitre control programme.

   (b) Vitamin A prophylaxis programme.

   (c) Prophylaxis against nutritional anemia.

3. **Others**

Integrated child development services (ICDS) programme.

1. (a) Applied Nutrition Programme

The Applied Nutrition Programme was launched by the Government of India in 1963 with the aid of UNICEF, FAO and WHO for improving the nutrition of the pregnant women and lactating mothers and children.

The chief aim of the programme is to stimulate the production of protective foods such as vegetables, fruits, milk, eggs and fishes etc., and by means of health education which is an important component of the programme, to promote their consumption by mothers and children who actually belong to vulnerable group. Actually Applied Nutrition Programme was launched to teach the villagers that how they can improve the production and consumption of the protective and nutritious foods. An important aspect of the programme is to train the personnels of various categories such as rural health workers, teachers, etc.

The Applied Nutrition Programme is one of the largest programmes assisted by UNICEF in many countries. In India it covers 1375 community development blocks, and serves 1.7 million women and children.

(b) Supplementary Feeding Programmes

The Special Nutrition Programme (SNP) was started in 1970 for the nutritional benefit of pre-school children (6 months to 6 years), pregnant women and lactating mothers, under the overall charge of the Ministry of Social Welfare, Government of India. This programme is beneficial mainly for the weaker section of the population. In the initial stages, children in tribal areas and urban slum areas were covered. Later on it was extended to the selected backward areas and chronically drought-affected areas.

The supplementary food supplies 300 Kcals and 10-12 gms of protein per child per day. The mothers receive daily 500 Kcals and 25 gms of protein. This supplementary food is provided to them for about 300 days in a year.

Balwadi Nutrition programme was started in 1970-71 under Social Welfare Department to provide primary education to children of 3 to 6 years of age. The supplementary food provided to the children supplies 30 calories and 10 grams of protein per child per day.

(c) Mid-day Meal Programme for school children

The Mid-day Meal Programme (MDMP) is also known as school lunch programme. This programme was started in the year 1961 throughout the country. The main aim of this programme is to attract more children for admission to the schools and retain them so that their literacy improvement may be brought about.

Main principles of Mid-day Meal Programme for school children are:—

1. The meal should be a supplement and not a substitute to the home diet.
2. The meal should supply at least one-third of the total energy requirement, and half of the protein requirement.
3. The meal should be such that it can be prepared easily in schools, no complicated cooking process should be involved.
4. The cost of the meal should be reasonably low.
5. As far as possible, locally available foods should be used, this will reduce the cost of the meal.
6. Menu should be frequently changed

***Table 35.* A mid-day school meal (model of menu)**

Food-stuffs	gram/day/child
Cereals and millets	75
Pulses	30
Oils and fats	8
Leafy vegetables	30
Non-leafy vegetables	30

The number of feeding days in a year should be at least 250 according to the National Institute of Nutrition, Hyderabad.

2. (a) National Goitre Control Programme

National Goitre Control Programme is in operation since 1962

There are four components of National Goitre Control Programme

1. Iodized salt or iodized oil
2. Iodine monitoring
3. Manpower training
4. Mass communication

1. Iodized salt or iodized oil — In India iodized salt is used to prevent the development of goitre. It is the common salt fortified with iodine by adding potassium iodide to it in very minute quantity (1 part of potassium iodide to 10,000 parts of common salt or 1 grm. of potassium iodide to 10 kg. of common salt) which is available in the market .

Iodized oil — An injection of iodized oil of 1 ml. (mostly poppy-seed oil) is administered intramuscularly in emergency, which provides protection for about 4 years.

Iodized oil, oral — Iodine is also administered orally as iodized oil or sodium iodate tablets but they are more costly than intramuscular injections.

2. Iodine monitoring — There are many laboratories in the country which monitor the goitre control programme by (a) Determination of iodine excretion (b) Determination of iodine in water, soil and food and (c) Determination of iodine in salt for quality control.

3. Manpower training — Health workers and others engaged in the goitre control programme are fully trained even to implement the programme forcibly and to educate the public.

4. Mas communication — Mass communication is the powerful medium in goitre control work.

2. (b) Vitamin A prophylaxis programme

Vitamin A prophylaxis programme is for the control of night blindness due to vitamin A deficiency in pre-school children in the community, by giving a single dose of oily preparation of vitamin A containing 200,000 i.u. or 110 mg. retinol palmitate orally every six months through health workers.

The above programme was launched by the Ministry of Health and Family Welfare in 1970 and it has revealed a significant reduction in vitamin A deficiency in children.

2. (c) Prophylaxis against Nutritional Anemia

A national programme for the prevention of nutritional anemia was launched by the Government of India during the IVth five year plan and it proved to be very important for the public health. Nutritional anemia has been defined by World Health Organization (WHO) as "a condition in which the hemoglobin content of blood is lower than normal as a result of a deficiency of one or more essential nutrients, regardless of the cause of such deficiency." The most frequently cause of nutritional anemia is iron deficiency and less frequently is folic acid and vitamin B_{12} deficiency.

Nutritional anemia generally occurs in developing countries like India. It is mostly found in women of child bearing age, young children, in pregnant women and lactating mothers and is more prevalent in rural areas.

Iron deficiency can arise either due to inadequate intake, due to excessive losses or poor absorption (less than 5%) from the intestine of the iron. Loss of iron in women occurs during menstruation. Malaria, hookworm infestations and hemorrhage from the body may cause anemia.

Treatment — (a) Mothers : One tablet of iron and folic acid containing 60 mg. of elemental iron (180 mg. of ferrous sulphate) and 5 mg. of folic acid should be given daily for 2 to 3 months after hemoglobin level has returned to normal. (b) Children : One tablet of iron and folic acid containing 20 mg. of elemental iron (60 mg. of ferrous sulphate) and 0.1 mg. of folic acid should be given daily.

Iron fortified salt—At the National Institute of Nutrition, Hyderabad it has been shown that when salt fortified with iron is consumed for 12 to 18 months, it reduces the prevalence of anemia.

3. Integrated child development services (ICDS) programme — The most important scheme in the field of child welfare is the ICDS scheme. It was initiated by the Government of India in the Ministry of Social and Women's Welfare in 1975, in pursuance of the National Policy for Children.

ICDS consists of the following services for young or pre-school (1-6 years of age) children, pregnant women and lactating mothers.

(1) Supplementary nutrition vitamin A prophylaxis, and iron and folic acid distribution

(2) Immunization

(3) Health check-up

(4) Medical referral services

(5) Nutrition and health education for women, pregnant women and lactating mothers in urban, rural and tribal areas to maintain their health and the health of their children.

The workers at the village level who provide the services are called Anganwadi workers. Each Anganwadi unit covers a population of about 1000. A network of Mahila Mandals has been built up in ICDS project areas to help Anganwadi workers in providing health and nutrition services. The work of Anganwadi is supervised by Mukhya sevikas. Field supervision is done by the Child Development Project Officer.

* * * * *

CHAPTER 17

DIET IN FEVERS, TUBERCULOSIS AND IN BURNS

FEVER

Fever is the rise of body temperature above normal (98.6°F or 37°C) taken orally. It is characterized by flushed face, hot and dry skin, headache, aching all over the body, anorexia, nausea and sometimes vomiting, constipation and sometimes diarrhea, scanty colored urine. Delirium may occur if the temp. is over 105°F. Convulsions may follow, especially in children, and may progress to coma.

Classification of fevers — Fevers may be classified as follows–

(1) Eruptive fevers — Fevers which are characterized by an eruption (or a rash) appearing on one of the first 4 days of the disease, as occurs in smallpox and chickenpox etc.

(2) Intermittent fever — Fever in which the temp. at sometime of the day is normal or sub-normal, and at the another time of the day, usually in the evening, it is raised to one, two or more degrees, as occurs in malaria.

(3) Continuous fever — Fever in which the temp. remains high continuously, it never comes down to normal and in which no eruption occurs during first 4 days, as occurs in pneumonia etc.

Fever may be (a) Acute or of short duration such as occurring in common cold, influenza, pneumonia etc. and (b) Chronic fever as occurs in typhoid and tuberculosis lasting for a long time.

Causes

- Infection or inflammation
- Hot environment
- Excessive physical labor.
- Following injury or surgery
- Following coronary occlusion
- Dehydration which occurs after excessive diuresis.
- Drug-induced fever as caused by atropine sulfate.

Metabolism in Fevers

The metabolic changes occurring in fever are as follows: —

1. Metabolic rate is increased by 7% for each degree Fahrenheit and 13% for each degree Celcius rise of body temperature.

2. There is increased restlessness which increases the requirement of calories.

3. Increased loss of body water due to increased perspiration as a result of high body temperature.

4. Increased excretion of sodium chloride and potassium salts from the body.

5. Increased catabolism (breakdown) of tissue protein.

Dietary Management

The nutritional requirement will depend on the nature, severity and duration of the fever and the duration of the convalescent period.

Calories — The requirement of calories is usually increased upto 50% due to increased metabolic rate, depending upon the rise of temp. It may be difficult to meet the requirements of calories during the peak of the fever but for more calories small foods containing high carbohydrate as gruels, porridges or sago etc. should be given frequently as soon as the fever is controlled. At peak of fever milk or fruit juice with sugar may be given. Intake of 18,00 calories will be sufficient.

Proteins — Since there is increased loss of tissue proteins due to their increased catabolism (breakdown) in fever, the daily intake of protein should be increased upto 50%. The protein should be of high nutritive value and easily digestible such as milk, milk products, pulses and egg protein. Beverages of high protein value are better than solid foods. Protein intake should be 70 gms./day.

Fats — Though fats as ghee, butter and vegetable oils etc., have double the energy to that of the carbohydrates, their intake should be reduced after the fever is controlled as they interfere with the digestion of food.

Carbohydrates — Glucose is rapidly absorbed from the intestine and does not require any digestion, it should be administered frequently, i.e., at 2 hourly intervals to provide energy to the body. Starch is present in the cereals (wheat and rice). Chapaties of wheat, bread or another preparation of cereals as porridge etc., can be consumed along with the milk and fruit juices.

Vitamins — The vitamins requirements are increased during convalescence period which can be met by intake of one multivitamin tablet daily.

Minerals — Plenty of minerals should be consumed through intake of vegetables, fruit and fruit juices and milk etc. The calcium and phosphorus requirements will be met by drinking one litre of milk daily.

Water — Water intake should be 3 to 5 litres per day in the form of plain water, milk, glucose water and fruit juices etc., for an adult depending on the climatic conditions to compensate the loss of water from the skin. Less water will be required during winter and more water during summer season. Small quantities i.e., 6 ounces of fluid as milk with glucose or fruit juice should be given 3 hourly.

The principle of the diet is that it should be high in protein, adequate in carbohydrate and low in fats and the diet should be bland and soft to be easily digested and absorbed. The foods should be given at frequent intervals, i.e., 2 to 3 hourly. The diet with excessive fibres should be avoided.

TUBERCULOSIS

It is an infectious disease caused by the tubercle bacillus, Mycobacterium tuberculosis which most commonly affects the lungs but other parts of the body such as gastrointestinal and genitourinary tracts, bones, joints, lymph nodes, nervous system and skin may also be involved. It is characterized pathologically by inflammatory infiltration, formation of tubercles, caseation, necrosis, abscesses, fibrosis and calcification. Symptoms and signs of pulmonary tuberculosis are as follows:—

Symptoms

- Cough persisting for several months, usually with expectoration and at times hemoptysis occurs.
- Fever— Evening rise of temperature, usually at 4 P.M. temperature is slightly raised, it becomes 99°F or more.
- Anorexia — Loss of appetite.
- Weakness
- Loss of weight
- Night sweats
- Palpitation or dyspnea on exertion.
- Pain in the chest

Signs

- A few scattered rales are heard at several points on ausculta-tion of the chest.
- The fingers are often clubbed, in the early stages, the nails are being curved like a parrot's beak.
- Sputum examination — Tubercle bacilli, i.e., Mycobacterium tuberculosis are found in the sputum.
- X-ray examination — There may be haziness in the lungs or small, soft, nodular shadows are seen scattered throughout the lung fields, in the early stages.

In later stages, cavitation is usually seen in X-ray film.

There may be evidence of pleurisy with effusion.

Causes — Tuberculosis is caused by the Mycobacterium tuberculosis. The bacteria may infect the body from dust or dried sputum, by droplet infection or contaminated food items, such as milk, cream, butter, cheese or meat etc. Contact with the person suffering from pulmonary tuberculosis is the most important source of infection.

Tuberculosis of the cattle caused by Mycobacterium bovis, transmitted to man through milk is called bovine tuberculosis.

Dietary Management

Calories — Since excessive weakness and weight loss occurs in tuberculosis, an adult should intake high caloric (2500-3000 Kcals) diets per day, to regain lost weight.

Proteins — Catabolism (breakdown) of the tissue proteins occurs in tuberculosis, a high protein (100-15 gms) diet should be consumed daily. It will promote healing. Milk is important because it contains excellent protein. At least one litre of milk per day should be consumed in any form, and eggs ,cheese, fish, meats and dals should be consumed freely.

Fats — By intake of fats in abundance, the weakness will be removed and the body weight will be increased.

Carbohydrates — Carbohydrates should be consumed in adequate amounts to provide the required calories.

Vitamins — Isoniazid in the treatment of tuberculosis generally causes Vitamin B_6 (pyridoxine) deficiency, so food-stuffs containing vitamin B_6 as fruits and vegetables, cereals and pulses, soyabean, groundnuts, milk, egg-yolk, fish, meat etc., should be included in the diet or a tablet of vitamin B_6 40 mg. should be given to the patient along with the anti-tubercular drugs or vitamin B Complex supplements should be administered. The diet should include food-stuffs rich in ascorbic acid (vitamin C) to promote the healing process of the tuberculous lesions. They include amla, lemon or lime juice, tomatoes, green leafy vegetables as spinach, cabbage, amaranth etc., root vegetables as radish and turnip etc., fruits as guava, orange, mango ripe, papaya ripe, apple and pine apple and germinating pulses as chana dal etc.

Minerals — Calcium and iron are more important to be considered.

Calcium — Calcium is necessary for the promotion of healing of the tuberculous lesions. The diet should include the food-stuffs containing calcium in excess, as milk (one litre of cow's milk provides about 1200 mgs. of calcium),milk products as cheese, curd, and butter etc., green leafy vegetables as spinach and amaranth etc., and other vegetables as radish, carrots, lady's finger and onion etc., cereals, pulses, millets, almond, eggs and fish etc.

Iron — It is necessary if there has been hemoptysis. The diet should contain iron-rich food-stuffs, as green leafy vegetables — spinach, bathua, legumes etc., fruits like apple, cereals, dry fruits, nuts, egg-yolk, poultry, fish and meat etc. Iron is also derived from cooking in iron utensils.

Fluids — Fluids upto 3 litres per day should be given to the patient, if there is no edema.

Generally the principle of diet for a person suffering from tuberculosis should be high caloric and high protein diet with fats in abundance for supplying energy and adequate amounts of carbohydrates.

Table 36. **Diet for an adult suffering from tuberculosis (gms.)**

(Calories 2900-3000 Kcals, Proteins 100-115 gms.)

Food-stuffs	Vegetarian	Non-vegetarian
Cereal and cereal products	300	300
Pulses or dal	100	80
Green leafy vegetables	100	100
Other vegetables	50	50
Potato and carrot	100	100
Fruits	200	200
Milk	1200 mls	800 mls
Butter and vegetable oils	40	40
Sugar	60	60
Egg	—	One
Nuts	50	30
Meat	—	50
Multivitamin tab.	One	One

BURNS

Large amounts of proteins, salts and fluids are lost when large areas of the body have been burned. Expenditure of energy after major burns is increased upto 200% above basic requirement and so more nutrients are required to supply the necessary energy for a couple of days or upto months.

Severe hypoproteinemia, edema at the site of injury, failure in skin growth and weight loss are the main problems of nutrition. Nutrition by intravenous route or tube feeding or both are required to provide the required energy. When oral feeds are tolerated, lot of milk and milk products should be given and then pulses and nuts being rich source of proteins should be included in the diet.

The principle of diet is that it should include high protein and high caloric (2900-3500) foods.

The energy requirements in a burn patient (Adult) : 25 Kcals × body weight in kilogram of the patient + 40 Kcals × percentage of burn

Children : 40-60 Kcals × body weight in kilogram of the child + 40 Kcals. × percentage of burn

Example—A person weighing 60 Kgs with 40 % burns will require 25 × 60+40 × 40 = 1500+1600 = 3100 Kcals.

The caloric requirement of the patient will be 3100 Kcals per day.

* * * * *

CHAPTER 18

DIET IN THE DISEASES OF THE GASTROINTESTINAL TRACT

Common Diseases of the Gastrointestinal tract are: —

(1) Dyspepsia or flatulence

(2) Vomiting

(3) Constipation

(4) Diarrhea and dysentery

(5) Peptic ulcer

(6) Ulcerative colitis

(7) Malabsorption syndrome

(1) DYSPEPSIA OR FLATULENCE

Dyspepsia or flatulence is the impairment in the process of digestion. It is not a disease in itself but a symptom of other diseases. It is characterized by discomfort and a sense of fullness in the abdomen after meals, eructation, heart burn, nausea and vomiting and loss of appetite.

Causes —

- Swallowing of the air
- Fermentation of the carbohydrates in the intestines.
- Some food-stuffs as onions, garlic, cabbage, cauliflower and preparation of dried peas and beans and high carbohydrate diet.
- Anxiety neurosis
- Strong emotional states.

Diet — Diet causing dyspepsia or flatulence as onions, garlic, cabbage, cauliflower and preparation of dreid peas and beans should be avoided. Diet rich in carbohydrates as potatoes, sweets, sugar, jaggery, juice of sugarcane, syrup (sharbat) of any kind should be reduced or avoided. If someone suffers from dyspepsia after taking one or more particular foods, that particular food or foods should be avoided.

(2) VOMITING

It is the condition of forcible ejection of the stomach contents through the mouth, and in cases of intestinal obstruction, of the intestinal contents.

Causes

- Intake of infected food
- Intake of food containing poisonous substances (food poisoning)
- Excessive intake of fatty and irritating foods.
- Excessive intake of alcohol.
- Acute gastritis

- Intestinal obstruction
- Dyspepsia
- Meningitis
- Cerebral tumor
- Migraine
- Specific fevers
- Pyloric stenosis
- Uremia
- Use of emetics
- Overdoses of some drugs, such as digitalis
- Pregnancy
- Carcinoma and simple ulcer, especially when they cause obstruction.
- Poisons such as arsenic, aconite and colchicum etc.

Diet — Whatever the cause, the diet of vomiting is the same. Since fluid is lost from the body in vomiting, it is important that this should be restored. Water with a little glucose or sugar and then fruit juices are given by mouth. Cold drinks are allowed, tea and hot drinks should be avoided. Then as tolerated, add other fluids and bland, soft solid preparations. For carbohydrate, sugar and well-cooked cereals and dry toast may be given. All fats should be eliminated from the diet. If vomiting continues, fluid may be given intravenously. 5% glucose with normal saline is given by transfusion.

In pregnancy (hyperemesis gravidarum) — If severe, fluid intake by mouth should be restricted but maintained by intravenous route. In less severe cases frequent small feedings of more or less dry foods are advisable.

(3) CONSTIPATION

It is the condition of infrequent and incomplete evacuation of the bowel by hard and dry stools difficult to pass. For maintenance of good health one should defecate once a day, though some people evacuate the bowel twice a day, while a few in spite of maintaining good health evacuate every second or third day.

Causes

- Lack of roughage in the diet
- Inadequate consumption of water.
- Failure to establish definite and regular times for defecation.
- Worry
- Anxiety
- Fear
- Intestinal atony (weakness of the intestinal musculature) as in elderly — Atonic constipation
- Excessive tonicity (spasticity) of the colon—spastic constipation
- To lead sedentary life
- Excessive use of laxatives
- Use of certain drugs as analgesics and antacids etc.
- Proctitis
- Anal fissure
- Intestinal obstruction
- Tumor in the intestine
- Diabetes mellitus
- Hypercalcemia
- Hypothyroidism

Complications of Constipation

Straining during defecation may lead to —

— Anal fissure

— Piles

— Prolapse of the rectum

— Inguinal hernia

— The distension of the bowels with accumulation of feces may produce headache and apathy.

— To strain during defecation in constipation is dangerous for the patient with coronary heart disease.

Diet

The diet plays a major role in the treatment of constipation. The diet should encourage bowel movement and improve the evacuation of bowels. The diet should contain foods rich in fibres (roughage) as whole cereals, whole legumes, raw green leafy vegetables in the form of salad, e.g., radish and carrots etc., onions and cucumber etc. may be added. Fresh fruits rich in fibres as guava, pear, apple, papaya etc., should be consumed. One should drink a lot of water along with the food.

Protein — Normal 1 gram per kg. of body weight should be given.

Fats — Ghee, butter and oils act as lubricant and cause evacuation of the bowel.

Milk — Intake of warm milk at bedtime is helpful in constipation.

(4) DIARRHEA AND DYSENTERY

Diarrhea — Diarrhea is the condition of frequent occurrence of loose or liquid motions. The amount of stool may vary from a few mls. to over a litre.

Causes

- Infection of the gastrointestinal tract with bacteria or viruses.

- Ingestion of undigestible food
- Ingestion of food containing toxins or poisonous substances (food poisoning)
- Bacillary dysentery
- Amoebic dysentery
- Psychogenic factors
- Use of certain drugs

Dysentery — It is a condition characterized by inflammation of the intestinal mucosa, especially of the colon with abdominal pain, tenesmus and passage of loose motions frequently containing mucus or blood.

Causes

- Bacterial infection
- Viral infection
- Protozoal infestation as by ameba
- Parasitic worms
- Chemical irritants

There are two main types of dysentery.

1. Bacillary dysentery — It is caused by the bacteria of the genus Shigella. It is characterized by sudden onset of colicky abdominal pain, tenesmus and passage of small loose motions with blood, 5 to 50 times daily.

2. Amebic dysentery — It is caused by the protozoon Entamoeba histolytica. It is characterized by cramping pain in the central and lower abdomen followed by passage of watery stools containing a large quantity of mucus. A small quantity of blood may be present.

Dietary Management of Diarrhea and Dysentery

Foods to be avoided :

- Salad and fibres or cellulose-containing foods

- Pickles
- Chutnies
- Spicy food items
- Excessively fried foods
- Sweets
- Dry fruits

In acute cases, when the dehydration supervenes, rehydration therapy is adopted in which in mild cases relydration solution is given orally and in severe cases fluid is administered intravenously. Composition of the oral rehydration solution — ORS is as follows —

Sodium chloride	3.5 gms.
Sodium bicarbonate	2.5 gms.
Potassium chloride	1.5 gms.
Glucose	20 gms.
Water	1 litre

In the market mixture of sodium chloride, sodium bicarbonate, potassium chloride and glucose is available in the powder form in the packets, which is known as oral rehydration mixture. It is dissolved in one litre of water , then the oral rehydration solution ORS is formed which should be consumed within 24 hours.

In severe cases, 5% glucose with normal saline is transfused intravenously, generally from the bottle.

Proteins — Proteins should be easily digestible. Food-stuffs rich in protein as soft boiled egg, butter milk, skimmed milk and milk preparations should be given to the patient. If the patient suffers from diarrhea due to lactose (milk sugar) intolerance, milk and milk products should be avoided.

Fats — Fats are usually restricted as they are not easily absorbed, when there is intestinal hurry, and they may aggravate the diarrhea.

Carbohydrates — Easily digestible carbohydrates should be given, especially in the form of sago, porridges or gruel etc. Foods containing roughage as whole cereals, millets and mature vegetables etc., should be avoided as these will cause irritation to the mucous membranes of the gastrointestinal tract and diarrhea may occur.

Vitamins — Vitamins are incorporated in the forum of oral or parenteral management.

Fruits — Banana is the best to be given to the patient. Apple can be introduced in the diet when the condition is improved.

(5) PEPTIC ULCER

It is an ulcer formed in the lower end of esophagus, stomach usually along the lesser curvature or in the duodenum, usually as a result of the action of excessive secretion of hydrochloric acid on the mucous membrane. It includes the following two types of ulcers :

I. Gastric ulcer — Ulcer present in the lower end of the esophagus, or stomach is known as gastric ulcer. It is characterized by pain in the epigastric region coming about half an hour after a meal which passes off before the next meal, loss of appetite, discomfort and flatulence in the upper part of the abdomen, fear of taking solid foods, nausea and vomiting. Antacids relieve the pain.

II. Duodenal ulcer — Ulcer present in the duodenum is called duodenal ulcer. It is characterized by pain in the epigastric region coming 3 to 4 hours after food when the stomach becomes empty—the so called "hungar-pain" which wakes the patient at about 2 a.m. in the night, and is almost immediately relieved by food. The pain lasts for a few minutes rather than hours.

Causes of peptic ulcer

- Excessive consumption of alcohol
- Excessive smoking or tobacco chewing

- Excessive consumption of spicy foods, pickles and condiments etc.
- Excessive consumption of strong tea and coffee.
- Inadequate chewing of food.
- It occurs in persons who do over work and eat food irregularly and hurriedly.
- Some occupations are contributory, as peptic ulcer may occur in bus drivers, medical practitioners and high-powered business executives.
- Fear
- Anxiety
- Other emotional disturbances
- Prolonged fasting — In this condition prolonged empty stomach may induce hypersecretion of hydrochloric acid which is the causative factor.
- Heredity

Dietary Management

The patient with peptic ulcer should avoid—

- Smoking or tobacco chewing
- Consumption of alcohol totally
- Excessively sour (acidic), salty or spicy foods
- Pickles and condiments
- Foods containing fibres or cellulose as raw vegetables in salad as radish, cucumber, onion and tomatoes etc., fruits with skin and seeds etc.
- Excessively hot food or drink
- Tea and coffee
- Heavy sweets

The aims in the dietary management of the patients with peptic ulcer are as follows —

1. To provide the food in small amounts frequently.
2. To provide adequate nutrition.
3. To give rest to the stomach and intestine.
4. To continuously neutralize the gastric acid
5. To inhibit the production of gastric juice.
6. To reduce the mechanical, chemical and thermal irritants.

Nutritional Requirement

Calories — The caloric intake should be adequate according to the age, sex and occupation. In case there is rapid loss of body weight, the calories should be increased choosing the correct type of foods.

Proteins — Normal protein requirement of 1 gm. per kg. of body weight, i.e., 60 gms. should be given. Milk should be included as a source of proteins, as it does not irritate the mucosa. Very small amounts of milk, or milk and egg mixture should be given frequently which is increased gradually. Meat should be avoided as its soup increases the acidity.

Fats — Fats like ghee, butter, cheese and cream etc., in moderate amounts are helpful as they suppress the gastric secretion, whereas fats of fried food articles are difficult to digest and may aggravate the symptoms.

Spices, Pickles and Condiments — Spices such as chillies (mirch), pepper (gol or kali mirch), ginger (sonth), cummin (Jeera) and amchoor etc., used in cooking, and pickles and condiments, all are chemical irritants and so these should be avoided. Soups of the meat etc., should also be avoided.

Diet Chart

Early morning (6.00 a.m.) — Milk 1 cup with 1 tea-spoonful of sugar

Breakfast (8.00 a.m.)	—	2 Slices of bread with 10 gms. of butter. Milk one cup with 1tea-spoonful of sugar.
Lunch	—	3 Small chapaties soft with ghee. Rice one medium-sized bowl, well-cooked dal 3/4 bowl. Vegetable 3/4 bowl without adding chillies (mirch) and cummin (Jeera)
4 p.m.	—	Milk 300 mls.
6 p.m.	—	Suji porridge 20 gms and milk 1 cup with sugar 2 tea spoonful.
Dinner	—	3 Small chapaties, rice 1 medium-sized bowl, well-cooked dal 3/4 bowl, soft bland vegetable 3/4 bowl.
Bedtime	—	Milk 1 cup and 1 tea-spoonful sugar

Diet will provide 2300 calories and 65 gms proteins.

(6) ULCERATIVE COLITIS

It is the condition of inflammation and ulceration of the colon characterized by cramping abdominal pain, rectal bleeding and frequent passage of small amounts of dark and offensive stools mixed with mucus and blood.

Causes

- Infection — Infection may be bacterial, viral or fungal.
- Nutritional — It may occur in some deficiency diseases as pellagra, and folic acid deficiency.

- Food allergy — Food allergy may be from cow's milk but other food-stuffs included are wheat, potatoes, tomatoes, oranges and eggs etc.
- Chemical food additives
- Emotional disturbance or emotional trauma.

Diet

Foods in small quantities are to be given frequently. An adequate diet with high protein and moderate fat is recommended. Supplementation of vitamins and minerals is essential.

Raw vegetables, cereal bran, dry fruits, nuts, spices. pickles and condiments should be avoided.

(7) MALABSORPTION SYNDROME

It is the condition of disordered or inadequate absorption of the nutrients as proteins, fats, carbohydrates, vitamins, minerals and water, from the intestinal tract, especially from the small intestine. It is characterized by diarrhea, steatorrhea (excretion of stools containing excess of fats—over 6 gms. of fat), distended abdomen, poor appetite, pallor, weakness, lassitude, weight loss, paresthesias, muscle cramps, edema.

Causes

- Infections affecting the intestinal mucosa.
- Tropical sprue which is characterized by steatorrhea, anemia, weakness and loss of weight.
- Gluten enteropathy or celiac disease — A disease caused by sensitivity to wheat gluten. It occurs usually in children.
- Pancreatic insufficiency
- Lactase deficiency
- Tuberculous iliojejunitis

- Regional enteritis
- Prolonged use of certain antibiotics
- Obstruction of the biliary duct due to stone or cirrhosis
- Malignant lymphoma
- Gastric resection and ileal bypass surgery.

Dietary Management

A high carbohydrate and high protein diet should be provided to the person suffering from malabsorption syndrome. In a few circumstances one or the other type of carbohydrate or protein may be avoided as in case of lactose intolerance. One may avoid milk and milk products or in case of sensitivity to the protein gluten of wheat, consumption of wheat may be reduced or avoided. A soft and fibre restricted diet should be used for a person suffering from persistent diarrhea. Fat intake should be reduced.

* * * * *

CHAPTER 19

DIET IN THE DISEASES OF LIVER AND GALLBLADDER

LIVER

Liver is one of the vital organs of the body which secretes bile and takes part in the metabolism of carbohydrates, fats and proteins and many other vital metabolic processes. Gallbladder stores bile and discharges it into the small intestine during the digestion of food. Bile is essential for the digestion and absorption of fat. Liver regulates the blood sugar levels by converting excess of sugar to glycogen which is stored in the liver.

Liver diseases may be as follows —

(1) Hepatitis

(2) Jaundice

(3) Cirrhosis of the liver

(4) Hepatic Coma

(1) Hepatitis

Inflammation of the liver which is caused by bacteria, viruses (Hepatitis A, B, C, D and E viruses but mostly by Hepatitis A virus and Hepatitis B virus. Hepatitis A virus enters the body through food or water and Hepatitis B virus through the use of infected blood products from the carriers, use of unsterilized needles and through sexual contact), parasites (Entameba histolytica causing amebic hepatitis as a complication of amebic dysentery) and toxic reaction to the drugs, alcohol and chemicals. The disease is characterized by general malaise, low-grade fever, anorexia, nausea, vomiting, muscle and joint pain, fatigue, headache, dark urine, clay-colored stool followed by jaundice (yellowness of the skin, conjunctiva, mucous membranes and body fluids), pruritus (severe itching), enlarged and tender liver.

Dietary Management — Normal feeding is difficult in the initial stages of hepatitis. The main purpose is to avoid further damage and strain to the liver and to provide nutrients for the regeneration of liver tissues. Generally a high protein, high carbohydrate and moderate fat diet is recommended.

Fluid and salt — Patients with liver disease often suffer from nausea and vomiting which may result in loss of fluid and salt, so these should be considered first. Transfusion of 5% glucose with normal saline (a solution containing 0.9 gm of sodium chloride per 100 c.c. of distilled water) may be required.

Energy (calories) — In the early stage, i.e., in nasogastric feeding stage, the requirement of calories should be 1000-1200 Kcals and later on during the convalescence stage 45 Kcals per kg. of body weight is advisable.

Proteins — The requirement of proteins varies according to the severity of the disease. Proteins are required for the regeneration of liver tissues. Vegetable proteins are best preferred. The diet should be rich in protein content. The recommended daily intake of protein is 60 to 80 grams.

Fats— A moderate intake of fat is recommended, as in severe liver failure the fat may not be metabolised if it is taken in excess. The intake of fat increases the calories without adding too much bulk and supplies essential unsaturated fatty acids and fat-soluble vitamins.

Fat should not be restricted unless the patient does not toterate it. Fat intake should be restricted if there is obstruction to the flow of bile which does not permit fat digestion and may produce fatty diarrhea.

Fats in the whole milk, cream, butter, ghee, egg etc. are easily digested and should be included in the diet. However, excessive amounts of fat in the diet should be avoided. The recommended daily intake of fat is 30 grams.

Carbohydrates — Diet should be rich in carbohydrates as high carbohydrate intake is advised because it is required to supply the energy needed and the proteins should not be used up for energy purposes. If adequate glucose and fluid cannot be tolerated by mouth because of vomiting, it must be given intravenously.

Vitamins — Vitamins are very important as they are required to generate liver cells. Vitamin B complex should be supplied in adequate amount to help in the metabolism of the high carbohydrate diet. Vitamin C and K also should be given to meet the daily requirement.

Minerals — Sufficient quantities of sodium chloride and potassium chloride should be consumed to maintain the electrolyte balance.

Fluids — In the presence of edema, ascites or abdominal distension the fluid intake should be restricted.

Foods to be allowed —

- **Cereals** — Wheat, soft-cooked rice and other cereals
- **Pluses or dals** — Well-cooked and mashed.
- **Fats** — Ghee, butter and vanaspati in moderation.
- **Vegetables** — Raw in the form of salad or well-cooked and thin soups of vegetables.Tubers like potatoes and yam may be consumed.

- **Fruits** — Fresh fruits and fruit juices without much fat.
- **Soup** — Clear soups and broths
- **Condiments** — In moderation
- **Beverages** — Milk, tea, coffee, cocoa and carbonated drinks
- **Sweets** — Sugar, jaggery, honey, jam, syrup
- **Desserts** — Ice-cream, custard, jellies and corn-flour puddings
- **Egg** — Soft-cooked.
- **Fish** — Fresh and well-cooked.
- **Meat** — Lean mutton, chicken.

Foods to be avoided

— Avoid well-cooked and mashed dals if abdominal distension occurs.

— Fried foods should be avoided.

— Gas-forming vegetables such as cabbage, turnips and onions are to be avoided.

— Soups and broths with fat should be avoided.

— Spices, pickles and chutneys should not be consumed.

— The patient should not drink strong tea or coffee.

— One should not consume chocolates and sweets with nuts.

— Alcohol should be totally abandoned.

— Excessive pepper and chillies

— Pastries

— Pies

— Dried fruits and nuts

— Fatty fish, meat or pork

— Eggs, fish and meat which are fried in ghee, butter or oil.

Diet chart

Bed tea — Light tea 1 cup with 10 gms sugar.

Breakfast — Fruit juice 150 ml + 15 gms sugar, 2 tablespoonful jams.

10 A.M. — Sugarcane juice 1 glass.

Lunch — Rice 2 medium-sized bowl, thin dal 1/2 medium-sized bowl, full-cream milk 1 cup with sugar.

4 P.M. — Light tea with 2 teaspoonful sugar, banana 1 of medium size.

Dinner — 2 chapaties of medium size, mixed fruits 250 gms, well-cooked vegetable 1 bowl.

Diet will provide about 200 calories and 35 gms of fat.

(2) Jaundice

It is a condition characterized by yellowness of the skin, whites of the eyes (the part of the sclera visible around the iris), mucous membranes, and body fluids, and excreta (feces and urine etc.) owing to the deposition of the bile pigment bilirubin, resulting from excess of bilirubin in the blood (hyperbilirubinemia)

Jaundice may be of the following types —

1. Hemolytic jaundice — Jaundice caused by hemolysis (break-down of the red blood cells with the liberation of hemoglobin in the plasma).

2. Hepatocellular jaundice — Jaundice occurring due to injury or disease of the liver cells.

3. Infectious jaundice — Jaundice occurring in infectious or viral hepatitis.

4. Obstructive jaundice — Jaundice resulting from some mechanical obstruction in the flow of bile from the liver to the duodenum.

Dietary Management

Calories — For an adult of 60 kgs body weight 1000 Kcals are required which may be provided by nasogastric tube or as intravenous glucose, during hepatic precoma and coma stage. In severe and moderately severe jaundice about 1600-2000 Kcals are provided.

Proteins — The quantity of proteins which can be given in the diet depends on the severity of the disease. I with hepatic precoma and coma, protein-containing foods are totally withheld and only high carbohydrate-containing foods are given by nasogastric tube feeding II with severe jaundice, in which serum bilirubin is 15 mgs/100 mls, protein intake should be 40 gms III when jaundice is mild, 60 to 80 grams of protein may be provided.

Fat — Fat intake will depend on the severity of the disease. In hepatic precoma and coma, due to the severe hepatocellular failure, fats are not metabolized by the liver and hence it should not be given at all. In severe jaundice about 30 gms of fat may be provided. In mild to moderate jaundice about 50-60 gms of fat may be given daily.

Carbohydrates — Glucose is the main carbohydrate which is administered in jaundice. Glucose is gven intravenously in the early stage of jaundice caused by viral hepatitis with severe nausea and vomiting. During hepatic precoma and coma, the foods are given through nasogastric tube. In severe cases of jaundice, fruit juices, porridge and puddings containing sugar can be administered. In mild to moderate cases, cereals may be given as the main source of carbohydrates, 300-340 gms of carbohydrates may be given daily.

Vitamins — A multivitamin and a vitamin C (500 mg) tablet should be administered daily. One tablet of vitamin K may be administered daily or vitamin K 1 mg may be administered by intramuscular injection. Food-stuffs containing the above vitamins can be consumed, as described in the chapter "Constituents of Food and their Functions."

Minerals — Sodium and potassium should be maintained at normal levels in the blood serum by adding sodium chloride and potassium chloride to the diet. Food-stuffs containing sodium chloride and potassium chloride, as mentioned in the chapter "Constituents of Food and their Functions", may be consumed.

Parenteral feeding — When the patient suffers from severe nausea and vomiting, 10% glucose should be abministered by intravenous route at the rate of 30 drops per minute. A total of 2000-2500 mls fluid should be given daily which provide 800-1000 Kcals each day.

Nasogastric feeding — When nausea and vomiting stop, nasogastric feeding should be strated. One litre of fruit juice (orange juice) is mixed with one litre of water and then 200 gms of sugar is added to them. This mixture is administered through nasogastric tube in divided doses (about 200 mls in each dose) at 2 hourly intervals, starting from 6.00 A.M. to 12.00 at night. A suitable dose of multivitamin can be added to each dose. This diet provides 1200 Kcals.

(3) Cirrhosis of the Liver

Cirrhosis of the liver is a chronic condition in which there is destruction of the liver cells due to necrosis followed by fibrosis and nodule formation. It results in loss of function of the liver cells and portal hypertension.

This disease is characterized by feeling of uneasiness and weight in the hepatic region, accompanied by enlarged liver which later on becomes small, hard and the surface becomes nodular, patient's facies showing dilated venules and capillaries in the cheeks, spider nevi in the neck, arms and trunk above the level of the nipples, palms of the hands showing a diffuse erythema (liver palms), ascites and jaundice in about one in 3 cases.

Causes

- **Alcohol** — Alcohol has a very toxic effect on the liver. Cirrhosis liver occurs due to regular intakes of alcohol for years in excess.

- **Viral hepatitis** — Hepatitis B virus may cause cirrhosis of the liver in majority of cases. Some cases are due to non-A and non-B hepatitis.
- **Malnutrition** — Deficiency of protein (PEM), especially of high biological value.
- **Toxins of foods** — Certain toxins which grow on certain food like aflatoxin (a toxin produced by Aspergillus flavus and Aspergillus parasiticus) on groundnuts, and certain fungi which thrive on cereals may be the causative factors.

Principles of diet — Diet should be rich in protein, carbohydrate, moderate or restricted fat (depending on the severity). Sodium is to be restricted in case of the presence of ascites.

Dietary Management

Energy (Calories) — The patient suffers from cachexia, so the diet should provide sufficient amounts of calories which should be 2000 to 2200 Kcals.

Proteins — A high protein diet should be provided because there is loss of considerable amount of protein (albumin) in the ascitic fluid. It will also help in regeneration of the liver cells. The protein should be given in the amounts of 1.2 to 1.5 gm. per kg. of body weight.

Fats — A moderate intake of fat is advised rather than complete restriction. Fat is given at the rate of .5 gm per kg. of body weight.

Carbohydrates — Carbohydrates provide more than 60% of the total calories in the diet so these should be given in adequate amounts.

Vitamins — The patients should be given one multivitamin tablet daily for providing the requirement of all the essential vitamins.

Minerals — Sodium intake should be restricted if edema and ascites are present. Potassium salts should be given to correct the potassium deficiency resulting from nausea, vomiting and diarrhea. Iron should be administered to cure anemia.

Consistency — Fibre content should be reduced in the diet in advanced cirrhosis when there is danger of hemorrhage from esophageal varices. A soft diet should be given frequently.

(4) Hepatic Coma

It is the condition of deep unconsciousness from which the patient cannot be aroused even by powerful external stimuli, due to liver failure. The causes in the liver may be I viral hepatitis II jaundice III cirrhosis liver.

Dietary Management

Calories — The calorie intake should be about 1000 Kcals and this should be in the form of glucose and fruit juices.

Proteins — Since the nitrogenous products of protein metabolism cause coma because of the liver damage, no protein should be given. So high carbohydrate diet should be given which spares protein. When the patient recovers from coma, proteins can be given in small quantity, i.e., 30-40 gms per day which can be gradually increased to the normal intake of 1 gm per kg of body weight.

Fats — Since fats are first metabolized in the liver, fat should not be given at all.

Carbohydrates — Since the chief source of energy are carbohydrates, these should be readily assimilable and so these should be in the form of glucose. Glucose is utilised by the tissues even when the liver is badly damaged.

Vitamins — The daily requirements of vitamins should be dissolved in the glucose-fruit juice mixture.

Minerals — The serum levels of sodium and potassium should be determined and any imbalance be corrected by adding their salts to the liquid diet. The diet is to be given by injections or through nasogastric tube.

Parenteral feeding — When parenteral feeding becomes essential, 10% glucose solution should be administered intravenously at the rate of 30 drops per minute. A total volume of 2000-2500 mls. should be administered daily. Vitamin B complex, vitamin C and vitamin K are also administered parenterally.

Nasogastric tube feeding — In most of the cases nasogastric tube feeding is carried out. The feed can be prepared as follows —

Orange Juice	1000 mls.
Glucose	200 gms.
Water	1000 mls.
Total volume	2000 mls.

The daily requirements of vitamins can be dissolved in the above fluid. The food should be given in 10 doses of 200 mls each at 2 hrly, starting from 6.00 a.m. to 12.00 at night.

GALLBLADDER

Gallbladder is a pear-shaped sac situated on the under surface of the right lobe of the liver holding and concentrating bile received from the liver until it passes into the duodenum through the cystic duct. The common diseases of the gallbladder are —

(1) Acute or chronic cholecystitis

(2) Gallstones

(1) Acute Cholecystitis

Inflammation of the gallbladder. It is characterized by sudden, severe pain in the right hypochondriac region, which is frequently referred to the back or to the right shoulder, fever, nausea and vomiting and mild jaundice in about 20% cases.

Causes — 1.Obstruction of the cystic duct or neck of the gallbladder on which infection is usually superimposed. 2. Infection from the teeth and tonsils, following influenza, pneumonia or typhoid fever etc. 3. Stagnation of bile. 4. Calculi in the gallbladder. 4. Foreign bodies, worms and ova in the gallbladder.

Dietary Management

Fluid diet is given. The composition of fluid is given below

Orange juice	1500 mls.
Glucose	200 gms.
Sucrose	200 gms.
Skimmed milk (fluid)	1000 mls.
	2500 mls

The above fluid is given in 10 doses of 250 mls. each at 2 hourly intervals starting from 6.00 A.M. to 12.00 at night.

Chronic cholecystitis — It is the chronic inflammation of the gallbladder and thickening of its wall. It is characterized by nausea, abdominal discomfort, flatulent dyspepsia or distension of the abdomen after meals, attacks of pain intermittently in the right hypochondrium or epigastric region radiating to the right shoulder or the back. There is intolerance of fatty foods as pain usually aggravate on taking fatty diet. Murphy's sign is positive.

Causes — Causes are the same as that of acute cholecystitis.

Dietary Management

Diet — The diet should be rich in readily available carbohydrates but low in fat and cholesterol. Fried foods, fatty meat, cheese, pastries, nuts, dry fruits, cabbage, cauliflower, cucumber, peas, beans, pickles, condiments and spices should be avoided.

Calories — Since the disease occurs mostly in obese persons, calories intake should be about 1500 Kcals.

Proteins — 1 gm of protein per kg. of body weight or 50-60 gms of protein per day are recommended.

Fats — Vegetable oils rich in essential fatty acids should be consumed. Animal fat and foods rich in cholesterol should be avoided.

Diet chart

Bed tea	Light tea 1 cup with sugar.
Breakfast	Toned milk without sugar, toast 2 with little jam.
Lunch	Rice 1 medium-sized bowl, 4 small and thin chapaties, thin dal 3/4th medium sized bowl, thin butter, milk, egg one, cooked beans and carrots, cooking oil one and half teaspoonful.
4 P.M.	Light tea 1 cup with 1 teaspoonful sugar Biscuits 3 to 4.
Dinner	4 small chapaties, cooked mixed vegetable 1 bowl, dal 3/4 bowl, orange — 1
Bedtime	Milk 1 cup without sugar and cream

Diet will provide about 1500 calories, 50 gms proteins and 30 gms fat.

(2) Gall-stones (Cholelithiasis)

It is the condition of the presence of stones in the gallbladder. Its symptoms are the same as that of cholecystitis.

Causes — The most common cause is stagnation of bile in the gallbladder from any cause or it may follow cholecystitis due to typhoid fever, or streptococcal infection. It may occur in stout persons leading sedentary life and who take diet rich in fat and sugar.

Dietary Management

Avoid foods containing cholesterol, animal fats, especially if cooked. A little butter is allowed but cream, egg-yolk and fat of the meat should be avoided. Foods containing potassium and magnesium should be consumed.

* * * * *

CHAPTER 20

DIET IN THE DISEASES OF THE CARDIOVASCULAR SYSTEM

Heart is a vital organ of the body which is supplied by the coronary arteries emerging from the aorta. Heart disease can affect people of all ages but it is most frequent after middle age. Arteriosclerosis is the condition of thickening, hardening and loss of elasticity in the arterial walls causing narrowness of the lumen of the artery.

Atherosclerosis is the degenerative disease of the arteries, chiefly of the coronary arteries, characterized by deposition of cholesterol or lipid in the intima (inner lining of an artery) of a coronary artery and followed by fibrosis and calcification, and the lumen of the affected artery is narrowed leading to the diminished blood supply to the heart which results in the onset of one of the following two ischemic heart diseases.

(1) Angina pectoris

(2) Coronary thrombosis or myocardial infarction.

(1) Angina pectoris — It is characterized by sudden severe sub-sternal pain and constriction of the chest which usually occurs during exercise or excitement and limits the physical activity, due to insufficient blood and hence the oxygen supply to the heart. The pain is increased on exertion, radiating usually to the left shoulder and down the left arm, or to the jaw. It is associated with hypertension (high blood pressure). Dyspnea may be present. Attack usually lasts for 30 minutes.

(2) Coronary thrombosis or myocardial infarction — It is also known as heart attack. It is characterized by thrombosis occuring in the coronary artery or a branch of a coronary artery, i.e., blood is coagulated in it. So, the blood supply is obstructed to that region of the myocardium which is supplied by the affected coronary artery or its branch, resulting in ischemia (deficiency of blood supply) in that region of the myocardium. Obstruction in the blood supply for a few moments only causes necrosis of that region of the myocardium, i.e., it becomes dead. Necrosed region of the myocardium is called infarct and the process of formation of infarct is known as infarction.

Coronary thrombosis or myocardial infarction is characterized by severe pain in the middle of the chest behind the middle and lower portion of the sternum (chest bone) in the night i.e., at the time of rest which goes on increasing rapidly. It is generally called heart attack. The pain may be localized or it may be referred to the shoulder, back, neck, jaw or to the arm (fourth and fifth fingers of the left hand) on the left side. The pain lasts longer than that of angina pectoris and not relieved on taking rest.

Causes of Atherosclerosis and Ischemic Heart Diseases

- Smoking or tobacco chewing
- Excessive intake of alcohol
- Excessive intake of saturated fat
- Physical inactivity or sedentary life

- Obesity
- Diabetes mellitus
- Hypertension
- Mental stress and strain
- Hypercholesterolemia

Dietary management in atherosclerosis and ischemic heart diseases.

Main purposes of the diet are as follows —

— Maintenance of good nutrition.

— To provide maximum possible rest to the heart.

— Prevention or elimination of occurrence of edema and other complications.

Principles of the Diet

The diet of the person suffering from atherosclerosis or any ischemic heart disease should be low in calories, low in saturated fats, low in cholesterol, moderate in carbohydrates, moderate in proteins and high in fibres.

Diet in atherosclerosis and ischemic heart diseases —

- **Calories** — The diet should provide 1000 to 1200 calories per day which is required for one who is in bed. This may be gradually increased to 1500-1800 calories.
- **Fat** — Fat intake should be reduced which is the main consideration of the diet. It should not be more than 20% of the total calories consumed. The consumption of saturated fats must be avoided as they stimulate the synthesis of cholesterol. Complete avoidance of fat may lead to mental and physical depression. Animal fats like ghee, butter, cream, margarine, egg-yolk, meat, lard (purified fat from the hog) are high in saturated fats and should be avoided. Olive oil and groundnut oil is recommended as they lower the low density lipoproteins.

It is better to consume vegetable diet as it will be low in calories and high in fibre content as fibres help in reducing cholesterol.

Reduction of Body Weight in Obese Patient

An obese patient should lose his body weight for the following reasons—

— The fat deposits in the myocardium reduce the efficiency of the heart.

— The fat in the abdominal region often interferes with the movements of the diaphragm and free action of the heart.

— Obese patients would have high blood cholesterol.

— The gradual reduction of body weight in an obese person reduces the work load of the heart because of the decreased BMR. With this there is slowing down of heart rate, a reduction in blood pressure which thereby improves the cardiac efficiency.

- **Cholesterol** — Cholesterol intake should be 200-250 mg. per day while normally it is 500 mg/day, which is attained by reducing fat intake of animal origin and consuming fruits, vegetables and cereals excessively. The plasma cholesterol level should be 20% less. Reduction of saturated fatty acids and cholesterol intake with fruit and vegetable fibre have a potent cholesterol lowering effect.
- **Carbohydrates** — Since the total calories intake is decreased, the carbohydrate intake should be reduced accordingly. Sugar intake should be specially reduced.
- **Proteins** — Proteins should be taken moderately, only animal proteins are avoided. Food in small quantity should be consumed frequently.
- **High fibre diet** — High fibre diet helps in the reduction of plasma cholesterol by preventing its absorption.

- **Vitamins** — Vitamin 'C' is required for capillary stability. Nicotinic acid reduces lipids in the blood, hence both are useful.
- **Minerals** — Adequate potassium and calcium in the blood are required to prevent arrhythmias.
- **Smoking or tobacco chewing** — Smokers and tobacco chewing persons are more prone to be afflicted with myocardial infarction due to following reasons and so the smoking and tobacco chewing should be strictly prohibited.

— A very poisonous alkaloid nicotine is found in tobacco which is vasoconstrictor, hence it constricts the coronary arteries.

— Nicotine causing the adherence of platelets increases the clotting of blood in the coronary artery.

— It reduces the oxygen supply to the heart and increases the heart rate.

— It reduces the high density lipoproteins.

- **Alcohol** — Consumption of heavy amounts of alcohol has the harmful effects on the heart and there is risk of ischemic heart disease.

— Alcohol has the toxic effect on the myocardium.

— It causes accumulation of fat in the myocardium, thinning and broadening of the heart muscles.

— It precipitates cardiac arrhythmias.

— It aggravates hypertension.

Diet chart for Atherosclerosis and Ischemic Heart Diseases

Bed tea	—	• Light tea without sugar.
Breakfast	—	• Milk one cup without cream and sugar.
Lunch	—	• Four small chapaties without ghee.
		• Rice one medium bowl
		• Oil for cooking 1½ teaspoonful
		• Cooked vegetables 3/4th bowl
		• Salad

4. P.M. — • Light tea without sugar
• Sweet lime (mausambi) and papaya
• Two medium-sized chapaties
• Pulse 3/4th medium bowl
• Curd 3/4 cup
• Salad

Dinner — • Oil for cooking 1½ teaspoonful
• Cooked vegetables 3/4 medium bowl

Diet provides about 1600 calories and 30 gms fats.

CONGESTIVE HEART FAILURE (CHF)

The condition is characterized by dilatation of the heart, cyanosis, engorged and pulsating neck veins, edema of the dependent (lower) part of the body resulting from the stasis of the venous blood and reduced outflow of blood from the left side of the heart, weakness and breathlessness.

Causes — (a) Infection as rheumatism, typhoid fever, influenza, pneumonia and diphtheria etc.

(b) Heart diseases — Myocardial infarction, atrial flutter, atrial fibrillation and paroxysmal tachycardia.

(c) Metabolic diseases — Hyperthyroidism, hypothyroidism, beriberi and scurvy.

(d) Hypoxia

Dietary Management

- **Calories** — The diet should provide 1000 to 1200 calories per day.
- **Proteins** — Normal requirement of 1 gm per kg. of body weight is adequate.
- **Fats** — Intake of fats should be reduced as they are difficult to be digested. Fried foods should be completely restricted. Fat intake should be 30 gms per day.

- **Carbohydrates** — Carbohydrates should be in such a quantity which may provide the rest of calories after the proteins and fats.
- **Fluids** — Intake should be reduced to 750-1200 mls. per day because of the presence of edema.
- **Sodium** — Sodium in the form of sodium chloride (common salt) should not be added to the food and should be avoided in cooking.

The patient is usually unable to eat himself and the rest is the most important requirement. The diet should be limited to fruit juice with sugar and water. Gradually as the patient's condition improves, soft, pureed, bland foods, soups etc., are given in small quantities as tolerated. Salt (sodium chloride) intake should be strictly restricted. As the patient's condition improves, a small semi-solid diet is given frequently. A normal solid food is allowed only when the patient is able to feed himself and can chew without excessive strain.

Sodium Restricted Diet

The food-stuffs in a full normal diet contain approximately 2-3 gms of sodium chloride (common salt) before any further addition is made in the daily preparation. A liberal intake of food to which salt has been added will increase the sodium intake. The retention of sodium in the body causes the development of edema.

Sodium restricted diet is of the following three types —

1. Moderately low sodium diet — In this type of food a limited amount of salt (1-2 gm) is consumed in cooking, but no salt is added to the cooked food. It is usually supplied to the patients suffering from mild type of congestive heart failure.

2. Low sodium diet — Salt is not consumed in cooking and it is not added to the prepared food even .5 gm to 1 gm of salt may be prescribed for the patients of congestive heart failure with edema, which is used carefully on his foods for the day.

3. Very low sodium diet — Less than 500 mg (½ gm) of salt is prescribed for the patients with congestive heart failure with severe edema, ascites or hypertension. No salt is added either during preparation or after preparation of food, it may be available from the raw food-stuffs.

HYPERTENSION

Hypertension is a condition in which the patient has a higher than normal blood pressure, systolic blood pressure above 140 mm. Hg. or diastolic blood pressure above 90 mm. Hg., which is caused by an increase in the peripheral resistance resulting from vasoconstriction or narrowing of the peripheral blood vessels.

Causes — Causes of hypertension are advancing age, excessive consumption of sodium (i.e., common salt) in the diet, smoking, obesity, diabetes mellitus, hypercholesterolemia, excessive use of alcohol, chronic emotional stress, sedentary life style, certain forms of renal disease, particularly when limited to one kidney, Cushing's syndrome, pheochromocytoma, adrenal tumors, hyperthyroidism with thyrotoxicosis, post menopausal state.

The condition is characterized by pain in the occipital region on awakening in the morning, diziness, palpitation, weakness, insomnia.

Dietary Modification in Hypertension

Low calorie, low fat, low sodium diet with normal protein and carbohydrate intake is advised.

- **Calories** — An intake of 20 Kcals per kilogram of body weight is the best. Obese persons must reduce the body weight to normal with a lower calorie intake.
- **Proteins** — Normal intake of protein, i.e., one gram per kilogram of body weight is advised.
- **Fats** — Intake of fats should be restricted as intake of fats in excess may cause atherosclerosis. Animal fats should be avoided. Vegetable oils should be used in moderation.

- **Carbohydrates** — Carbohydrates should be consumed as specified in balanced diet.
- **Salt (sodium chloride)** — Salt intake should be restricted. It must be 2-3 gms per day or less depending upon the severity of hypertension.
- **Smoking or tobacco chewing** — Smoking or tobacco chewing should be strictly prohibited.

  Preserved foods like pickles, canned foods, ketchup and sauces should be avoided.

  Salted food like peanuts, nuts, potato chips, banana chips, popcorn and biscuits should be avoided. Baking powder should not be consumed. Soft drinks containing sodium benzoate should be avoided.

* * * * *

CHAPTER 21

DIET IN THE DISEASES OF THE URINARY SYSTEM

The most important work of the kidneys is to filter the blood and after reabsorption of glucose and amino acids etc., wich are essential substances for the body, to form the urine from the rest of the filtered fluid. Urine passing through the ureters is carried to the urinary bladder whence it is excreted.

The dietary management of the following diseases is considered in this chapter.

- Nephritis
- Nephrotic syndrome
- Acute renal failure
- Chronic renal failure
- Renal and vesical calculi

NEPHRITIS

Nephritis is the inflammation of the kidney due to bacteria or their toxins, or toxic substances as alcohol. The glomeruli, tubules and interstitial tissues may be affected. The condition may be acute or chronic.

Acute nephritis — It is an inflammatory form of nephritis involving the glomeruli, the tubules or the entire kidney. It is also called diffuse, suppurative, interstitial or parenchymatous nephritis. The condition affects mostly children and young adults. The glomeruli are affected by inflammation, so the renal blood flow and the glomerular filtrate volume are reduced, hence volume of excreted urine is also reduced. Urea and other end products of protein metabolism are retained in the blood. Urine contains blood, albumin and casts.

Dietary Management — The diet of low proteins, rich in carbohydrates, low sodium and restricted fluids should be advised.

- **Calories** — The calorie intake should be about 10% less than that of a sedentary person as the afflicted person will be in bed at rest. An intake of 1700 Kcal per day for adult males and 1500 Kcal per day for adult females may be adequate.
- **Proteins** — The intake of proteins should be reduced to the minimum, i.e., about 30 gms per day, by excluding high protein foods, especially milk products and non-vegetarian foods. The pulses should be consumed. If the individual is passing 500 to 700 mls urine, then 0.5 gm protein per kg. of body weight is allowed. The daily intake can be gradually increased to the usual intake. Prolonged restriction of proteins may cause nutritional anemia. Excess of protein intake will give rise to increase the blood urea.
- **Fats** — Fats can be consumed in moderate amounts i.e., 20-30 gms. per day.

- **Carbohydrates** — Carbohydrates act as the main source of energy, so the diet should be rich in carbohydrates.
- **Sodium chloride (common salt)** — Common salt is restricted as long as the edema persists. As edema subsides common salt can be gradually consumed.
- **Potassium** — Intake of potassium is restricted when the flow of urine is scanty. At this time fruit juice as orange juice, tomato juice or vegetable soups containing potassium should be avoided.
- **Vitamins** — Vitamins intake should be adequate. One multivitamin tablet providing the daily requirements of vitamins may be included.
- **Fluid** — Apart from the water excreted in the urine, about 100 mls is lost daily through perspiration, respiration and defecation. The fluid intake should be 100 mls. plus the volume of water lost in the urine, which is usually 400 to 600 mls. per day, i.e., the fluid intake should be equal to output of fluids and it should be maintained daily.

Chronic nephritis — It may involve glomeruli, the tubules or the entire kidney. It is also known as chronic interstitial or chronic parenchymatous nephritis. It affects the individuals of all age groups but adults are mostly affected. There is no history of kidney or urinary tract infection. It is characterized by severe albuminuria, edema and reduced volume of the excreted urine.

Dietary Management — A salt free diet containing high protein, high carbohydrate and moderate fat with restricted fluid intake is recommended.

- **Calories** — Calorie intake should be adequate, i.e., 2000 Kcals for adult males and 1700 Kcals for adult females.
- **Proteins** — Protein intake should be 100-120 gms. per day and it should be of high nutritive value, e.g., protein of milk,

eggs, fishes and meat for the replacement of serum albumin which is lost daily in the urine and may be 10-20 gms., depending on the severity of albuminuria.

- **Fats** — Fat intake should be 30 to 50 gms per day, half of the fats should be of vegetable oils rich in essential fatty acids, e.g., sesame oils and sunflower seed oil, as this helps to lower the cholesterol level in the blood.
- **Carbohydrates** — Diet should be rich in carbohydrates as they supply a major part of the calorie requirements.
- **Vitamins** — The intake of vitamins should be adequate. For this purpose one multivitamin tablet should be given daily to the patient.
- **Sodium chloride (common salt)** — It should not be added to the diet as it will aggravate the edema.
- **Fluids** — Fluid intake should be 100 mls. plus the volume of water lost in the urine excreted daily. The water content of the diet should be taken into consideration for calculating the extra fluid needs.

NEPHROTIC SYNDROME

Nephrotic syndrome is the disease of glomeruli of the kidneys characterized by severe proteinuria (excretion of protein in the urine more than 3 gms. per day or more than 0.5 gm per kg. of body weight in children), generalized edema and hypoalbuminemia (less than 30 gms. of albumin per litre of blood serum). It causes increased susceptibility to infection, wastage of the tissues, malnutrition and fatty liver.

Dietary Management — A high calorie and high protein intake is required for the replenishment of the damaged tissues. Intake of sodium chloride or common salt should be restricted to prevent further accumulation of fluids. It should be 2 gms. or less per day as this may prevent the recurrence of, or increase in edema.

Diet Chart

Bed tea	Light tea with 2 teaspoonful of sugar and 50 mls. milk.
Breakfast	Milk one glass (200 mls.) with 2 teaspoonful of sugar. Bread 2 slices with 10 gms of butter Egg 1 fried.
Lunch	2 Chapaties of medium size Rice 1 medium bowl, Dal 1 medium bowl. Curd 1 medium bowl
Evening	Roasted groundnut 30 gms, chana 30 gms. Milk one glass +2 tea-spoonful protinex
Dinner	3 Chapaties of medium size with ghee, matar paneer 3/4th bowl or 2 eggs as egg curry etc., dal 3/4th bowl, sweet dish 100 gms.
Bedtime	Milk one glass+2 teaspoonful sugar.

Diet provides 2,600 calories and 95 gms. proteins.

ACUTE RENAL FAILURE

Acute failure of the kidney to perform the essential functions. The blood flow of the kidneys is impaired in this condition by bacterial toxins, glomerulonephritis, acute destruction of the urinary tract, following trauma, shock from some operation, inhalation or ingestion of poisons such as carbon tetrachloride or mercury. It is characterized by oliguria (scanty urine containing tubular casts and albumin) and uremia (condition caused by retention of the end products of protein metabolism as urea etc., which are normally excreted by the kidneys). Blood urea level in uremia becomes 150 mg. to 500 mg. per 100 ml. of blood (Normal blood urea level is 30 mg/100 ml of blood). Urea is reduced in the urine. The main symptoms of uremia are persistant dull headache, diziness, hypertension, dimness of vision, nausea, vomiting, convulsions or coma.

In cases of acute renal failure mortality rate is nearly 50% Dialysis is usually employed, till kidney resumes normal function.

Dietary Management — Dietary treatment is mainly concerned with the correction of fluid and electrolyte balance and there should be nutritional balance in order to reduce the endogenous catabolism (breakdown) which would subsequently lead to uremia.

The catabolism or the breakdown of tissue proteins can be prevented by the administration of glucose orally, or intravenously if injury at the mouth, vomiting or diarrhea causes hinderance in oral administration.

Diet — 400 gms. glucose and 100 gms. of refined groundnut oil made into an emulsion in one litre of water with vitamins (daily requirement) is to be given through nasogastric tube. Only 200 gms of glucose in one litre of water may be given if diarrhea occurs in some cases with the above regime. As soon as the flow of urine is resumed, the patient may be given more fluids in the form of milk, fruit juice, etc.

CHRONIC RENAL FAILURE

Chronic renal failure occurs as a result of glomerulonephritis, chronic pyelonephritis and nephrotic syndrome. In this condition glomeruli and renal tubules are severely damaged. The glomerular filtration rate (GFR) is reduced and becomes inadequate to excrete the nitrogenous waste products. The glomerular filtration rate becomes less than 5 mils. per minute while normal glomerular filtration rate is 120 mls. per minute. The blood urea nitrogen (BUN) is more than 80 mgs. per 100 mls of blood while normally it is 8 to 18 mgs. per 100 mls of blood.

The condition is characterized by oliguria or anuria, uremia, water retention, high serum sodium (hypernatremia) and potassium level (hyperkalemia). The patient suffers from anorexia, nausea and vomiting.

Even the sight or smell of food may provoke to be nauseating. Ulceration of the mouth may interfere with food intake. The patient is irritable, drowsy and eventually coma may develop. Congestive heart failure may develop when heart failure is associated with the retention of sodium and water. Death may occur due to high serum potassium.

Dietary Management — The diet in chronic renal failure should be of adequate calories, low in protein, in adequate amounts of all the amino acids, low in sodium, potassium and fluid.

Energy — Adequate calories should be provided by carbohydrate and fat. If energy (calories) intake is inadequate, the catabolism of endogenous protein tissue takes place to supply energy which would further aggravate the existing anemia.

Protein — Protein intake is reduced to 0.5 gm per kilogram of body weight per day. Very low protein diet as 0.25 gm per kg. of body weight per day or 15-20 gms. protein is advised in severe chronic renal failure.

Sodium and potassium — Sodium is restricted by seeing the existing edema and blood chemistry. Sodium in the form of table salt should be avoided. Potassium is restricted according to the blood potassium levels. Potassium intake is reduced by soaking the vegetables for half an hour and boiled and then drawing away the water, i.e., by leaching process. Fruits and vegetables as orange and tomatoes should be avoided.

Fluids— Fluids are restricted keeping the input and output ratio in view. Daily intake of fluid is usually 500-700 mls. which can be increased with the improvement of the condition of the patient.

Diet Chart

Bed tea	Light tea with one teaspoonful sugar
Breakfast	Milk 1 cup with 1 teaspoonful sugar, Bread 2 slices with 10 gms of butter, cheese 25 gms or one egg.

Lunch	4 small-sized chapaties with ghee, rice one medium bowl, dal one medium bowl, curd one cup +1 teaspoonful sugar.
Evening	Preparation of 50 gms. groundnut, fruit juice 1 glass, banana 1.
Dinner	2 small-sized chapaties with ghee. Fried rice 2 bowls, curd 3/4 cup, dal fried 3/4 bowl, mixed vegetable 1 bowl, ice cream/sweet 50 gms.
Bedtime	Milk one glass.

Diet provides 2800 calories, 85 gms. proteins and 105 gms. of fats.

Renal and Vesical Calculi

Any abnormal concretion which is usually composed of mineral salts in the kidney, ureter, urinary bladder or urethra is called calculus (plural is calculi) It is usually formed of crystalline urinary salts held together by viscid organic matter. It is also known as stone. Calculi or stones may be of the following types—

Calcium oxalate — It is popularly known as mulberry stone. It is very hard with rough surface and covered with sharp projections. It may cause the kidney to bleed, and altered blood is deposited on the surface of the stone, so it seems to be black. It is found single.

Calcium phosphate — It is smooth and dirty white. In an alkaline urine it enlarges rapidly and often fills the renal calyces, taking on their shape.

Sodium urate — They are usually multiple and they are hard and smooth. Their color varies from yellow to raddish brown. They are usually found in children. Such stones are yellow, soft, and friable, and unless they contain impurities, they do not cast an X-ray shadow.

Cystine calculi — These are found in the urinary tract of the patients with cystinuria. Crystals of cystine are white, translucent, perfect hexagons which appear only in the acid urine. Cystine calculi are usually multiple and may assume a caşt of the renal pelvis and calyces. These calculi are soft, like bees wax, and pink or yellow when first removed. On exposure the color changes to a greenish hue. Cystine stones are most commonly found in young girls.

Causes

Following factors may contribute to the formation of calculi or stones.

- **Climate** — In warm climates, the urine volume is reduced and the urine is highly concentrated with urates, oxalates and calcium.
- **Occupations** — Individuals who work hard in the direct sun perspire a lot and so they pass concentrated urine leading to the formation of urinary calculi.
- **Infection of the urinary tract** — Frequent infection of the urinary tract may be one of the contributory factors. Pus cells and epithelial cells may form a focus around which the stone may be formed.
- **Dietary habits** — Persons consuming habitually foods rich in calcium, oxalates, phosphates and purines, e.g., milk (rich in calcium), leafy vegetables (rich in calcium and oxalates), whole cereal flours and fish (rich in phosphates) and meat (rich in purine and phosphates) are more prone to the formation of urinary calculi Excessive consumption of tea may be an important causative factor.
- Deficiency of Vitamin A and B complex
- Hyperthyroidism

Dietary Management in Prevention of Urinary Calculi

A diet intended for the prevention of urinary calculi should be low in calcium, phosphates, oxalates and purines. A list of the food-stuffs rich in calcium, phosphates, oxalates and purines is given below which should be consumed in small quantity to prevent the formation of urinary calculi. Foods rich in oxalates and purines should be completely avoided.

Calcium — Milk and milk products as cheese, curd and butter etc., green leafy vegetables as spinach and other vegetables as radish, carrots, lady's finger and onion etc., eggs and fishes are rich sources of calcium.

Phosphates — Fishes are the richest source of phosphates. Vegetables as spinach, cabbage, radish, carrots etc., wheat, rice, maize, nuts, groundnuts and almond etc., and animal foods as milk, cheese, egg-yolk and organ meat etc., are also rich sources of phosphates.

Oxalates — Green leafy vegetables, tomatoes, tea, coffee, cocoa, chocolates, cashewnuts, beet root etc. are the rich sources of oxalates.

Purines — Purines are the end products of nucleoprotein digestion which breaks down to form uric acid. Fish, meat of organs of the animals as of the kidney, liver and brain etc., are good sources of purines.

The patient should consume a large quantity of fluids so as to increase the output of urine to 2 to 2.5 litres per day, thereby preventing the formation of concentrated urine and then urinary calculi.

* * * * *

CHAPTER 22

DIET IN DIABETES MELLITUS

Diabetes mellitus is a metabolic disease which occurs as a result of the disturbances occurring in the metabolism of the nutrient carbohydrate taken with the food, due to inadequate production or utilisation of insulin produced by the β cells of the islets of Langerhans of pancreas. It generally occurs in people of 50 to 60 years of age and is characterized by polyuria (excessive urination), glycosuria (presence of sugar in the urine), hyperglycemia (sugar in the blood above normal), polydipsia (excessive thirst), polyphagia (excessive hunger), weakness and loss of body weight. Fasting (following going without food for 12 hours after the dinner at night upto the morning) blood sugar is 80 to 110 mg. per 100 mls. of blood and postprandial (2 to 2½ hrs. after the lunch) is 110-170 mg. per 100 mls. of blood.

Causes —

- Excessive intake of food, especially carbohydrate as potatoes, rice and sweets etc., and lack of physical labor. It is the main cause of diabetes mellitus.

- Obesity — The more is the obesity, the more will be the possibility of the occurrence of diabetes mellitus.
- Heredity — If mother or father is suffering from diabetes mellitus, there are great chances of occurrence of diabetes mellitus in the offspring also. Family history of being diabetic is obtained in about 25% patients of diabetes mellitus.
- Infections — Generalized infections, especially virus infection may cause diabetes mellitus. If may occur after coryza, smallpox and mumps etc. Localized infections as boils, abscesses and carbuncle etc., may also cause diabetes mellitus. Infection causes the damage of the cells of the pancreas.
- Anxieties existing since a long time.
- Mental tension
- Malnutrition
- Undernutrition
- Following some injury or accident
- Drug-induced diabetes mellitus as caused by Adrenocorticotrophic hormone.
- Pregnancy.

Diabetes mellitus includes mainly the following types of diabetes.

(1) Juvenile onset diabetes — JOD, or insulin dependent diabetes mellitus — IDDM, or type I diabetes. This type of diabetes mellitus develops abruptly before the age of 25 years, mostly at the age of 5 years and early adolescence in which insulin is required to be injected to survive, i.e., this type of diabetes is dependent on insulin.

(2) Maturity onset diabetes — MOD,or non-insulin dependent diabetes mellitus — NIDDM or type II diabetes. This type of diabetes mellitus develops after the age of 40 years in which insulin is not required to survive, i.e. it is not dependent on insulin and it may be controlled by oral medicines. This type of diabetes mellitus is of the following two types according to the obesity.

1. **Obese non-insulin dependent diabetes mellitus (Obese NIDDM)**
2. **Non-obese non-insulin dependent diabetes mellitus (Non-obese NIDDM)**

Other types of diabetes mellitus :—

1. **Malnutrition related diabetes mellitus** — Diabetes mellitus occurring in malnutrition before the age of 30 years.
2. **Secondary diabetes mellitus** — Diabetes mellitus developing as a secondary to some diseases.
3. **Gestational diabetes mellitus** — GDM — Diabetes mellitus developing during pregnancy.

Dietary Management

Food-stuffs containing excess of carbohydrate, such as sugar, sweetmeat, sweet drinks, rice, potatoes and cakes etc., should be avoided.

Calories — Requirement of the calories depend on the weight of the diabetic patient. The weight of the diabetic patient is calculated by the following formula—

Height of the patient in centimeters — 100 = weight of the diabetic patient in kgs.

Depending on the body weight the required calories are calculated as follows —

Category	Calories requirement
Over weight	20 Kcal/kg. body wt/day
Normal weight	30 Kcal/kg. body wt/day
Under weight	40 Kcal/kg. body wt/day

An elderly person above 50 years of age may require 10% less calories for each decade.

Carbohydrates — Simple carbohydrates as glucose, sucrose, fructose and lactose etc., are not usually advised as they are very quickly absorbed and raise the blood sugar level immediately. Complex carbohydrates as cereals (wheat and rice etc.), pulses, vegetables as potatoes, and fruits etc., on the other hand, are digested and absorbed slowly. Less than 250 gms of complex carbohydrates should be consumed. But there should be no drastic reduction as it may result in excessive metabolism of fat resulting in ketoacidosis.

Fats — Foods rich in saturated fats and cholesterol should be limited.

Proteins — The protein intake should be in normal amount, i.e., 1 gm. per kg. of body weight. There should be an additional intake of protein, especially during pregnancy, in elderly people and the people inflicted with some injury or undergone an operation.

Fibres (cellulose) — Diet should be rich in fibres as they delay the passage of food through stomach and small intestine, thus delaying the absorption of carbohydrate.

Vitamins — Diet should be rich in vitamin B complex as it will avoid the development of diabetic neuritis.

Minerals — Foods rich in potassium as tomatoes etc., should be taken as it helps in releasing insulin from pancreas.

Sweetening agents — (1) Saccharine — It is 300 to 350 times sweeter than sugar used as an artificial sweetner in the form of tablet, granules or liquid, but it may cause cancer, so its use is now restricted. 2) Sorbitol— It is hydrogenated glucose which does not cause glycosuria.

Diet Chart

Bed tea	1 cup of tea or coffee.
Breakfast	1 cup of tea and 2 toasts with little butter.
Lunch	2 chapaties, rice 1 medium-sized bowl, dal 3/4 medium-sized bowl, leafy vegetables 1 bowl, oil for cooking 1½ teaspoonful

Afternoon	1 cup of light tea without sugar
Evening	Fruit one
Dinner	2 small chapaties, rice 1 medium-sized bowl or 2 more chapaties, dal 3/4 medium-sized bowl, salad, other vegetables 1 medium-sized bowl.
Bedtime	1 glass toned milk without sugar calories about 1500.
	Carbohydrate less than 250 gms.

*****

CHAPTER 23

GERIATRIC NUTRITION

The aging process brings about many physiological, mental and sociological changes which affect the nutritional requirements. Geriatric nutrition deals with the nutritional requirements of the old people.

PHYSIOLOGICAL CHANGES IN AGING

The important physiological changes which affect the nutritional requirements in old people are as follows: —

- **Basal metabolism** — There is diminution in the metabolism of the tissue cells as a result of aging. Hence, basal metabolic rate (BMR) is decreased.
- **Calories or energy** — In old age, due to diminution of physical activity, calories or energy requirement is decreased. It becomes 25% less.

GASTROINTESTINAL TRACT

1. Loss of appetite for many foods. 2. Loss of teeth due to decay of the teeth and gums which causes improper mastication. Inability to chew the food properly may diminish the tolerance of certain types of food. Hence such hard foods are avoided, but softer food may lead to constipation. 3. Saliva is diminished and so the starch is not digested properly. 4. Gastric juice is diminished and the secretion of digestive enzymes by the stomach (pepsin, lipase), pancreas (amylase) and intestines (enterokinase, trypsin, invertase or sucrase, lactase and maltase) usually diminish in advancing age, so the ability to digest food is diminished. 5. Atrophy of the intestinal mucosa results in diminution of absorption of nutrients in old people. 6. Transportation of food nutrients from the intestinal tract to the different tissues is adversely affected by the changes in the circulation and diminished oxygen uptake.

- **Malnutrition** — Due to loss of appetite and poor digestibility of food, old people suffer from protein deficiency, i.e., protein energy malnutrition (PEM).
- **Diabetes mellitus** — It is a long term disease which generally occurs in old age due to defective carbohydrate metabolism.

RESPIRATORY ILLNESSES

Chronic bronchitis, asthma and emphysema generally occur in old age.

CARDIOVASCULAR SYSTEM

Atherosclerosis — It occurs in old people in which the lipid is deposited on the intima (inner wall) of the large and medium-sized arteries, especially the aorta and coronary arteries causing narrowing of their lumens, and eventually the fibrosis and calcification occurs in lipid deposition. Atherosclerosis in the coronary artery leads to the diminished blood supply to the heart, thrombus formation, high blood pressure and rupture of the coronary artery.

Heart rate — Heart rate becomes slow.

Blood pressure — There is a tendency of hypertension in old age. The rate of rise of systolic arterial pressure is greater than that of diastolic pressure.

URINARY SYSTEM

Kidney functions are deficient and blood urea is raised.

REPRODUCTIVE SYSTEM

Impotency — Occurrence of impotency in old men, mainly due to deficiency of testosterone hormone and partly due to diminution of sexual power.

Enlargement of the prostate — Prostate gland is generally enlarged in old age characterized by dysuria, nocturia, frequent and urgency of micturition.

Leukoplakia vulvae — Atrophy (thinness) and dryness of the skin and mucous membrane of vulva (labia minora, labia majora and clitoris) with stenosis of the vaginal orifice. Severe itching and a white marble-like appearance of the skin, frequently with excoriations are its characteristics. Frigidity (coldness or non-arousal of the sexual desire) even on stimulation in the women occurs after menopause. Dyspareunia (pain during sexual intercourse) occurs in older women, i.e., after menopause. All the above changes occurring in older women (after menopause) are due to deficiency of the estrogen hormone. If untreated, malignancy may develop.

NERVOUS SYSTEM

Following changes take place in the nervous system due to aging-

1. Deafness

2. Dimness of vision
3. Diminution of sense of taste
4. Diminution of sense of smell.

SKELETAL SYSTEM

Osteoporosis — It is the condition of increased rarefaction or porosity of bones due to their decalcification, occurring most commonly in old people, characterized by deformity, localized pain and fracture.

LOCOMOTOR SYSTEM

Osteoarthritis — It is the degenerative disease of the joints, usually of the knee joints marked by the destruction of joint cartilage and overgrowths of the bones at the margin in the joint, with pain and stiffness.

SKIN AND HAIR

Skin— Dry, rough, scaly and wrinkled skin with decreased elasticity.

Hair— The hair become grey and rough in old age.

MENTAL CHANGES

1. Impairment of memory.
2. Rigidity of outlook and dislike of change.
3. Change in behaviour.

EMOTIONAL DISORDERS

Bitterness, inner withdrawal, depression, weariness of life and even suicide resulting from social maladjustment.

Vitamin deficiency — Mild deficiencies of several vitamins occur frequently in old people.

Accident — Fracture of the neck of the femur generally occurs due to decalcification of the bones in elderly, usually on slipping over the smooth floor.

Cancer — Cancer generally occurs in old age. Cancer of the prostate gland is common after the age of 65.

Nutritional Requirements

Calories — As a result of decreased basal metabolic rate and physical activity, the calories requirement is lessened by about 25%, as compared with the normal adults doing light work. In the persons having normal body weight, calories intake should be adjusted to maintain the body weight constant. In obese persons the calories intake should be adjusted to reduce the body weight gradually as described in the chapter on obesity. In the persons whose body weight is below normal, the calories intake should be adjusted to increase the body weight bringing it to about normal level.

Proteins — As old people generally suffer from protein deficiency, their diet should include adequate amounts of protein-rich foods such as pulses, nuts, milk, eggs, fish and meat etc. The daily protein intake should be 1.5 gm per kilogram of body weight.

Fats — Fat is concentrated source of energy, the diet should not contain more than 50 grams of fat per day. At least half of this quantity should be in the form of vegetable oils rich in essential fatty acids.

Vitamins — Signs and symptoms of deficiency of several vitamins are usually seen in old people. So if the diet taken does not provide sufficient quantity of all the vitamins, a multivitamin tablet providing half the daily requirement of different vitamins may be taken daily. An addition of 400 IU of vit. 'D' will help to increase the absorption of calcium and prevent osteoporosis.

Minerals — Since the absorption of calcium and iron in old people is less than that in normal adults, the intakes of calcium and iron should be increased to meet the requirements. The daily requirement of calcium is 0.8-1.0 gram and iron is 30-40 mg. in old age.

Roughage — The diet of old people should contain tender vegetables and fruits containing fibres, to avoid constipation, but they should not consume mature vegetables, and whole cereals and pulses or their bran in excess as these contain large amounts of fibres and hence may irritate the intestinal mucosa and cause digestive upsets.

Water — Water intake should be liberal to ensure that the volume of urine excreted is not less than 1.5 litres per day. This will cause elimination of waste metabolic products such as urea and uric acid etc.

Serving good food — The old persons generally think that they are not being needed by their family or by the community. The frustration and isolation from the people and feeling of being rejected and unwanted may be expressed as complaints against food and refusal to eat or they may indulge in eating their favorate foods such as sweets, so serving good food in pleasant atmosphere may indicate the older person that some one is caring for him and he is an important person.

***Table 37.* Nutritional requirements for old people**

Nutrients	Man	Woman
Calories	2100	1700
Protein (gm)	80	70
Calcium (gm)	0.8	0.8
Iron (mg)	30	40
Vitamin A (IU)	5000	5000
or in μg	750	750
Thiamine (mg)	1.2	1.0
Riboflavine (mg)	1.4	1.2
Nicotinic acid (mg)	16	13
Folic acid (μg)	100	100
Vitamin B_{12} (μg)	1.0	1.0
Ascorbic acid or Vitamin C (mg)	50	50
Vitamin D (IU)	400	400
or in mcg	10	10

Table 38. Balanced diet for old people over 60 years (in grams)

Food-stuff	Man		Woman	
	Veg.	Non-Veg.	Veg.	Non-Veg.
Cereals	350	350	250	250
Pulses	85	55	85	55
Green leafy vegetables	85	85	100	100
Roots and tubers	75	75	50	50
Other vegetables	55	55	55	55
Fruits	55	55	30	30
Milk	300	200	300	200
Fats and oils	35	40	30	55
Eggs	—	30	—	30
Fish and meat	—	55	—	55
Sugar and jaggery	30	30	30	30
Multivitamin tablet	1	1	1	1

* * * * *

CHAPTER 24

DIET OF THE PREGNANT WOMEN AND LACTATING MOTHERS

During pregnancy it is essential to maintain the health of the woman. If pregnant woman would be healthy, a healthy child will be born. If she would be unhealthy, a weak and unhealthy child will be born, or abortion, miscarriage or premature delivery may occur. Sometimes a deformed child is delivered.

An optimum weight before conception should be considered for normal pregnancy and delivery. In obese mothers toxemias of pregnancy may occur frequently. If the mother is under weight, there are chances of premature birth. The optimum weight gain during pregnancy is about 1.5 kg in the first trimester. In the second trimester the average weight gain should be about 1.5 kg per month, i.e., about 4.5 kgs in three months. The weight gain should be a little more in the last trimester. At full term the total gain in weight is about 10-12 kgs., with persistent vomiting during early pregnancy slight loss of weight may occur. Sudden change in body weight (either gain or loss) may also be harmful.

The weight gain should not be less than 9 kgs, and more than 13.5 kgs at full term. If it is less than 9 kgs, the weight of the pregnant is to be increased by providing her nutritious foods. If weight gain is more than 13.5 kgs, it should be reduced by reducing the quantity of ghee, oils and carbohydrate-containing foods as rice and sweets etc.

A pregnant woman requires a well-balanced diet due to the following reasons—

1. To maintain the health of the pregnant woman.
2. To fulfil the demands of the uterine fetus. A fetus is a parasite to the mother and draws nourishment from her diet. If the nutrition of the mother is inadequate, her body reserves are depleted, so there are chances of premature delivery, hence the mother should take a good nutritious diet during pregnancy.
3. To prepare the mother for lactation.
4. To remove the minor disorders of the pregnancy.
5. For the repair of wear and tear occurring daily in the body.

Nutrition During Pregnancy

Energy — There should be an increase in energy intake during pregnancy in order to support the growth and development of the organs and systems of the mother, fetus and placenta.

The increase in calories for trimesterwise is as follows —

1st trimester — 10 Kcals per day

2nd trimester— 90 Kcals per day

3rd trimester— 200 Kcals per day

Non-pregnant woman requires about 2000 calories, while pregnant woman at full term requires more calories, i.e., 2200 Kcals per day.

Proteins — The normal protein requirement for an adult is about 60 gms per day. It is increased during pregnancy about 20 gms per day, i.e., about 80 gms of protein should be provided daily. There are two sources of proteins.

A. Animal sources — Proteins of animal origin are found in milk, cheese, eggs, fish and meat etc. 1/2 litre cow's milk contains about 20 gms protein.

B. Vegetable sources — Vegetable proteins are found in cereals, millets, pulses, nuts, oilseeds, vegetables and fruits.

Pregnant woman should be given about 350 gms. cereals, 90 gms. pulses and 800-900 gms. milk. Vegetarian woman can be provided 80 gms. kernels of groundnuts and non-vegetarian one egg and about 90 gms meat and fish.

The additional protein requirement is needed for the following reasons —

- For rapid growth of the fetus.
- For the enlargement of the uterus, placenta and mammary glands.
- For the transfer of amino acids from the mother to the fetus.
- For the formation of amniotic fluid to facilitate the delivery.
- For increase in maternal circulating blood volume and subsequent demand for increased plasma protein.

In case the demand of protein during pregnancy is not fulfilled, the following conditions may occur —

- The required growth of the baby is not achieved.
- The baby in the uterus may grow at the mother's expense.
- The cells of the tissues, especially of the brain of the baby may be under developed.
- The deficiency of calories and protein during pregnancy may result in poor utilization of food by infant after the birth.

Fats — Pregnant woman should take 40 gms of ghee or butter daily.

Carbohydrates — Pregnant woman should consume 80 gms potatoes, 100 gms rice and 60 gms gur in addition to 350 gms cereals, per day. If the pregnant woman is diabetic, gur should be avoided and quantity of carbohydrate should be reduced.

Vitamins— Fat-soluble vitamins

Vitamin A— Vitamin A is an anti-infective vitamin, i.e., it protects the body from infection and it is necessary for the growth of the body of the baby. Its daily requirement for pregnant woman is 3500 IU. Pregnant woman should consume carrots, spinach, cabbage, tomatoes, ripe papaya, ripe mango, milk, cheese, butter or ghee for Vitamin A. In addition to these, Vitamin A can be obtained from egg-yolk, fish liver oil as from shark liver oil or cod liver oil and meat etc. Fish liver oils are the richest source of Vitamin A. One teaspoonful of cod liver oil or shark liver oil contains about 6000 IU of Vitamin A.

Vitamin D — It helps in the absorption of calcium and phosphorus from the intestine and hence it is necessary for the formation and development of the bones of the baby in uterus. Its requirement is increased during pregnancy, 10 mcg. or 400 IU of vitamin D are required per day. When pregnant woman is not given extra vitamin D, her uterine baby would become deformed and rickety after birth. Vitamin D is found in milk, cheese, butter, egg-yolk and fish oil etc. So the pregnant woman should be given milk and eggs and she should be advised to take a capsule of cod liver oil daily.

Vitamin E — It is also known as anti-sterility vitamin, and it cures sterility. Its deficiency causes infertility or if fertilization occurs, there is possibility of abortion to occur. It is found especially in germinating wheat, and green vegetables. It may be provided to the pregnant woman as supplement in the form of tablet of 100, 200 or 400 mg.

Vitamin K — It is also known as anti-hemorrhagic factor. Its deficiency may cause melena neonatorum or hemorrhagic disease of the newborn. It is found in dark green leafy vegetables and tomatoes, soyabean, milk, egg, fish liver and meat etc. The pregnant woman should consume these food-stuffs. During childbirth the mother is usually given an intramuscular injection of 1 mg. of vitamin K because there is always a risk of hemorrhage in cases of prematurity.

WATER-SOLUBLE VITAMINS

Vitamin B complex — Vitamin B includes many factors, so it is known as Vitamin B complex.

Vitamin B_1 (Thiamine hydrochloride) — It is essential for the maintenance of health of the nerves, so it is administered in pregnancy in the treatment of paresthesia. It is found in cereals (wheat and rice), pulses, vegetables, legumes, fruits, oil seeds, nuts, especially groundnuts, milk, yeast, egg, fish and meat. Daily requirement of Vitamin B_1 for pregnant woman is 1.5 mg.

Vitamin B_2 (Riboflavine) — It is concerned with the growth and development of the fetus, and its deficiency in the mother causes the deformities in the fetal bones, and cleft palate in the infant. It is found in abundance in green leafy vegetables, milk and milk products, groundnuts, yeast, egg, poultry, fish and meat etc. Its daily requirement for pregnant woman is 1.7 mg.

Vitamin B_6 (Pyridoxine hydrochloride) — It is concerned mainly with the normal functioning of the central nervous system. Its deficiency causes mental irritability, convulsions, depression and vomiting. It is given in pregnancy usually in case of vomiting. Its sources are cereals, pulses, vegetables, fruits, soyabean, legumes, milk, cheese, egg-yolk, groundnuts, fish and meat etc. Its daily requirement for pregnant woman is 2.5 mg.

Vitamin B_{12} (Cyanocobalamin) — It is essential for the formation and development of red blood cells in the bone marrow, so it is also called hematinic principle or anti-anemic factor. It is concerned with the capacity of the nerves for transmission of the impulses. Its deficiency causes pernicious anemia and subacute combined degeneration of the spinal cord. Vit B_{12} is found in foods of animal origin. It is found in milk, cheese, egg. fish, liver and meat etc., and is also synthesized by bacteria in the intestine. It is not found in foods of vegetable origin. Its daily requirement for pregnant woman is 1.5 mcg.

Niacin or nicotinic acid — Its deficiency causes pellagra, so it is also known as pellagra-preventing factor. It is essential for the normal functioning of the skin, so the skin diseases do not occur when niacin is present in the diet in sufficient quantity. Its deficiency causes a skin disease pellagra. It is also essential for the normal functioning of the nervous system. Its deficiency in excess may cause the symptoms of schizophrenia and paralysis. Niacin or nicotinic acid is found in cereals (whole wheat, rice), pulses, milk, yeast, groundnuts, poultry, fish, liver and meat etc. The pregnant woman requires about 16 mg. of niacin daily.

Folic acid — It is necessary for the erythropoiesis or formation of red blood cells in the bone marrow. During pregnancy it increases the birth weight of infants and decreases the incidence of low birth weight babies. In about 1/3 of pregnant women folic acid deficiency occurs in the last weeks of pregnancy, which causes megaloblastic anemia in which the red blood cells are large, immature and fragile. In addition to this, the growth and development of the uterine baby are impaired due to folic acid deficiency. Folic acid is found in fresh green leafy vegetables, soyabean, peas, fruits and pulses and liver etc. in abundance. About 400 mcg of folic acid are required during pregnancy. To prevent the anemia during pregnancy, it is given to the woman in the form of tablet or capsule, usually the tablet of folic acid contains Vitamin B_{12} also.

Vitamin C or ascorbic acid — It is also known as Anti-scorbutic vitamin because its deficiency causes scurvy and it acts against scurvy. In deficiency of vitamin C local hemorrhages occur and the bones are fractured easily. It protects the body from infection. It helps in wound healing. It has an important role in the absorption and metabolism of iron. Low intake of vitamin C during pregnancy may cause premature rupture of the fetal membranes and hence the death of the fetus. Vitamin C is found in amla, lemon or lime juice, tomatoes, green leafy vegetables as spinach and cabbage etc., root vegetables as turnip and radish etc. Fruits as guava, orange, mango ripe, papaya ripe, apple and pine apple also contain vitamin C. Germinating pulses, as chana dal contains vitamin C. Mother's milk contains a good amount of vitamin C. Amla or Indian goose berry is one of the richest sources of vitamin C, both in the fresh as well as in the dry condition, guava comes next. Daily requirement of vitamin C in pregnancy is 75-80 mg.

Minerals

Iron— The requirement of iron during pregnancy is increased due to the following reasons—

- During pregnancy the blood volume of the woman is increased and hence the total number of red blood cells is also increased for which more iron is required.
- Demand of iron is increased also for the growing fetus in the uterus and iron content in the placenta.

Sources of iron are vegetable foods, e.g., cereals, green leafy vegetables as spinach and legumes, fruits like apple etc., oil seeds, nuts, dry fruits, animal foods as egg-yolk, poultry, fish, meat and liver etc. Daily requirement of iron for pregnant woman is 38 mg per day while for non-pregnant woman it is 30 mg per day.

Calcium — During pregnancy the woman requires 1.5 gm of calcium per day in comparison to the non-pregnant woman who requires 500 mg to 1000 mg calcium per day, for the formation and development of the bones of the baby in the uterus. Calcium is found in milk and milk products as cheese, curd, skimmed milk and butter etc., green leafy vegetables as spinach etc., and other vegetables as radish, carrots, beet root, lady's finger and onion etc., cereals, millets, pulses, eggs and fishes.

The pregnant woman should be given calcium in the form of tonic from 3rd to 8th month of pregnancy. Usually Vitamin D is also being added to the calcium in calcium tonic for facilitating the absorption of calcium. Use of calcium and vitamin D supplements reduces the muscular cramps during pregnancy.

Magnesium—It is essential for the proper functioning of the brain, spinal cord and all the nerves. Its deficiency causes sleeplessness in pregnant woman. She suddenly becomes deranged on hearing a slight noise, hands and legs begin to tremble and the heart begins to palpitate. Magnesium is found in cereals, milk, cheese, eggs, green vegetables and fruits. In fruits banana is the richest source of magnesium. Daily requirement of magnesium for pregnant woman is one half of the calcium requirement, i.e., 750 mgs.

Fluid—A pregnant woman should drink 1 to 1.5 litres of water daily according to the weather.

Diet—A pregnant woman requires more food, for herself as well as for her uterine baby, but even then she should not take too much food. A balanced diet should be consumed which should be taken in little amounts frequently. An excess of food causes the overdevelopment of the fetal body which causes the difficulty in labor. Overfeeding may cause eclampsia in the pregnant. Increased intake of the food items containing excess of ghee or oil causes burning sensation in the abdomen, body weight is also increased and there is possibility of occurrence of heart disease. There is the danger of occurrence of diabetes mellitus if diets containing food-stuffs with large amounts of carbohydrates are consumed, or sweets are taken in excess. Pregnant woman should be encouraged to take fresh fruits and vegetables in excess. These do not allow the constipation to develop.

In deficiency of food, the fetus does not develop and a weak and lean child is born, premature child is born and anemia occurs in pregnant woman.

The pregnant woman should take 4-8 gms common salt (sodium chloride) daily. In case of hypertension, kidney disease and in the later half of pregnancy it is not good to provide excess of salt to the pregnant woman.

Pregnant woman should not drink tea in excess. It causes the heart burn and urination is increased.

Diet of the Lactating Mother

The daily nutritional requirements of the lactating mother should be for —

1. Her own daily requirements
2. Providing sufficient nourishment for the growing infant.
3. Providing the energy for the milk production.

The average daily milk production in a lactating mother is about 650 mls. though some women may secrete even more. The dietary pattern used during pregnancy is to be continued during lactation. The diet during lactation should be well-balanced to meet the increased requirements. No specific food is needed to be avoided unless it causes distress to the mother. Consumption of alcohol and tobacco chewing should be avoided as they may have an adverse effect on the child.

* * * * *

CHAPTER 25

NUTRITIONAL REQUIREMENTS OF INFANTS

Nutrition plays an important role during infancy and the growth and development is rapid, if proper nutrition is provided.

In the early infancy most of the nutrient requirements are fulfilled by the breast milk and weaning foods should be started by 4-5 months.

Energy — The energy requirements of an infant are much higher. Infants require 120 Kcals/ kg of body weight. The energy requirements of an infant are as follows —

ICMR recommended energy for Indian infants

Less than 3 months	120 Kcals/kg fo body wt.
3 – 5 months	115 Kcals/kg of body wt.
6 – 8 months	110 Kcals/kg of body wt.
9 – 11 months	105 Kcals/kg of body wt.
1 year	112 Kcals/kg of body wt.

Protein — In an infant protein requirements are higher. In the initial months, the mother's milk provides the essential amino acids needed for growth.

The protein requirements of an infant are as follows—

- 0 – 3 months 2.3 gms/kg (in terms of milk protein)
- 3 – 6 months 1.8 gms/kg (" " ")
- 6 – 9 months 1.8 gms/kg (partly vegetable proteins also)
- 9 – 12 months 1.5 gms/kg (" " ")

If the protein and calories requirements are not fulfilled adequately, it may lead to Protein Energy Malnutrition (PEM)

Fats—About 35-45% of calories are provided by fats in the initial stages of infancy and in the later stages inclusion of supplementary (semi-solid or solid) foods also provide the required amount of fats.

Carbohydrates—Carbohydrates provide 35-45% of calories in infants where lactose in milk accounts for it.

Vitamins — Vitamins are essential for the rapid growth and development of the infant. Breast - milk provides almost all the vitamins which are sufficient for the infant. Cow's milk contains small quantity of vitamin C and D which are often consumed during weaning stages. Vit C and D are provided to the weaning infants as supplements.

Minerals—For raipd growth and development of the infant, a large quantity of minerals, especially of calcium and phosphorus is required. Though mother's milk contains less calcium but it is absorbed satisfactorily from the breast-milk. The intake of cow's milk leads to hypocalcemia due to its high phosphate content.

Fluid—A full term infant requires about 60 mls of fluid per kg of body weight on the 1st day which is increased to 100-120 mls. per kg. of body weight on the 2nd and 3rd day. Premature baby requires 70-100 mls of fluid per kg. of body weight on the 1st day which is increased to 150-170 mls. per kg. of body weight for the next 3 or 4 days. As the weaning starts, boiled and cooled water should be given to the baby along with the fresh fruits and fruit juices or vegetable soups.

Composition of human milk, cow's milk and buffalo's milk (per 100 mls.)

Table 39

Nutrients	Human Milk	Cow's Milk	Buffalo's Milk
Water (mls)	88	87	81
Protein (gms)	1.1	3.2	4.3
Fat (gms)	3.4	4.1	6.5
Sugar (gms) (lactose)	7.4	4.4	5.1
Calcium (mgs)	28	120	210
Phosphorus (mgs)	11	90	130
Iron (mg)	—	0.2	0.2
Thiamine (mg)	20	50	40
Riboflavine (mg)	20	290	100
Niacin (mg)	—	100	100
Vitamin A (mcg)	42	52	48
Vitamin C (mgs)	3	2	1
Calories	65	67	117

BREAST FEEDING

The main food of most infants is breast milk. Most of them start feeding by first few hours of birth. A thin yellowish fluid is secreted from the breast in the first few days after delivery, which is called colostrum which has an excess of protein, vitamin A and calories in addition to immunoglobulin gamma A, IgA (Immunoglobulin gamma A) which confers immunity to certain infections during the first few months of the infant's life.

While suckling, the baby pulls the nipple and a part of the breast into her mouth, she bites at the breast with her jaws and squeezes the nipple against the roof of the mouth and then colostrum or milk is carried into her stomach.

Production of milk starts from 3rd or 4th day after delivery. When the breasts are filled up with the milk, they are engorged. Baby takes milk by suckling the breasts and thus the breasts are emptied and their engorgement is vanished. It is very necessary to relieve the pressure of milk in the breasts by expressing any milk that baby does not take. If the breasts are allowed to remain full, the milk present in them will be dried and there will be chance of infection.

Indian mothers secrete 450 to 750 mls. of milk per day. During early months the baby requires feeding 8—10 times a day, whereas at the end of second month, her feedings will be 5—6 times a day, then she takes sound sleep.

Advantages of breast feeding

- Infant derives the sense of security and belonging by the comfort of being held in the arms during the process of breast feeding. There is unbreakable bond created between the two.
- Breast milk is clean and hygienic as it is free from contamination, so there are no gastrointestinal problems in breast-fed infants. Mortality rates are lower in them.
- Breast milk is available at correct temperature and needs no time for preparation.
- Breast feeding is economical.
- Breast milk contains all the nutrients in right form and in the right proportion to be digested by the baby.
- Breast-fed babies are not likely to develop constipation.
- Breast-fed baby is not likely to suffer from allergy as proteins of human milk do not cause allergies.

- Jaws and teeth are properly developed and they are not crowded together as the infant must suckle hard to extract the milk.
- Breast feeding helps in reducing the weight of the mother.
- Breast-fed children rarely become obese.
- Proper emptying of the breasts reduces the chances of mastitis.
- There is the risk of occurrence of cancer of breast in the women who have never used their breasts for feeding.
- Breast feeding has contraceptive effect, so it helps in birth control. A hormone called prolactin is secreted from the anterior pituitary gland in response to babys' suckling, which postpones ovulation by decreasing the synthesis of ovarian hormones, thus causes contraception for some days after child birth.
- Breast feeding stops the bleeding from the uterus.
- Baby's suckling the breasts causes the secretion of oxytocin hormone from the posterior pituitary gland which helps the uterus to contract to its normal size.
- Breast milk contains—

I. Immunoglobulin, gamma A, IgA. — It is an antibody which protects the surface of the mucous membrane of the gastrointestinal tract from bacterial and viral infection.

II. Lysozyme — It is an enzyme that destroys bacteria by breaking down their walls, so provide protection against diarrhea and respiratory infections.

III. Lactoferrin — It is an enzyme that combines with the iron in the blood of the infant. As a result iron is not available to the invading pathogenic micro-organisms, that require iron for their reproduction.

Restrictions to Breast Feeding

These are certain conditions in the mothers in which they are not advised for breast-feeding their infants.

— Marked inverted nipples.

— Presence of fissures or cracks of the nipples.

— Septicemia

— Malaria

— Nephritis

— Renal failure

— Active tuberculosis

— Typhoid fever

— Severe neurosis

— Post partum psychosis

— Eclampsia

— Grade IV cardiac failure

Underfeeding — The baby should gain 30 gms of weight daily, i.e., 200 to 250 gms. weekly. If she is not gaining weight at this speed, she will be supposed to be underfeeding. Constipation may develop in underfed babies. A baby who is deprived of milk feeds may pass frequently small, dark, greenish mucous stools which are known as "Hunger stools."

If underfeeding is present, it should be corrected by increasing the supply of breast-milk or by supplementary feeding.

Regurgitation and vomiting are signs of overfeeding.

Increasing the Supply of Breast Milk

1. By regular emptying of breast — The baby must suckle the breast when she becomes hungry. If anyhow she cannot empty the breast by suckling, milk should be expelled bimanually or by breast-pump, and should be given to the child.

2. By improving the mother's general condition — Lactating mother should drink plenty of fluids as milk and fruit juices etc., and she should consume food rich in protein, and calcium (as milk etc.) Her diet should provide at least 3000 calories. The diet reducing weight should be avoided by the lactating mother. Worries and unhappiness of the mother decrease or abolish the secretion of breast milk.

ARTIFICIAL FEEDING

Though there is no substitute of mother's milk but due to the conditions mentioned under the head "Restrictions to breast feeding" and due to the following conditions artificial feeding is essential.

- When pregnancy occurs during lactation period.
- When the child is too weak to suckle the breast due to cleft palate or hare lip.
- When the breast milk is available in small quantity and eventually stops.
- When the mother is not available for feeding, especially if she is a working lady or she died after childbirth.

Usually cow's milk is given to the infant. It is richer in fat than mother's milk. Hence it is to be diluted with clean water and a litle sugar is to be added, because mother's milk contains more sugar. Two parts of clean water are added to one part of milk which is given to the infant in the first week of life, by bottle. Later on, water should be gradually reduced so that at the age of six months the infant gets the pure cow's milk with 4 teaspoonful of sugar in a day.

The milk to be given to the infant should be boiled and the bottle should be properly sterilized.

On boiling the vitamin C is destroyed so it should be supplemented from the 3rd month. Five mgs of vitamin C may be obtained from 3 teaspoonful of orange juice or tomato juice. Children fed exclusively on milk may develop anemia which can be prevented by giving pediatric iron drops to the infant.

Methods of sterilization of bottle

- The cap, nipple and bottle should be separated and kept in boiling water for 10 minutes.
- Bottle should be rinsed with warm water and then with cold water to remove the milk particles.
- Bottle should be cleaned with a brush.
- No soap or detergent should be used.
- Bottle should be sterilized every time before use.

Disadvantages of bottle feeding

Infant sickness and mortality rate are increased due to—

- Ignorance of sanitation rules and sterilization of the bottle.
- Lack of even clean water for cleaning, especially amongst poor people.
- Lack of knowledge of milk formula and the preparation of milk.
- Frequent inadequacy of nutrients in formula of milk.

Weaning

It is the process in which an infant's diet pattern is gradually changed from liquid food like breast-milk to solid foods which are supplementary foods to the breast-milk. These can be added after six months of infant's life because breast-milk alone cannot provide the required amounts of nutrients and so can not sustain the growth of the infant after this age. Hence, most important aspect of weaning is the introduction of solid foods and not to stop the breast-milk. The body has to maintain the expected growth rate, it has to remain well nourished and healthy. Therefore, the supplementary feeds should be started from 4 to 5 months of infant's life.

Amongst poor people, breast-feeding continues for even 1 to 2 years.

Types of Supplementary Foods

5-6 months—mashed banana, apple and sapota, 7 months—vegetables (boiled, mashed, soups and purees), fruits as banana, mango and papaya after being smashed and strained, semisolid foods in the form of the gruel or paste, khichadi, rice idly, and suji halwa may be given. Well-cooked potato, carrots and pumpkin with rice may be given.

Eggs and starchy foods are introduced. Hard cooked egg-yolk is given initially, which is given in small quantity. It is gradually increased in quantity. Bread may be given by one year which at first may be mixed with milk, curd, butter or dal soup.

Factors to be considered while introducing weaning

- Feeding schedule should be based on the signs of hunger rather than fixed hour of feeding.
- One kind of food should be introduced at a time so as to know the tolerance of the child. The number and kinds of food are slowly increased as the child approaches the first birthday.
- The infant should become familiar with the foods before giving new one.
- Any new food should be initially given once a day in small quantity, i.e., 1 to 2 teaspoonfuls of new food should be given.
- Consistency of food should be very thin and should not contain fibrous material.

Note — Food is frequently pushed out by the tongue of the baby rather than going back because the baby cannot yet swallow well and not due to dislike to the food.

By the end of second year the child is able to eat the normal adult diet.

Problems of Weaning

Diarrhea — Weaning may cause acute diarrhea which may be associated with indigestion when weaning food is introduced too early or there may be lack of digestive enzymes which may cause diarrhea.

Unhygienic feeding conditions like unclean bottles etc., may also be responsible for diarrhea.

Regurgitation and vomiting — Weaning food may cause regurgitation and vomiting which usually occur during the first 6 months.

Constipation— It occurs due to insufficient feeds. Fluids or sugar should be increased and in older babies fruit juices, cereals, pulses and vegetables should be increased.

Refusal to take new food — If the child does not like a particular new food, she would refuse to consume it.

Obesity— Diet rich in fat or carbohydrates and too frequent feeds can produce obesity.

Underweight — Ingestion of less quantity of food and less concentrated foods may lead to underweight babies. Frequent illness and repeated diarrhea may lead to weight loss. Symptoms are irritability, excessive crying, failure to sleep and constipation.

Allergy — The foods generally found allergic with the children are wheat, milk, certain fruit juices and egg, fish and meat etc.

Choking — Hard and big pieces of fruits like apple or vegetables should be avoided for children below 3 years of age which would otherwise lead to death due to choking.

Nutritional management in infants suffering from diarrhea.

Withdrawal of food during diarrhea is harmful and leads to malnutrition. They should be encouraged to continue feeding during diarrhea and increase thereafter. Breast-feeding should be continued without interruption. Other foods including undiluted cow's milk, cereals and vegetable extracts should be given if the baby is over 3 months. Food should be mashed to make it easily digestible. Banana is very useful. Child should take small foods frequently, i.e., 6-7 times daily.

Infants may consume milk in the form of condensed milk, evaporated milk, dried or powdered milk as artificial feedings but vitamin C should be supplemented to such babies.

* * * * *

INDEX

A

D

E

F

G

H

T

U

V

W

Z